NORTH WARWICKSHIRE COLLEGE
00067669

KT-144-584

The Library in the Twenty-First Century

By the same author

Peter Brophy *The Academic Library*, 2nd edn, 2005, ISBN 978-1-85605-527-8

Peter Brophy, Shelagh Fisher and Jenny Craven (editors) *Libraries Without Walls 5: The distributed delivery of library and information services*, 2004, ISBN 978-1-85604-511-7

Peter Brophy, Jenny Craven and Margaret Markland (editors) *Libraries Without Walls 6: Evaluating the distributed delivery of library services*, 2006, ISBN 978-1-85604-576-6

Peter Brophy *Measuring Library Performance: principles and techniques*, 2006, ISBN 978-1-85604-593-3

The Library in the Twenty-First Century

Peter Brophy

Published by Facet Publishing,
7 Ridgmount Street, London WC1E 7AE
www.facetpublishing.co.uk

Facet Publishing is wholly owned by CILIP: the Chartered Institute of Library and Information Professionals.

British Library Cataloguing in Publication Data
A catalogue record for this book is available from the British Library.

ISBN 978-1-85604-606-0

First edition 2000
This second edition 2007

Typeset from author's disk in 11/13 Elegant Garamond and Franklin Gothic by Facet Publishing.
Printed and made in Great Britain by MPG Books Ltd, Bodmin, Cornwall.

Contents

Preface to the first edition ix

Preface to the second edition xiii

Part 1 What is a library? 1

1 Libraries in the modern world 3
Introduction 3
The information society 6
The loss of the core business? 9
Libraries: unprepared for change? 17
Beyond technology 18
Conclusion 19

2 What is a library? The view from the sectors 21
Introduction 21
The view from the sectors 1: national libraries 22
The view from the sectors 2: academic libraries 27
The view from the sectors 3: public libraries 34
The view from the sectors 4: school libraries 42
The view from the sectors 5: workplace libraries 45
Conclusion 52

3 What is a library? Cross-sectoral models 53
Introduction 53
Alexandria: the enduring collection 55
The resource-sharing model 58
The access model 61
The immersive library 63
Conclusion 64

4 What is a library? The profession's view 67
Introduction 67
CILIP's view of the profession 68
The American Library Association's *Library Bill of Rights* 70
The Society of College, National and University Libraries 72
The Society of Chief Librarians 74
Benchmarking librarianship 75
Conclusion 76

5 What is a library? Digital libraries 77
Introduction 77
Knowledge mediators 78
Moving to Distributed Environments for Library Services 79
Objects, handles and repositories 80
Core digital library services 81
The JISC Information Architecture 82
The Digital Library Federation 84
User workflow and the digital repository 84
Summary of digital library concepts 85
The real-world library 87
Conclusion 87

6 What is a good library? 89
Introduction 89
The library as a system 90
International standards 91
Public library performance in the UK 94
Demand for library services 96
Quality management 97
Impact 106
Conclusion 108

Part 2 Future libraries 111

7 Linking users to resources 113
Introduction 113
The library as expert intermediary 114
Disintermediation 116
Library users 118
User populations 119
Collections 120
Intelligence 122
Using information intelligence 125
The user interface 125
The source interface 126
Conclusion 127

8 Beyond the intermediary 129
Introduction 129
Library functions 133
Conclusion 137

9 The library user 139
Introduction 139
The personalization of services 141
Data protection and privacy 145
Information behaviour 146
Library use 148
Libraries and learning 152
Networked learning 154
Lifelong learning 156
Information literacy 157
Conclusion 160

10 The information universe 163
Introduction 163
Information policies 164
Information infrastructures 167
Web 2.0 169
Organization of content 172
Information environments 173

Open access 176
Supporting creativity 179
Content 180
Information objects 181
Document formats 185
XML 185
Metadata 187
Managing objects and metadata 192
Finding and delivering the content 194
Preservation 199
Summary 202
Conclusion 203

11 Envoi 205
Introduction 205
Move from being user-centric to being lifeflow-centred 206
Learn the language 207
Support creativity 207
Join the broader literacy movement 208
Understand learning 208
The library as place 209
Put technology in its place 211
Form alliances 212
Conclusion 212

Bibliography 213

Glossary 233

Index 239

Preface to the first edition

Libraries are one of the marks of civilization. A nation uninterested in the truth of its past, unconcerned with developing its citizens' potential and inimitable to freedom of expression, does not need libraries. Libraries may be maintained in the collective mind, as in oral traditions, or may have physical presence in the city, town or village. They may be large or small. What they contain may, indeed should, be contradictory, puzzling, at times shocking and frequently outrageous. Above all, their contents must stimulate the mind, provoke original thinking and suggest new ways of looking at the world.

But libraries are under threat. If the world is really being built on information and knowledge, transmitted almost instantaneously from anyplace to anywhere, what role is left for yesterday's fusty mausoleums of print? Perhaps they will survive as museums, becoming just one stop on the country house tour, preserved in the state in which they were left as the world moved on and now trampled through by thousands of feet on their way to the teashop. And what of the profession of librarianship, is that any better? It bemoans the poor public perception of librarians, yet never quite shakes it off. As a House of Commons Select Committee put it recently: 'The image of an imposed silence has been perpetuated, and the most pervasive image . . . is the hissed "shh" in response to the slightest noise' (House of Commons, 2005). Already the library seems to belong to a bygone age.

This book was conceived because, after years of working in libraries, I have come to believe that there is a real danger that libraries and librarians will be left behind. I believe in libraries, but I fear for them. They have so much to offer, yet could so easily become backwaters.

I do not intend to engage in polemic or special pleading. Rather this is an attempt to understand what a successful, relevant, dynamic library must be in the Information Age and to communicate that, inevitably partial, understanding to others. It concentrates on technological change, because that is where the biggest challenges lie. No one needs reminding that we live in an increasingly digital world or that information is at the heart of economic and social development –

however defined, the Information Age is now very much a reality. While all organizations, from manufacturing firms through voluntary support groups, are rethinking their strategies and approaches, it is surely stating the obvious to claim that those which have long been involved in information processing are likely to be among the most profoundly affected. Libraries, among the most information-intensive organizations in existence, will have to change. Although there continue to be numerous differing views as to whether or not libraries will be transformed or even destroyed by the changes taking place around and within them, there are relatively few publications that have taken a broad and systematic approach and attempted to set out the challenges to libraries across the different sectors. As Greenberg (1998) has put it: 'we have not thought as systematically as we should about the characteristics of the print library and how and whether they can, or should be, duplicated, transformed, or abandoned in a digital world'.

This book is the result of an attempt to think systematically and strategically about the future of libraries. That it is partial and ultimately inadequate is inevitable given the breadth of issues which must be considered and the rate of change in the information arena.

The perspective from which it is written needs stating in order to explain its starting points and concerns. For the last two years I have occupied the Chair in Information Management at the Manchester Metropolitan University, a position which has enabled me to reflect on and engage in some of the more theoretical and strategic debates which are ongoing. Prior to that I spent 15 years as the 'chief librarian' (with the usual variety of job titles) of academic libraries, having also worked as a systems librarian and as a subject librarian. By the time I moved on from such positions, in 1998, I had also experienced the challenges of responsibility for cross-university IT services and for a Learning Technology Centre. In 1998–99 I was privileged to serve as President of the UK's Institute of Information Scientists, to which body I am grateful for giving me insights into a number of other sectors, including in particular commercial and industrial information service concerns. I am grateful also for the knowledge which colleagues from other disciplines have shared with me down the years. Finally my involvement in international research and development projects, primarily although not exclusively in Europe, has broadened my horizons and given me some inkling of different cultural and societal concerns and approaches.

In Part 1 of the book (Chapters 1 to 6) the aim is to analyse the changing environments in which libraries operate and to answer the fundamental question, 'What *is* a library?' In Part 2 the emphasis switches to synthesis, presenting firstly a model of the 'library' in Chapter 7, and then considering the major issues which need to be addressed in building such libraries in Chapters 8 to 10. Finally, Chapter 11 suggests emphases beyond technological and operational competence which will help to shape tomorrow's libraries within their societal and individual contexts, and draws general conclusions.

I remain a believer in the importance of libraries to societies and individuals. Of course I am biased: I haunted the public library as a child and I have relied on academic institutions for employment since graduating from one in 1971. But it is more than that. To repeat the sentiment of the first paragraph above, for me libraries are symbols of civilized societies. The burning of the national library in Sarajevo was not just the loss of a fine building and a unique collection: it symbolized a decline into barbarism. A library makes a statement about the value which a society places on knowledge and learning, and thus on truth. It is no accident that in the past, and hearteningly in recent years, library buildings have been designed to make statements about their parent bodies – whether it is the Ruskin Library at Lancaster University, the SCONUL Award-winning Aytoun Library at Manchester Metropolitan University or the public libraries in Vancouver or the London Borough of Peckham.

But symbols are not enough. Without descending into technological determinism, we must acknowledge that information and communications technologies have started to change the whole nature of publication, transmission and use of information. The world wide web is, as a public resource, less than a decade old yet has utterly transformed information behaviours. It is not obvious or inevitable that libraries, even if transformed from their present state, have a future. While some initiatives are positive – the UK's *New Library* process for example – the public image of librarians remains poor and distinctly old-fashioned, while technologists lay claim to so-called digital libraries that will apparently replace traditional place-based libraries with a few simple keystrokes.

For everyone involved in libraries these are confusing times. If this book helps to elucidate some of the foundations on which future libraries can be built it will have more than served its purpose.

Peter Brophy
June 2000

Preface to the second edition

When I came to revise this book I fully intended to rewrite the preface which appeared in the first edition completely, not least because what had started as an exercise in 'updating' the text turned into a wholesale rewriting. Yet, I find that almost all that I wrote in my earlier preface holds true. In seven years there has been a huge amount of change, especially in the technological environment. Nonetheless, libraries have survived – some have prospered – but most remain under threat from new technologies, new ways of working and, sadly, sometimes from neglect.

The structure of this book is similar to that of the earlier edition. Again, Part 1 (Chapters 1 to 6) examines different perspectives on libraries, seeking to understand what different viewpoints have to offer in answer to the question: 'What *is* a library?' Part 2 begins by exploring two different models of the library, one traditional in depicting its role as an information intermediary, the other broadening out the conception to a much wider range of functions. It explores both users and information in order to highlight critical issues, and ends with a synthesis consisting of eight critical issues which I believe libraries need to address as they move forward.

I remain grateful to the many colleagues who have contributed, sometimes unwittingly, to the research on which this book is based. I recognize that in trying to cover a huge field I have undoubtedly omitted matters which others would regard as significant, and may well have described with less than perfect felicity topics about which others are far more expert than I can claim to be. Such omissions and errors are, of course, entirely my responsibility.

Peter Brophy
June 2007

Part 1

What is a library?

1

Libraries in the modern world

> Until recently, the status of a research library was defined by the extent of its collections, so the question raised by the late-twentieth century flood of information and information formats struck at the heart of the academic library's sense of importance and identity.
>
> (Sapp and Gilmour, 2003)

Introduction

Libraries emerged soon after the invention of writing. In the third millennium BCE, clay tablets were used in Mesopotamia to create records of commercial and administrative transactions, personal correspondence and literature – most famously the Epic of Gilgamesh. They were stored in centralized collections and acted as reference libraries for the leaders of society. The scribes of the kings of Assyria, notably those working for Ashurbanipal, used different shapes and sizes of tablets for different types of record, thus creating a crude classification system. In ancient Greece, 'public' libraries were established by Pisistratus and his successors, although of course the term 'public' referred only to the elite citizenry. A similar development, serving a similar clientele, was to be found later in Rome. The papyrus scrolls of the Alexandrian Library, founded by Ptolemy I some time around 300 BCE, represented an attempt to gather together the whole of the world's knowledge for the use of scholars. Callimachus created a catalogue of the library's holdings, listing works alphabetically by author. In medieval Europe, parchment manuscripts, in codex format, were jealously guarded in monasteries. Each monastery built up its own collection, resulting in what was in effect a large distributed library, with scholars travelling to read the manuscripts they wished to consult.

When printing with movable type was invented there was a flood of literature and previously tiny libraries began to grow. As the scientific revolution took hold university and royal libraries started to become significant, taking on many of the characteristics that are recognizable in today's libraries. The purpose of the library started to change, with greater emphasis moving to the communication of ideas. As time went on, its social role became prominent – it was noteworthy, for example, that a library formed the central service of most of the Mechanics' Institutes established in Britain in the early 19th century. Later, in Victorian Britain, the new public libraries gave widespread access to a wealth of literature which had previously been available only to the privileged upper and middle classes. In the 20th century new information-handling technologies appeared in rapid succession, from punched cards through microfilm to digital objects of myriad types. Libraries found themselves challenged to organize and exploit these technologies.

Today we are awash with information objects, from web pages through books, newspapers, video and audio to immersive multimedia packages. Economic activity is increasingly dependent on the trading and utilization of information and knowledge: it is reported that 'exports of knowledge-based services trebled from 1995 to 2005, while knowledge-based employment has risen from 30% of employment in 1990 to 41% today' (Hutton, 2007).

In these circumstances it might be expected that the role of libraries would have been strengthened. Whether that role is seen in terms of collecting and preserving valuable cultural artefacts, the provision of access to information sources, putting in place the infrastructure needed to enable people to access resources for themselves, or enabling people to develop the skills needed to be proficient information users, surely the place of the library is assured?

Yet, somehow, this doesn't seem to be the case. Libraries are challenged as never before. Decades of public endorsement during which the accepted rhetoric spoke almost without question of libraries as 'a good thing' (the academic library, for example, was 'the heart of the university') have given way to uncertainty and a sense of vulnerability.

Libraries are changing. Many changes are driven by technology, but others are responses to societal opportunities and governmental pressures or are a result of deliberate attempts to reposition library services in relation to those serving similar needs.

This book is concerned both with documenting significant changes which are taking place in librarianship and with the process of achieving change. It is not a 'how to do it' manual for library managers. What it attempts to do is to sketch out the critical theoretical and practical underpinning for future libraries and to suggest ways in which new kinds of service can be built on these foundations.

It has been noticeable during the early years of this century that much discussion about libraries has been focused on their place in their broader environments rather than on their internal organization and structures. Thus the library as a way of providing access to information debates how it can compete with Google and other search engines. The library as a cultural centre positions itself alongside other cultural agencies, including museums and galleries, and defines itself within that broader spectrum. The library as an enabler of learning leans heavily on formal institutions, be they universities, colleges or schools, and tries to define its contribution with reference to pedagogical principles. The library as the preserver of information sources becomes heavily involved in digital curation. The library as a social space draws on architectural concepts of space, contests the relevance of the example of retail outlets like bookshops and debates virtual approaches such as social networking, typified by services like MySpace and YouTube.

The driving forces behind these ways of thinking about libraries are many and varied. They arise in part from the ways in which technology has insinuated itself into everyday life, so that for many people to search for information is to Google, and to connect with friends is to text. They arise through a worldwide search for new types of community and thus the urge to re-establish community identity. They arise because of the huge strides made in gaining acceptance of inclusion as a guiding principle for civilized societies. They arise because of the emphasis on learning throughout life, as a means of maintaining work and life skills.

There is also considerable evidence that the potential users of libraries are changing and approaching the use of information in new ways. This is most obvious in the case of younger people, among what is sometimes referred to as the Net Generation. Young people are now emerging from tertiary education having grown up with digital technologies. John Seely Brown addresses this generation in the following terms:

> As members of the Net Generation, you are entering a world that needs you. But be aware that much of this world will find your ways of working, learning and socializing quite bizarre. You are digital natives. We – the grey beards, the baby boomers and the gen X-ers – are digital immigrants and our practices will need to evolve rapidly to keep up with yours. . . . You breathe bits of information as easily as my generation breathes air.
>
> (Brown, 2005)

Nor is this generation homogeneous. A recent Demos report suggests that there are at least four identifiable 'types' of technology user among young people:

- *Digital pioneers* were blogging before the phrase had been coined

- *Creative producers* are building websites, posting movies, photos and music to share with friends, family and beyond
- *Everyday communicators* are making their lives easier through texting and MSN
- *Information gatherers* are Google and Wikipedia addicts, 'cutting and pasting' as a way of life.

(Green and Hannon, 2007)

It is also important to recognize that there is significant 'leakage' of technology usage between generations. While most young people are heavy users of texting, for example, this does not mean that text communication is limited to this generation. Furthermore, some of this generation do not or rarely use text. Libraries can use these analyses to identify some relevant trends but few new developments are pervasive and they rarely displace older technologies. What results is a complex web of content creation, information behaviours and enabling hardware and software infrastructures which are continually interacting and modifying expectations and demands.

The information society

The set of theories and observations which underpins much discussion of the transformation accompanying technological change generally goes by the term 'the information society'. While this is, in many ways, a simplistic tag to apply to a complex situation, it has to be acknowledged that hardly a day goes by without further evidence emerging of the revolutionary changes across all sectors of society being introduced by the impact of information and communication technologies (ICTs). The word 'revolutionary' is used here deliberately to convey the idea that this is not a process of gentle evolution, nor even one of carefully planned change. Revolutions involve massive change, the adoption of totally new paradigms, the loss of much that has been taken for granted and the introduction of innovations which were never thought possible. Instant, pervasive access to the world's information from the home, from the workplace and while on the move raises questions about the structures which have been developed to organize and make available information in the past. Why does the world still need libraries? Are they not the 21st century's equivalent of the 19th century's canals – an intermediate technology to be consigned to near oblivion: canals by the railways, libraries by the world wide web?

Bell's *The Coming of the Post-Industrial Society* (1973) is often cited as the foundation text for this view, the first comprehensive analysis of the changes which are destroying industrial society and replacing it with the post-industrial, variously described by epithets such as 'information', 'knowledge' or 'learning'. Bell wrote that 'knowledge and information [have] become the strategic and transforming resources'. His contribution has been recognized as 'the dominant context for thinking about information and society' (Schement and Curtis, 1995) and, while some have criticized the coherence of his theories – Duff (1998), for example, concludes that 'his theory fails as a synthesis . . . failing to assimilate each of the elements properly (and leaving) some parts of the theory overblown and others underdeveloped' – his place in information society development is assured.

Many writers since Bell have echoed his theme, and many have stressed that what is happening is not simply the effect of a single new technology. It is the convergence of a variety of technologies – which together may be termed 'digital' – that provides the opportunity to develop new forms of relationships between people and organizations, largely independent of time and place. It is easy to forget that it is little more than a century since the telegraph displaced the ocean liner as the fastest way to do business across the Atlantic. De Kerckhove (1997) writes thus:

> Whether we call it the Net, the Internet, or the Information Highway, the growing synergy of networked communications is, with the exception of language itself, the communication medium par excellence – the most comprehensive, the most innovative, and the most complex of them all. . . . In the mega-convergence of hypertext, multimedia, virtual reality, neural networks, digital agents, and even artificial life, each medium is changing different parts of our lives – our modes of communication, entertainment and work – but the Net changes all of that and more, all at once. The Internet gives us access to a live, quasi-organic environment of millions of human intelligences perpetually at work on anything and everything with potential relevance to anyone and everybody.

Castels (1998) echoes these thoughts:

> Networks constitute the new social morphology of our societies, and the diffusion of network logic substantially modifies the operation and the outcomes in processes of production, experience, power and culture.

An important characteristic of digital technologies, which arises through networking, is that they are interactive rather than unidimensional. Users expect to be able to interact with services, at the simplest level by repeated querying, but increasingly by becoming 'immersed' in the experience. By engaging both with services and with one another, users become producers of content as much as consumers of it. They become arbiters of quality and of what is acceptable and useful. Social networking services have built huge popularity on this concept. As Green and Hannon (2007) comment:

> There is nothing new about young people being creative and expressive – you certainly do not need a computer to decorate your bedroom, form a band or decide which clothes to wear. The difference is that by digitizing their creative efforts this generation of young people can share the fruits of their labour with a worldwide audience.

The emergence of the approach and group of technologies loosely characterized as Web 2.0 (discussed in more detail in Chapter 10) is also of critical significance. While it is difficult to find a consensus on exactly what Web 2.0 means, there is general understanding that it refers to the shift towards a perception of the internet as a platform (in place of Web 1.0's reliance on the individual workstation's operating system) with applications being served from the website to the end user, collating content in accordance with the individual user's wishes and interests. Web 2.0 is sometimes used synonymously with the *semantic web*, in which the focus is on content containing descriptions which enable it to be processed by machine, thus enabling software applications to display a measure of intelligence. Once content is tagged with meaning, software can build new products without human intervention. Service-oriented architectures (SOA) enable components to perform their tasks without prior knowledge of a particular functional requirement, thus opening up content and services to new applications. Instead of monolithic systems, Web 2.0 supports a vast, ever-changing and almost anarchic array of customized end-user services, constrained only by compliance to agreed technical standards and developers' imaginations and ingenuity.

As a result, these developments shift us away from passive services towards approaches which are highly adaptive to individual wants, needs and desires. The intelligence becomes wrapped up in the service, rather than in the human intermediary. The significance of this for traditional services, like libraries, which rely heavily on human expertise, cannot be overstated.

Libraries can seem to be falling victim to these changes, unintended casualties of the information revolution. The term 'library' is either lost or changes its meaning beyond recognition. After all, if 'connected intelligence' (the title of De Kerckhove's book) underpins the future, is there any place for old ways of recording and organizing intelligence, knowledge or human memory? Would it perhaps be best if librarians bowed to the inevitable and found themselves new skills and new niches in the information society?

> Five years ago, the library at my laboratory used to occupy several large rooms and employ 30 people. It has been replaced by a digital library that is now ten times bigger – and growing fast. This digital library is staffed by only 12 of the original librarians who are now amongst the best html programmers in the company. This digital library has become an essential part of our lives and the work output has gone up tenfold in 10 years.
>
> (Cochrane, 1999)

So, at the outset, it should be stated that libraries as we have known them are under threat; however, it does not look like it. To enter any academic or public library in almost any part of the world is to be greeted by a scene not that different from what would have met a visitor half a century ago. Admittedly the serried ranks of card catalogue cabinets have been replaced by computer screens, but the bulk of the space is still occupied by books and journals on shelves, by reader tables and by staff areas where books are issued and returned, new books acquired and added to the collection and reader enquiries answered. What is more, despite some decline in usage statistics in some sectors, libraries remain popular. The public library, we are constantly told, is among the most heavily used of local public services. But, underneath all this activity, the ground is shifting.

The loss of the core business?

Technological change is incredibly fast – the PC is little more than 25 years old, the world wide web less than 15. The threats are significant, and their impact on libraries as they currently exist could be devastating – their core business could be about to disappear. Consider the following:

1 New publishing paradigms

Scientists, engineers, social scientists and researchers in the humanities, who together provide the vast majority of content for academic journals, now take electronic publication as a matter of course and are starting to make serious use of alternative publication methods, based on electronic archives and various e-print services. Institutional and subject repositories are becoming established and work is ongoing to provide 'seamless' access to their content. While the academic journal is hardly likely to disappear altogether, the role of the library is changing – and thus under threat – in two ways:

- As more and more journals switch to electronic publication, the library's role is reduced to providing pointers to content held elsewhere, thus losing its custodial role. Increasingly, mechanisms used to direct users to such resources are outside the individual library's control – witness Google Scholar as an example. One recent study concluded that there were 'no significant differences between sources obtained through Google Scholar and the university library's catalogue of electronic resources' (Helms-Park, Radia and Stapleton, 2007).
- The maintenance of the repository may become someone else's responsibility unless libraries lobby hard for it to remain part of their remit (as, to be fair, many are doing). However, with subject and national repositories this is not easy. The latter model has been adopted in some fields, for example with the UK's higher and further education learning objects repository, the Jorum (www.jorum.ac.uk). As Van de Sompel and Lagoze (2000) state: 'the explosive growth of the Internet has given scholars almost universal access to a communication medium that facilitates sharing of results', while 'the slow turn-around of the traditional publishing model [is] an impediment to collegial sharing'. As that impediment is removed, libraries' positions become vulnerable.

2 Expansion of bookshops

Bookshops are more successful than ever before. They fall into three types:

- The high street bookshop has been taking business away from the public library for years – by providing a wide range of *new* books which customers are encouraged to *own* as opposed to the grubby specimens libraries allow them to borrow; by providing pleasant surroundings, including comfortable armchairs, where customers can linger; and by providing ancillary services like coffee shops with a large choice of lattes, cappuccinos and espressos to attract an affluent clientèle. Of course some libraries are adopting these models and doing so successfully, but most have not.

- Every charity shop in the high street has entered the business of second-hand bookselling. Virtually all mass market fiction and non-fiction is as readily available from this source as from the public library. Because the unit price is low, and in any case represents a charitable donation, the effective price advantage the library offers is reduced. Given that most charity shops manage to operate from prime high-street locations, it is not surprising that they have captured significant market share.
- Internet bookshops are providing access to an enormous range of discounted stock which they deliver direct to the customer's door. Amazon and other internet retailers are adept at targeted marketing to their established clientèle, and also encourage customers to contribute reviews and thus create an interactive experience. What is the lesson for libraries from the idea that Amazon's founder implemented? Jeff Bezo realized that not only does the internet allow a retailer to interact directly with a customer wherever that customer happens to be – and particularly from the comfort of home or office – and not only can an online retailer offer stock before acquiring it from the wholesaler, but as the business grows it does not have to invest more in bricks and mortar: 'If a chain of 1,000 stores wants to double sales . . . it has to open *another* thousand stores, with all the land and manpower costs that that entails. But once an online operation gets past the fixed cost of its Web site and distribution channel, it can handle bigger sales with very few extra expenses' (Levy, 1999). Contrast this with the UK public library experience where space devoted to stock, and thus choice, has been seriously reduced, not least to make way for PCs (which customers can use to order from Amazon!).

3 E-commerce

What is true of online bookshops holds good for the wider world of e-commerce. Of course, as yet it represents only a fraction of the total economy, but it is growing rapidly and it is reasonable to suppose that once people become used to e-shopping for one commodity they will have few inhibitions about adopting it for others. Given the efforts being made by banks to switch their customers to electronic accounts, which are far cheaper to service than either high-street or postal accounts, the knock-on or trickle-down effects are unlikely to be much delayed. With the constant promotion of e-government, a further boost is given to the habit of transacting personal business online. Add to that the renaissance of grocery deliveries to the home (sadly no longer by a lad on a bike!) and the trend is clear.

Where e-commerce scores heavily is in the service sector, the very sector which most libraries occupy. Finance, travel and information are particularly suited to transactions in cyberspace. Of course not everyone has internet access at home – yet. But this is again a transitional issue. It is unlikely to be long before internet access is as pervasive as television. So there is little future in building a business on the assumption that customers will continue to visit a physical building – unless there are other services there to attract them.

The main difficulty for the individual library is that of scale. Successful e-commerce services are almost always large scale – at least national and often global. Individual libraries can compete only if they work together to develop, deliver and constantly improve attractive and useful services. Can they do so?

4 Interactive television services

As yet digital television has made only a limited impact, doing little more than replace analogue broadcasts and expand the number of channels, and thus the amount of content, offered. Truly interactive services alongside the convergence of technologies are, however, starting to change the picture. In early 2007, Virgin launched an integrated digital video, broadband and telecommunications service in the UK consumer marketplace. The whole nature of television programming is changing with a move away from the idea of 'channels' broadcasting programmes at set times; instead there are databanks ('libraries') of available programmes for each viewer to choose from at will. The DVD recorder will soon be seen as an interesting example of an intermediate technology whose purpose has disappeared. Where will libraries fit into such a world, especially if video on demand expands to include text and audio on demand?

5 Social networking

One of the most significant recent developments has been the rise of social networking. Although the term has been in use for over 50 years to describe individuals' relationships with others, depicting each individual as a node with multiple ties to others, it has more recently been used for the ways in which people, and young people in particular, use technology to build relationships within a global virtual space.

There is now a significant number of social networking websites, with many millions of registered users. Initially, they developed from a circle of friends who sent out invitations to their friends and so on, building up a large user base very rapidly. The best known example is probably MySpace (www.myspace.com) which began in mid-2003 and was bought by News Corporation in July 2005. A much noted feature of this site was the way it went from an internet start-up to a $500 million corporation within two years. Each MySpace user has a profile containing personal information such as images, interests and school attended, and can include a blog. By inviting friends the user builds up a network of users who can view each others' profiles and blogs, exchange messages and bulletins etc. in privacy, i.e. user information (unless set to public) cannot be viewed by anyone who has not been invited to join. In addition to these circles of friends, it is possible to set up a 'group' with a common page, moderated by an individual who controls membership. The result is a huge number of small and large social networks, exchanging a vast amount of information every day. More recent developments include access via mobile devices and instant messaging.

A related development is exemplified by YouTube. Here the emphasis is on creating objects (usually video) and making them available to anyone who wants to view them – a showcase for individual creativity. Objects become popular, through mechanisms that are attracting considerable interest from researchers, and receive huge numbers of downloads. While quality is a real issue, the particular importance of YouTube and services like it lies in the way it closes the gap between content creation and use.

Why should libraries feel threatened by these developments? There are at least three reasons. Firstly, social networking is a new way of creating communities which are not based on physical proximity. If libraries focus on their physical presence there is a mismatch between their understanding of community and that of their potential users. Secondly, social networking services are widely used by some potential library users, such as students, to share information and discuss school, college or university assignments. Because they are operating in cyberspace, such use will tend to include the sharing of electronic resources which are freely available rather than offline or restricted access materials. Thirdly, sites which support the creation of content, such as YouTube, are also presenting commercial content under licence which might previously only have been available on subscription or through a library service. While most of this content is currently entertainment oriented, it seems inconceivable that the opportunity to deliver ever broader ranges of content will be neglected for long.

6 Online learning environments

Learning environments are being developed which deliberately integrate all kinds of learning support. Whether these are to be found in schools, in colleges, in universities, in local learning centres or in cyberspace, they are built on the foundations of modern pedagogical principles which imply that the student is at the centre and is learning actively rather than absorbing information passively. Support no longer means a separate library but rather the integration of largely online, multimedia resources into the learning experience. The role of the librarian, as expert in information sources and information skills, becomes an integral part of the role of the tutor. Librarians may, and do, claim that they have a vital role to play as a part of the tutorial team, but remarkably few teachers are on record as sharing a similar view of libraries. And how many librarians are qualified teachers? Is it not more likely that teachers will develop their own information and information skills expertise? If this happens, the library will lose any direct role in teaching and will have to rely on tutors to point students to its services. Since learning objects may become increasingly self-contained and wrapped in purpose-built presentations, it could become very difficult for 'external' services to expose their content within the virtual learning environment (VLE).

7 Mobile communications

The explosive growth of mobile telephone usage can be seen as an indicator of one of the most likely technological developments of the next few years, namely the replacement of place-based by place-independent telecommunications, and thus services. Without suggesting that fixed line and wireless technologies will not have a future, what is clear is that more and more products – by which we must mean information products – will be delivered over mobile communications channels. In April 2000 major global telecommunications companies bid £22 billion – something approaching 10% of the size of the UK's total national debt – for the third generation of mobile communications licences, equivalent, on optimistic forecasts, to about £14 per month per expected subscriber over a ten-year period. While companies have yet to turn a profit on this investment, it illustrates the anticipated value and anticipated market penetration of the services to be delivered.

Investment in hardware devices also demonstrates the trend that major international corporations perceive. At the time of writing in 2007, Apple had just announced the iPhone, a clear attempt to move away from dependence on computer and music playback devices to more integrated technologies with mobile communications at the core. In making this move the company is responding to a market described by the Demos report in the following terms: 'the generation of young people who do not remember life without the instant answers of the internet or the immediate communication of mobile phones . . . [were] slightly bemused by our questions. Why would anyone want to ask about computers and mobile phones? Aren't they just part of everyday life?' (Green and Hannon, 2007). Again we have to ask: do libraries' business models fit with this communications paradigm?

8 Print on demand

There has been a trend among publishers in recent years towards 'print-on-demand' approaches, especially where titles are expected to sell slowly and/or in small numbers. Digital printing technologies are now mature enough to enable a book to be printed from an electronic file when it is required, rather than in anticipation of demand. The technology is not entirely stable yet, of course, and the products do not have the sophistication of full colour reproduction and designer bindings – otherwise presumably there would be no one left publishing 'just in case'. It is also true that the technology is taking much longer to mature and achieve significant market penetration than was expected, yet there is clear movement. For example, Cambridge University Press reports that it 'has responded to the burden of printing costs and the growth of demand for backlist titles, stimulated by online bookselling, by placing more than 7,000 titles in a Short-run Printing Programme with specialist printers. These books, almost entirely academic titles, comprise both those which are too expensive to reprint conventionally and a growing number of titles that were out of print and have now been brought back into print with limited stock. The quality of the short-run printing has steadily improved to approach that of conventional printing' (Cambridge University Press, 2006).

While the implications for libraries are as yet unclear, it does look as if serious competition could arise from this source. Some booksellers are currently able to offer a limited service of this type and it must be expected that this will increase. A major factor in determining the impact on libraries could be the penetration of this approach in the student textbook (academic libraries) and popular fiction (public libraries) markets.

9 Dynamic and transitory information sources

Libraries' roles in collecting and preserving the heritage of the world are threatened on a number of fronts, and not only by pervasive technologies which favour instant communication. Lehmann (2004) has observed:

> Four major developments can be noted that favour momentary memory as opposed to collective memory:
>
> - globalization accompanied by world-wide networking and opportunities for communication that generate a flood of images and information – entirely independent of place and time;
> - media transience, which fosters simultaneity, interactivity and openness to anything and everything but cannot communicate permanence, public openness and selectivity;
> - the disappearance of a shared canon of cultural and intellectual heritage, the body of literature and art from which collective memory draws its identity;
> - the unmistakable tendency to favour economic rather than cultural perspectives.

Libraries are struggling to determine what their roles and responsibilities should be in a world where so many information sources are place-independent, dynamic and transitory. The question, not yet satisfactorily answered, is why any one library should take responsibility for any particular globally available information product.

10 The unknown

Finally, there is the threat of the unknown:

- In the 1960s, when it became apparent that libraries could use mainframe computers for their administrative processes, few were predicting that within 30 years computers with greater power would be on every user's desk and in every user's briefcase.
- In the 1970s few recognized that the future lay in end-user searching of remote databases.
- In the 1980s no one predicted the impact of the web, with its matter-of-fact interlinking of users and information sources, based on the principle that, in the words of its inventor, 'once someone somewhere made available a

document, database, graphic, sound, video or screen at some stage in an interactive dialogue, it should be accessible . . . by anyone, with any type of computer, in any country' (Berners-Lee, 1999).

- In the 1990s the rise of Google took everyone by surprise – a commercial information retrieval service able to make huge profits from its 'killer' application.
- In the first decade of this century, social networking services, as already described, seemed to appear from nowhere to engage almost everyone under 25 in the developed world.

It is (by definition!) impossible to know what the next unexpected, ground-shifting invention will be; all that can be said with certainty is that there will be one. However, given that all the other inventions in this sphere have posed at the least challenges and more usually threats to traditional libraries, it would be surprising if the unknown did not follow the same course. Will libraries respond by installing the technology and marketing these as-yet-unknown products themselves? Past experience would suggest that they are more likely to allow another player to capture the market.

These ten points are deliberately presented as threats and are deliberately couched in provocative terms. They are presented in this way to reinforce the point that there is a real crisis for libraries and that it is very close. They could also be reinforced by the observation that most of these points are in essence step changes and qualitative effects. However, what may be of even more importance are the gradual quantitative effects which, because they have become familiar, may appear to have been allowed for already. Internet usage is doubling every six, nine or 12 months – depending on how it is measured and who is doing the reporting, although the period doesn't really matter. The fable of the Chinese emperor who managed to lose his kingdom by offering to give away a grain of rice on the first square of a chessboard, two on the second, four on the third and so on – before realizing that by the end of the first half of the board he would have given away more than a thousand million grains – is a useful reminder of how doubling can have an unexpected large-scale impact.

Libraries: unprepared for change?

These are not the only threats to libraries; others are of librarians' own making:

- The technology is complex and librarians have not developed the skills to understand it, exploit it or create it. Those few who do have such skills find they have a very marketable commodity and can make a much better living elsewhere.

- Libraries are expensive and becoming more expensive. The competition, at least in some of its forms, is cheap: the whole of the world wide web, including complex multimedia, is available for a very modest outlay. For example, in the UK the annual cost of a home broadband connection is now less than that of an annual TV licence. What is more, web content looks good even if in the end much of it is disappointing. In the glamour stakes, libraries haven't yet reached the starting-gate!
- Libraries are their own worst enemies. While the competition hots up they find themselves closing branches and reducing opening hours. Grandiose claims to be 'the people's universities' are simply not borne out by the facts. In this case it is the Emperor's new clothes that provides the apposite fable.

Over 20 years ago Lancaster wrote:

> Ultimately . . . libraries as we know them seem likely to disappear. Facilities will still exist to preserve the print-on-paper record of the past, of course, but they will be more like archives, or even museums, providing little in the way of public service. As for the electronic sources, libraries may have an interim role to play . . . In the longer term, it seems certain that the libraries will be bypassed. That is, people will have very little reason to visit libraries in order to gain access to information sources.
>
> (Lacaster, 1983)

Beyond technology

And yet, one is left asking whether all this technology-based analysis is adequate. Is it simply a case of the now discredited 'technological determinism', the belief that technology will determine the future? Is what we are seeing simply another step in a process of human and societal evolution which is far less pervasive and far less influential than technology acolytes would have us believe? The demise of paper as a medium of communication, to take one example, has been prophesied again and again. Not only has it failed to happen, but world consumption has in fact increased many times over. In their extensive treatment of this issue, Harris and Hanna (1993) remark:

> While it seems undeniable that we are dealing with a new 'social framework' in Bell's sense, it also appears clear that we must find some way to transcend the two most common reactions to the information society – 'the complacent (yet delirious) camp-following celebration' or the 'moralizing condemnation' so common in our literature . . . we must find a way to confront critically and intervene intelligently in the process of change sweeping our society and, more explicitly, our profession.

Toffler (1980) commented, in his influential volume *The Third Wave*, that even today we cannot reach agreement on the causes of the first Industrial Revolution over 300 years ago:

> Each academic guild or philosophical school has its own preferred explanation. The technological determinists point to the steam engine, the ecologists to the destruction of Britain's forests, the economists to fluctuations in the price of wool. Others emphasise religious or cultural changes, the Reformation, the Enlightenment, and so on.

The sociology of the Information Revolution is a massive subject with its own extensive literature which goes far beyond the scope of this book. But it is right, at the outset, to acknowledge that the forces shaping the profession of librarianship and the design of libraries are not solely technological. There are massive cultural, social, psychological and philosophical forces at work: our views and understandings of the world are very different from those of our predecessors. The users of libraries come now with expectations far removed from those of their forebears, and technology is only partly the explanation. It is also true that a proportion of our understanding of the foundations of librarianship is based on myth: libraries have never given access to anything more than a small proportion of the world's information. Perhaps their continued inability to do so will not after all mean that they are doomed to irrelevance.

Conclusion

However the present role of libraries may be defined, and this is the issue which will occupy the first part of this book, it must be clear that as participants in the information 'business' they will be deeply affected by the changes that are taking place around them. They are among the best examples of 'information-based organizations' – selecting information, acquiring it, organizing it, storing it, making it available – at the present time. Does this signify a central role in the new dispensation? Or are they becoming anachronisms, the 21st-century equivalent of the Zeppelin? Many writers have commented on these issues, and many of these contributions will be examined later. But before those questions can be answered it is necessary to explore in greater detail what it is that libraries do, and why, and how, before turning to consider what roles they might usefully be able to play in the future.

2

What is a library? The view from the sectors

> Libraries play a vital role in the world's systems of communication and education. The numerous resources and services that libraries provide help people carry out their work, studies, and leisure-time activities. Libraries rank among society's most important and useful cultural institutions. . . . Libraries provide access to knowledge and information that has been accumulated throughout history. People of all ages and all walks of life – including students, teachers, scientists, business executives, and government officials – use library resources for their work. In addition, large numbers of people turn to libraries to satisfy a desire for knowledge, to pursue a hobby, or to read in their free time.
>
> (*World Book Encyclopedia*, 2007, www.worldbook.com/wb/Article?id=ar322340&st=library)

Introduction

The key concepts in the above description are *communication*, *education*, *information* and *knowledge*, but it also makes clear that libraries provide a very wide variety of activities and services for people of 'all ages and all walks of life'. The aim of this chapter is to explore in some detail what it is that libraries are actually *for* – what purpose they serve in society – as perceived by practitioners and policy-makers in the various sectors, and to begin to examine how external influences are forcing a rethink of these roles.

Because libraries seek to serve groups of users, it is not surprising to find that they are most usually organized sectorally. For example, members of universities form a large user group and the academic library has been developed with their needs in mind. School libraries are different because they focus on the needs of children in their learning environments. Libraries serving commercial and industrial organizations differ again, as they usually have a much tighter subject focus and a closely defined clientele. So we could continue, but the critical point is that the nature of the library is influenced, more than anything else, by its user group.

Examining what each sector regards as the key role of the library therefore helps us to identify both what libraries of different types have in common and their significant differences.

The view from the sectors 1: national libraries

The development of national libraries has, not surprisingly, followed a variety of patterns, although a common route in Europe has been through royal collections: the Kungliga Biblioteket or Royal Library in Stockholm provides a typical example of this development. King Gustav Vasa is usually credited with starting the collection in the 1520s. His sons, Erik XIV, Johan III and Karl IX, added to it, and by 1587 a corridor lined with bookshelves, known as the 'Green Corridor', had been set up in a Palace attic. In 1661 legal deposit was enacted with all publishers in Sweden required to deposit two copies, one in the Royal Library and the other in the Royal Archives. The main reason for this appears to have been nothing to do with preservation or national bibliographic completeness but simply as a means of censoring, or at least checking up on, publishers and authors. Further additions to the Library came as a result of Swedish conquests abroad (the *Codex gigas*, or *Devil's Bible*, dating from the 13th century, perhaps the Library's greatest treasure, was acquired from Prague in this way) and the confiscation of books owned by religious houses during the Reformation.

In a similar vein, the British Museum Library's foundation collection, that of Sir Hans Sloane, was greatly enhanced when the royal collection was added in 1757 and then further enhanced with the collection of George III in 1823. Republics have taken a slightly different route, with the national library often developing as an adjunct of government, as with the Library of Congress in the USA, established in 1800 as a legislative library. The Australian National Library had similar antecedents, being separated from the Commonwealth Parliamentary Library in 1961.

The role of the modern national library was established during the 19th century, with the then librarian of the British Museum, Antony Panizzi, providing leadership. His key achievements may still be seen as marking out the ground that a national library should occupy. He:

- secured an annual block grant from the Treasury, thus establishing the principle that the national library should be funded on a permanent basis through general taxation

- enforced legal deposit, the system whereby the national library was entitled to a copy of every book published in the country
- employed a network of agents to purchase foreign works for the library, thus establishing that while the collection would not be comprehensive in such works, it was a function of the national library to provide access to a representative selection of non-indigenous works
- established the formal '91 rules' for the construction of the library catalogue
- fought for, and established, the principle of access for all who needed it
- established that the fundamental purpose of a national library was educational
- secured appropriate accommodation for the national library and ensured that this was of high status – the Round Reading Room in Bloomsbury came to stand for the concept of a national library for many, leading eventually to a strong rearguard action by readers when the Library transferred to its new and modern building at St Pancras.

The functions of national libraries have been set out in a number of guideline documents by the United Nations Educational, Scientific and Cultural Organization (UNESCO) in association with the International Federation of Library Associations and Institutions (IFLA). Although these probably do not give the prominence they should to the impacts of information technologies, they usefully give due weight to the needs of developing countries. For example, Lor (1997), drawing on the work of Line and Line (1979) and IFLA (1992), establishes three 'dimensions' to the work of a national library, identifying functions concerned with:

1 Heritage
   - acquisition, comprehensive bibliographic recording and preservation of a complete collection of material published in and relating to the country
   - document access through direct services to in-house and remote users based on its own collections
   - reference and information service (primarily relating to the library's collections)
   - research and development relating to its own collections, systems etc.
   - heritage promotion: raising awareness of the library's collections, including exhibitions, conferences, publications, etc.
2 Infrastructure
   - serving as a national preservation centre, including planning and

co-ordinating preservation activities in the country's libraries and providing a conservation service
- serving as the national bibliographic agency
- national collection management
- national availability of publications, including national and international interlending systems
- national reference and information services
- professional and technological leadership
- national planning and co-ordination, with an emphasis on resource sharing, standardization and international liaison
- formal and informal education and training (depending on the LIS educational facilities available in the country)
- commissioned and sponsored research and development on matters of national importance
- assisting other libraries in the country in heritage promotion
- promotion of information awareness among the broad population, including literacy promotion, information literacy, etc.

3 Delivery of a comprehensive national library service
- acquisition and processing of library material for other libraries
- recycling and disposing of material acquired for other libraries
- central support of reference, consultation, loan and document delivery services by other libraries
- system-wide professional and technological leadership
- advice to other libraries
- system-wide planning and co-ordination
- research and development relating to the development of the service
- literacy programmes: using constituent and affiliated libraries as centres for literacy promotion.

Most national libraries still enjoy the benefits (and of course disadvantages) of legal deposit of printed materials. In some cases, the privilege has been extended to new media and in particular electronic objects. In the UK the Legal Deposit Libraries Act 2003 is still, at the time of writing, being implemented. As 'enabling legislation' its provisions can only come into force once the government publishes regulations: so far these have not appeared. However, the Act does introduce the principle that all publications should be subject to legal deposit, and until it is fully in force a voluntary code is being operated by the legal deposit libraries. The focus is on offline electronic materials, although national libraries are also collaborating on selective archiving of websites. They are also involved in initiatives like the Internet Archive (www.archive.org) and the European Web Archive (http://europarchive.org).

The question of preservation and conservation looms large on the national library agenda since a core responsibility is to ensure that the national bibliography is preserved for future generations. Clearly it will continue to be essential to conserve and preserve valuable objects from the past. The relationship of this national library function to those of other heritage institutions, such as museums, has been stressed in the strategic planning of IFLA's National Libraries Section. Thus in the 2006–7 Strategic Plan, the first goal is:

> To promote the universal availability of information by such activities as encouraging the creation and building of national libraries, the development of national legislation for national libraries – especially legal deposit dispositions and preservation activities – and to promote the convergence of information and heritage institutions.
>
> (IFLA National Libraries Section, 2007)

The role of providing bibliographic access, in effect that of describing the contents of the national bibliography, is one which has become more difficult with increasing numbers of publications, globalization and the explosion of non-print media. It is hard to see that the justification for concentrating, in bibliographic terms, on paper-based products can be sustained even in the medium term. Further, it is by no means obvious, at a time when other agencies have taken on – albeit imperfectly – the task of describing electronic resources, that the national library is the only appropriate focus for this work. While the production of the national bibliography of 'traditional' materials may be a continuing and necessary role, it is questionable whether that will be enough to justify the investment. Even the work of most national libraries of acting as 'honest broker' in the development of appropriate standards is under threat as the globalization of MAchine-Readable Cataloguing (MARC), and standardization on USMARC for most purposes, continues on the one hand while the standardization process for descriptions of non-print materials is pursued in other fora such as the W3C's Resource Description Framework (RDF).

Because the volume of publications – even counting only traditional media – continues to grow, national libraries continue to face the problem of how to cope with all the material they receive and select. For them the option of withdrawing material and discarding it is rarely open – they provide national back-up services and other libraries treat them as libraries of last resort. As a result it is not surprising that recent decades have seen a spate of building – the British Library finally opened its new premises at St Pancras in 1998, to be followed a year later by the Bibliothèque Nationale in Paris, while a spectacular new national library opened in Singapore in 2005. Die Deutsch Bibliothek opened in Frankfurt-am-Main in 1997. At the opening ceremony Hermut Kohl, then German Chancellor, said:

> Libraries have always been a kind of memory for mankind. If the human race did not collect and organise knowledge it would forever lack history. For more than 3,000 years the great libraries have been the manifestation and a basic component of advanced civilizations . . . Libraries have always been the focal point of national identity as well. They provide a polyphonic sounding board for language. Here culture lives in the rhythm of the past and the beat of the present day. Here we can sense the melody of the future.
>
> (Kohl, 1997).

This brings us to an important conclusion from the perspective of the national library. In terms of function – leaving aside medium and content – the national library provides a cultural focal point which transcends the present and reaches into the past, in terms of the 'stuff' it secures, and into the future, in terms of transmitting human knowledge to future generations. It fulfils these roles by collecting a representative, although never comprehensive, set of records and by ensuring that they are organized and preserved so as to remain of use into the future. A national library which fails to build the representative collection or fails to secure its permanence has failed in its duty.

Of course, national libraries cannot shoulder all of this responsibility on their own, and they are joined by major academic and other libraries in a co-operative endeavour which builds on specialisms which have developed over the centuries. In the UK the concept of a 'Distributed National Collection' has been raised a number of times in the past. With the increased importance of electronic resources the emphasis now is more on creating the national infrastructure which can ensure that users can access the full range of resources, and the national libraries play a significant role in this. Good examples of this approach include the Consortium of Research Libraries (CURL), Online Public Access Catalogue (COPAC, http://copac.ac.uk) and the Serials Union Catalogue (SUNCAT, www.suncat.ac.uk). The Research Information Network (RIN), established in 2004 and focused on the needs of researchers, defines its primary purpose as 'to give the strategic leadership required to establish a national framework for research information provision'

(Research Information Network, 2005). It is also charged with leading 'the development of a programme to sustain and enhance management and development of the aggregate UK collection of published hard copy research resources' (ibid.).

Looking to the future, then, it appears that the comprehensiveness of access to published information which national libraries sought to provide is likely to be achieved more through collaborative networks than by individual national libraries. However, this does not downplay the critical role of collecting and preserving the national published heritage and making that heritage available in innovative ways. The British Library has shown, in recent years, how the function of preserving the national published memory and that of broadening and deepening access can be combined, with innovative products like Turning the Pages (www.bl.uk/onlinegallery/ttp/ttpbooks.html) and the Business & Intellectual Property Centre (www.bl.uk/bipc).

The view from the sectors 2: academic libraries

Academic libraries emerged with the modern university during the early middle ages, but were a somewhat neglected part of their parent institutions until at least the 18th century and in many cases much later. The medieval college or university library was small and grew very slowly. Cambridge University Library had only 122 volumes in 1424, but the number was starting to grow – by copying, by purchase, but most importantly by donations and gifts. Scholars would travel from library to library to consult rare and valuable manuscripts, as indeed they still do. This sense of the academic library's role as a centre for scholarly research has persisted to the present.

Fremont Rider described the research library as:

> A vast aggregation of all sorts of book and periodical and manuscript materials, assembled together, not for sustained, or for pleasurable, reading . . . but for 'research', that is, for the purposes of scholarly investigation. Research libraries are, primarily, the stored-up knowledge of the race, warehouses of fact and surmise.
>
> (Rider, 1944)

Writing in 1964, Vernon Clapp observed that academic libraries do not rely solely on their own collections, even if in times past it tended to be the readers rather than the books which moved from place to place:

> [F]rom earliest times two principles have controlled the growth of libraries – the principle of local self-sufficiency and the principle of sharing the resources . . . [Their role is] to enable inquirers to identify library materials relevant to their inquiries and to supply them with copies of these materials for their use.
>
> (Clapp, 1964)

But he noted the impossibility of any academic library achieving self-sufficiency and suggested that the solution might lie in:

> the assignment of specific responsibility for certain conspicuous subjects to particular libraries, each of which would be obliged to acquire comprehensively in the subject, organize and publish its bibliography, and render a nationwide (or perhaps even international) backstopping lending or photocopy service in the subject.
>
> (ibid.)

Such ideas were taken up from time to time, for example, in the 1960s many British university libraries accepted limited responsibility for a particular range of subjects. In this way, each academic library would contribute to the library wealth of the nation. However, such schemes have fallen out of favour, largely for economic reasons. Firstly, when budgets became tight, each library needed to retain the flexibility to manage its acquisitions budgets as it saw fit. Secondly, the over-riding concern of each library had to be to serve its parent institution, reflecting its academic and, in particular, its research strengths.

Nevertheless the idea of the research library as the centre of scholarly activity has persisted; Lyman, for example, has written:

> Research libraries are homes for scholarly communities. . . . Since the turn of the twentieth century, research libraries have provided a sense of order for scholarly research – a center for teaching and research that is local and yet extends across time and even national boundaries.
>
> (Lyman, 1997)

An enduring metaphor for the academic library is that it is the 'heart of the university'. The exact origins of this phrase are unclear, although Grimes (1998) suggests that it was used first by the then President of Harvard University, Charles William Eliot, who was in that post from 1869 to 1909. The image was picked up in the UK and appeared in various reports, including the influential Parry Report of 1967 (University Grants Committee, 1967). However, as Grimes points out, the metaphor has been used loosely and with little evidence that it reflects institutional realities:

> The metaphor implies that the academic library is of unparalleled importance. Despite its persistence for more than one hundred years, there is a considerable distance between the relationship it implies and institutional opinion and practice. Evidence of this difference is found in a number of areas. . . . Students and faculty alike fail to involve library resources and services in regular learning and instruction, turning to the library primarily as an undergraduate study hall or reserve book room. . . . National initiatives . . . fail to mention, much less to plan, improvement of library resources. . . . [There is] a disheartening decrease in academic library share of institutional funding. . . . they remain, for the most part, on the periphery of decision-making and innovative processes. . . . librarians are often not involved in information policy development. . . . In all, the 'library is the heart of the university' metaphor leads librarians and academics to erroneous conclusions about the real relationships between the library and the university.
>
> (Grimes, 1998)

Many other commentaries on the academic library as the centre of scholarly activity neglect the fact that for most university researchers such notions simply do not reflect reality, if they ever did. In fact, the proportion of the scholarly population which relies on access to physical libraries for its raw material – in the sense outlined above – is actually quite small. It is true that scholars in the humanities need to access physical collections which contain original objects – manuscripts, incunabula and the like – but the same is certainly not true in the sciences, in engineering, in professional disciplines and in many of the social sciences. Many scholars in these latter disciplines place a far higher priority on immediacy – on access to the very latest results – and some are developing their own mechanisms to achieve this.

Firstly, e-print archives have mushroomed in popularity in recent years. The tradition of exchanging pre-prints has existed in many of the sciences for a long time. It can be regarded as the foundation of the scientific journal, since the original *Le Journal des Savants* in France and the *Philosophical Transactions of the Royal Society* in the UK were created in 1665 as a means of circulating 'letters' containing scientific results among the research community. More recently the pre-print has been used to counter the problems of long publication lead times in traditional print publications. Such usage is starting to expand not only in quantity but to embrace 'final' versions of papers including peer-reviewed contributions. A considerable impetus was given to this movement by the publication of the Budapest Open Access Initiative (www.soros.org/openaccess/read.shtml) in February 2002 which recommended a dual strategy: open access journals and self-archiving by scholars of their research outputs. Further initiatives followed, including the 2003 Berlin Declaration on Open Access to Knowledge in the Sciences and Humanities (http://oa.mpg.de/openaccess-berlin/berlindeclaration.html) and the UN World Summit on the Information Society Declaration of Principles in December of the same year (www.itu.int/wsis/docs/geneva/official/dop.html). This stated (paragraph 28) that 'we strive to promote universal access with equal opportunities for all to scientific knowledge and the creation and dissemination of scientific and technical information, including open access initiatives for scientific publishing'. The associated Plan of Action (www.itu.int/wsis/docs/geneva/official/poa.html) spoke of encouraging 'initiatives to facilitate access, including free and affordable access to open access journals and books, and open archives for scientific information'. In 2006 and 2007, many influential organizations, including the European Commission, put their weight behind the concept of self-archiving of the final published version of research papers (see, for example, European Commission, 2007).

A small number of e-print repository infrastructure systems, notably DSpace (www.dspace.org) and ePrints (www.eprints.org), became available in the early part of the current decade and have been taken up widely. The adoption of the Sante Fé Convention, later superseded by the Open Archives Initiative Protocol for Metadata Harvesting (OAI-PMH), provided a standards-based framework for this expansion and more widespread adoption of these approaches (see Chapter 10).

These developments call into question the long-term future of the academic journal. Ginsparg's comment is still apposite: 'it is difficult to imagine how the current model of funding publishing companies through research libraries . . . can possibly persist in the long term' (Ginsparg, 1997).

A second issue for academic libraries arises from the wealth of vital information that is simply not published – it appears in what librarians would call the 'grey literature'. This includes reports and papers produced while projects are in progress and, perhaps most important of all, conversational transcripts and raw datasets. For example, most of the information exchange which takes place in major international research projects is now conducted by e-mail, either privately within the research team or using closed or open discussion lists. Much research data is held in shared databases. The mechanisms to facilitate, organize and maintain these media are virtually uninfluenced by libraries and they rarely find their way into library catalogues.

However, there is a third, still more important issue. The massification of higher education has led in recent years to much greater prominence being given to the academic library's role in supporting learning and teaching. It is worth reviewing the events of the last few decades to explore how this has come about.

In the UK, the 1963 Robbins Report (Committee on Higher Education, 1963) set the stage with its mould-breaking statement of principle: 'higher education opportunities should be available to all those who are qualified by ability and attainment to pursue them and who wish to do so'. Robbins recommended massive expansion; the beginning of the end of higher education for the élite and the start of mass higher education. As a result new universities were founded, colleges of advanced technology turned into universities, the Open University was created and, before the end of the 1960s, polytechnics were established as the second half of a binary higher education system. By the mid-1990s the system had been transformed: in 1963 there were only 120,000 students in UK higher education, by 1997 there were 1.6 million.

A similar expansion had occurred somewhat earlier in the USA, as Osburn (1997) noted:

> The Industrial Revolution made it clear that knowledge and education presented an avenue to advancement for those not satisfied with the lot of the assembly line worker. Education became the doorway to options for one's future. The general public in America began to see higher education as useful – thus breaking with European tradition then – and, to varying degrees, this vision has significantly influenced colleges and universities ever since. . . . Unprecedented numbers of those who once would not reasonably have aspired to higher learning and to a place among the professions were attracted to, and accommodated by, the universities.

Back in the UK, the Follett Report (Higher Education Funding Council for England, Scottish Higher Education Funding Council, Higher Education Funding Council for Wales and the Department of Education for Northern Ireland, 1993), set up to examine the impacts of this massive expansion on academic libraries and to recommend solutions, saw the future partly in terms of traditional services – for example, recommending funding for expansion of buildings – and partly in terms of new services delivered through information and communications technologies (ICTs). It also set in train strategic thinking which has enabled libraries to take an institutional lead in some areas, for example in the development of broad, cross-organizational information strategies.

The UK higher education Electronic Libraries Programme (eLib), funded as a result of the Follett Report's IT-related recommendations, was highly significant. A summative evaluation of phases 1 and 2 of the three-phase programme (ESYS, 2000) remarked:

> In 1993 it might have been possible to dismiss the impact of electronic information services on libraries as marginal. This was no longer the case by the end of 1998 by which time the impact on many areas, including the concept of universities themselves, could not be ignored.

The eLib Programme was structured to address what, in 1993, were seen to be the key areas for academic library service development, a view which was largely vindicated by subsequent developments. The major strands of work were:

- electronic document and article delivery
- electronic journals
- on-demand publishing
- access to network resources
- training and awareness.

In phase 3, attention was directed towards hybrid libraries, clumps and preservation of digital objects. Alongside this research and development, the establishment of national agreements enabling all members of UK higher education institutions to access a large range of major datasets, based on the all-important 'free at the point of use' principle, ushered in an era of real resource-sharing and co-operation. At the same time, evidence from statistical returns and other sources demonstrated a continuing high level of demand from students for traditional materials: user satisfaction surveys continued to produce demands for 'more books'.

It was rapidly realized that the next phase of development had to be much more integrated than the project-led approach of eLib. As a result the Joint Information Systems Committee (JISC) launched the Distributed National Electronic Resource (DNER) development programme. The DNER itself was described by the JISC as:

> a managed environment for accessing quality assured information resources on the Internet which are available from many sources. These resources include scholarly journals, monographs, textbooks, abstracts, manuscripts, maps, music scores, still

> images, geospatial images and other kinds of vector and numeric data, as well as moving picture and sound collections.
>
> (JISC, 1999)

The DNER vision was based on the idea that there are four major components which are needed to make electronic resources useful in learning, teaching and research. These are:

- the network technology, including the physical networks that link academic institutions, as well as the internet itself and the world wide web
- digital content, the 'stuff' which can be delivered to the users
- complementary networks: since the academic sector cannot be self-sufficient, developing these networks in a co-ordinated fashion would enable interoperability and hence enhanced services
- a learning society: a broad social environment that places learning (a term which in this context includes research) at the head of its list of priorities.

The DNER was soon renamed the JISC Information Environment (IE) and a series of development programmes was launched to tackle key themes. The overall problem identified was described in the following terms:

> An Information Environment can be characterised as the set of network or online services that support publishing and use of information and learning resources. At the moment online services providing digital resources tend to operate in a stand-alone manner. The user is therefore required to navigate a complex set of different websites with different search interfaces in order to locate relevant resources. Similarly the resources offered tend to be characterised by a lack of mediation to provide vital signposts to explain context and relevance to the user. It has been recognised that this is one of the key features limiting take up of digital resources.
>
> (JISC, 2007a)

The answers to this problem had therefore 'to offer the user a more seamless and less complex journey to relevant information and learning resources' (ibid.). Programmes focused on the development of appropriate infrastructure components (middleware and shared services), resource discovery, digital repositories and digital preservation.

As these programmes progressed it became clear that not only had the information environment itself to be integrated, but information services needed to be made integral to users' working environments. This has led to considerable work on the relationship between information services and e-learning and e-research. Further discussion of this area of work will be found in subsequent chapters.

The above description has focused on the effects of information and communications technologies on the academic library, with good reason, but it has to be recognized that there are other drivers for change. These include the role of library staff in the direct delivery of teaching, especially in relation to information literacies (a topic discussed in Chapter 9), accountability and pressure on resources with the consequent requirement for robust performance measurement (discussed in Chapter 6) and the whole question of the design of the physical library in an age of electronic communications.

The role that academic libraries will play in the future is far from clear. They retain institutional expertise in information organization even if the recognition of this expertise is patchy. Their legacy collections are important and recognized as such. The integration of their services into learning, teaching and research provides perhaps the greatest challenge, with the possible loss of large numbers of researchers as direct users as alternative patterns of scholarly communication emerge. And there remains the question as to what a physical academic library should look like in an age of e-learning and e-research.

The view from the sectors 3: public libraries

Public libraries have a proud heritage. In Britain the key event in the development of public library services was the 1849 report of the Select Committee on Public Libraries. The Committee took evidence from a wide range of interests, although it is notable that, as Murison (1971) has pointed out, many of the proponents of public libraries were concerned more with social control than with the development of individuals' potential or the enhancement of their leisure: 'where witnesses [to the Select Committee] approved the need for the public library they almost unanimously showed themselves to be concerned with its effect as a counter-agent to evils rather than as a positive force for educational or recreational benefit'. Typical was James Buckingham, Member of Parliament for Sheffield, whose hope was that public libraries would 'draw off, by innocent pleasurable recreation and instruction, all who can be thus weaned from habits of drinking, and in whom those habits may not be so deeply rooted as to resist all attempts at this moral method of cure' (ibid.). Public libraries, funded from local authority rates, opened in many towns and cities in the following half-century. The system developed slowly although the

1919 establishment of county libraries was significant in raising standards and, of course, Andrew Carnegie was highly influential in providing funding for buildings. By the time of his death over half the library authorities in Britain had Carnegie libraries.

By the second half of the 20th century there was general agreement around the proposition that the public library fulfilled three interconnected roles: education, information and entertainment. It enabled its users to undertake informal learning as well as providing a place for study, it provided access to organized sources of information on all subjects, and it provided entertainment, primarily through lending fiction. Within these roles libraries developed all manner of specific services: children's libraries; business information services; music libraries; audio and video collections; even toy libraries and at least one example of a pet lending library. However, as budgetary cuts started to bite, and Carnegie's buildings started to show their age, it became apparent that public libraries were struggling to define what this tripartite role really meant in an age of mass communication and mass formal education. Furthermore, while the potential roles they could fulfil were almost numberless, there was little guidance on how they should prioritize their activities so as to be good at doing a limited range of things rather than overstretched trying to do everything.

In recent years there has been a number of attempts to define the role of the public library more precisely. It is interesting that users themselves tend to take a conservative view and to see the public library in quite mechanistic terms. During the VITAL research project, for example, public library users were asked to state their main reason for using the library. Interestingly, even in libraries with relatively well-developed IT facilities, the answers were overwhelmingly 'to borrow books' (Eve and Brophy, 2001).

Policy level studies have, of course, delved much more deeply into the role of the public library and the contribution it makes to society. For example, in 1993 the Comedia consultancy issued a report under the title *Borrowed Time* which concluded that:

> Public libraries are currently making an impact in five main areas of public life:
>
> — EDUCATION Support for self-education and lifelong learning . . .
> Responding to the impact of educational reform, providing space in libraries as homework centres.
>
> — SOCIAL POLICY Acting as an entry point into the wider culture for many of Britain's ethnic minority communities . . . playing a leading part in preserving

> local identities . . . supporting the emotional needs of particular disadvantaged groups in local communities – providing a quiet haven or refuge in the midst of the noisy city.
>
> — INFORMATION Providing more and more information services in a society in which individual rights and the need to know are at a premium . . . Yet unsure of its role in a society in which information is capital and an increasingly expensive commodity.
>
> — CULTURAL ENRICHMENT Providing a choice of books, recorded music, videos across a range of interests; acting as an entry point for children into literacy and 'the book of life', story telling, after school activities, offering a home to art exhibitions.
>
> — ECONOMIC DEVELOPMENT Libraries play a role in developing local business information services and in a wider context, act as a focal point in the town centre mixed economy where retailing alone cannot sustain liveliness and vitality.
>
> (Comedia, 1993)

In 1995, UNESCO issued its *Public Library Manifesto* (IFLA, 1995) which stated that 'the public library, the local gateway to knowledge, provides a basic condition for lifelong learning, independent decision-making and cultural development of the individual and social groups'.

The UK Audit Commission's 1997 report *Due for Renewal* (Audit Commission, 1997) stated that public

> libraries find themselves tackling needs in a number of separate areas:
>
> - recreation and culture (for example, by lending books to people to read for pleasure)
> - learning (for example, by making study materials available for reference and loan)
> - social welfare (e.g. by taking materials to housebound people, or offering a safe and warm place where people can relax)
> - economic development (e.g. by providing business information or by helping individuals with training and jobseeking).

Also in 1997 there was a response from government to a review of the public library service carried out by Aslib two years earlier. *Reading the Future* (Department of National Heritage, 1997) saw ICTs as a means of restoring public libraries' importance in society, though offered little hard advice and even less in the way of resources. In any case, the Government which had produced it was about to be defeated in a general election.

The new Government received a much more influential source of advice with the publication in mid-1997 of *New Library: the People's Network* by the Library and Information Commission, arguing:

> for the transformation of libraries and what they do; it makes the case for re-equipping them and reskilling their staff so that they can continue to fulfil their widely valued role as intermediary, guide, interpreter and referral point – but now helping smooth the path to the technological future.
>
> (Library and Information Commission, 1997)

Its core recommendation was for the establishment of 'a UK-wide information network made available through (public) libraries and implemented on the basis of a high-specification central core'.

The network was to be known as 'The People's Network'. The *New Library* report made five distinct claims for the new libraries:

- they would be agents to enable people of all ages to acquire new skills, use information creatively and 'improve the quality of their lives'
- they would be integrated parts of the national educational system – and hence it was not long before even government ministers were referring to them as 'street-corner universities'
- they would be truly inclusive, being 'open and accessible to all' and offering access to both print and online resources
- they would be 'at the hub of the community', offering leisure and cultural opportunities and making available information about every aspect of life
- they would provide access to official and government information so as to enable people to become more involved in the democratic process.

The People's Network (PN) was rolled out on time and within budget, something of an accolade for any government-led IT project. A number of evaluation reports gave testimony to its initial success in providing internet access to disadvantaged groups and individuals. For example, one user commented:

> Mohammed is a refugee and speaks very little English – he has been in England for just a few months. He uses the computer to access the internet so he can follow

> events in his own country . . . it gives him encouragement to be able to read about things from home.
>
> (Brophy, 2003)

Co-ordination of the People's Network and associated initiatives has been the responsibility of the Museums, Libraries and Archives Council (MLA). Although covering the three domains of libraries, archives and museums, the MLA does maintain specialist briefs for each and, since its role is to advise the relevant government department (the Department for Culture, Media and Sport, DCMS) on library issues, it is useful to examine in some detail its view of this area of responsibility. Its five-year strategy, published under the title *Investing in Knowledge* in 2004, states that 'museums, libraries and archives collect and interpret knowledge about the past and the present, for the future', an interesting statement in itself because of the emphasis on collecting. This emphasis is repeated later in the document where it is expressed in the following terms: 'museums, libraries and archives lie at the heart of our society, both as storehouses of knowledge and as trusted sources of expertise and scholarship' (MLA, 2004a). There would seem considerable logic to this approach, since the common feature of libraries, archives and museums is surely an organized collection. However, the 'collections' part of the MLA website (at www.mla.gov.uk), while claiming that 'MLA supports or contributes to a variety of initiatives to provide comprehensive advice and information for everyone involved in developing and managing collections', provides this advice via the MDA (previously the Museum Documentation Association but now known only by its former acronym) in partnership with the Institute of Conservation and National Preservation Office. So 'collection' doesn't seem to feature strongly in its view of libraries after all!

The educational role of the public library has been emphasized repeatedly in the last ten years. MLA has set up the 'Inspiring Learning for All' framework which aims to:

> - provide more effective learning opportunities
> - create inspiring and accessible learning environments
> - build creative learning partnerships
> - place learning at the heart of the museum, archive or library.
>
> (www.inspiringlearningforall.gov.uk)

The framework is supported by a methodology for assessing the impact of public libraries, museums and archives on learning using Generic Learning Outcomes (GLOs). These are intended to assess:

- knowledge and understanding
- skills
- attitudes and values
- enjoyment, inspiration and creativity
- action, behaviour, progression.

(MLA, n.d.)

Bearing in mind that these are related to learning activities and not necessarily to the whole range of public library services, these statements nevertheless reveal a considerable amount about public library purpose – at least from the national government perspective – at the current time.

Perhaps the most useful conclusion is that public libraries continually try to contextualize information usage – using 'information' in the wide sense to include works of the imagination – within the concerns of their local communities, reinterpreting needs in terms of international, national, regional and local priorities. In the past they have proved flexible in response to external change; the key question may be whether they can change quickly enough to remain relevant to the emerging information society and cement a place in the overall learning landscape. For the moment they retain overwhelming public endorsement: a survey in Northern Ireland carried out in 2002 reported that '89% of people think that the Public Library Service is important to the community. In the survey an overwhelming 93% of people, both users and non-users of the service, agreed that "every community needs a library". A similarly high proportion, 84%, agreed that public money should be spent on libraries; three quarters of non-users would also agree with this' (Department of Culture, Arts and Leisure, 2002).

The library-specific ten-year vision was published in 2003 with the title *Framework for the Future* (DCMS, 2003). Again, it is striking that this vision of the future does not emphasize the collection focus of the later *Investing in Knowledge*, but neither does it say much about what is *distinctive* about libraries. Thus when speaking of public libraries' future it says:

- The vision has to start from a well thought through understanding of the modern needs of users and non-users
- The modern services libraries should offer increasingly depend on partnerships with education, learning, leisure, health and e-government

- Libraries are places: their tangible look and feel still matters hugely to people
- Libraries need to be seen as open, welcoming places
- Successful libraries are not standalone services. They thrive when they play a clear role within local authority strategies to promote learning and social cohesion.

The obvious reaction to these statements would be to ask whether they do not apply equally to other local authority services. Equally, it is noticeable that while there is stress on partnerships within the local authority there is little about working with libraries in other sectors.

A new round of consultation on the future of UK public libraries was launched in early 2007 with the publication of a discussion paper by John Dolan, Head of Library Policy at the MLA. The title of this document, *A Blueprint for Excellence: public libraries 2008–2011: connecting people to knowledge and inspiration*, is interesting in its own right with its emphasis on the role of the public library as an interface between the people it serves and knowledge resources. This is followed up in a section on the purpose of the public library:

> to be a trusted community resource providing a universal entitlement to:
>
> - The skills and joy of reading.
> - Knowledge in all its forms, including print, audio, visual and digital media.
> - Essential information, learning and knowledge at all stages of life.
> - Involvement in the social, learning and creative life of the community.
>
> It will achieve this by being at the very heart of the community, engaging with local people, offering informed guidance to them and supporting their needs, interests and aspirations.
>
> (Dolan, 2007)

While this is only a consultative document at this stage, it may well turn out to be something of a landmark in the development of the public library service, not least because it starts to answer the criticism that so many other statements have been imprecise, often with more emphasis on advocacy than hard thinking about what it is that is distinctive about the public library. Thus it is *reading* that is now the first purpose, bringing libraries back both to the key skill they have always been based upon and to a commitment to the sheer joy, as well as utility, of not only being able to read but becoming a voracious reader:

> I grew up in libraries. My mother was a voracious reader and took me to the library whenever she went. When I was old enough to have a library card, my mother got me two!
>
> (Barbara Taylor Bradford in the 'Love Libraries Campaign', 2007)

Coupling this with ensuring access (which is presumably what the use of the term 'entitlement' means) to information, and supporting it with services which help sustain community learning and creativity, paints a clear picture of what public libraries need to strive to become.

Perhaps because public libraries are locally accountable, there has been an emphasis on a small number of 'spectacular' redevelopments, such as those at Peckham and Norwich – one observer commented of them that these 'flagship public libraries . . . combine a welcoming exterior and interior, with a feeling of inclusion, comfort, safety and refuge to the user' (Davies, 2003). For these library authorities and their communities, as Berndtson (2003) has remarked in the context of Scandinavian public libraries:

> [A]s in the initial phases of their history, public libraries are becoming prominent and esteemed by virtue of their building structures. Nobody can deny that the magnificent Carnegie library buildings, built in the United States and England in the late 1800s, played an important role in elevating the esteem attributed to public libraries. Large, prominent libraries have a symbolic value, or serve as icons for the entire institution of the library and its status.

What is less clear is the extent to which such innovations have permeated through the majority of public library services in the UK. Critics argue that 'many public libraries throughout the country are drab and dismal. It is as if there were an assumption that any attempt to create an attractive space is a waste of taxpayers' money. Yet it is a far greater waste to offer an unwelcoming service in an unpleasant environment resulting in no visitors' (Coates, 2004). Lending figures have continued to fall, and while IT provision has brought in large numbers most usage seems to be general web surfing and e-mail – though the Tavistock Institute remarked that 'users are overwhelmingly positive about ICT in libraries, especially the free internet access, speed of the connection and state-of-the-art technology' (Sommerlad et al., 2004). The House of Commons Select Committee, however, issued a timely reminder: 'We are in no doubt that, while libraries are about more than books (and newspapers and journals), these traditional materials must be the bedrock upon which the library services rest no matter how the institution is refreshed or re-branded' (House of Commons, 2005). Picking up on that comment, recent investment in showcase public libraries has brought books back to the fore: 'the newer dominant feature of many libraries, the free People's Network terminals, have been tucked away. Instead, there are books just inside the door – in a new Quick Choice book exchange section for customers in a hurry, with bestsellers and titles in the news on bookshop-style cabinets and tables, and a fast automatic checkout terminal for borrowers' (Ezard, 2006). Goulding (2006) summarizes the situation in saying:

> On the optimistic side, we can say that the ICT equipment and reader development services introduced into libraries have had a positive impact on services provided and visitor numbers. On the other hand, the two vital aspects of books and buildings have suffered and are starting to show the effects of years of underfunding.

The view from the sectors 4: school libraries

Until fairly recently even the best school libraries were fairly limited affairs, with a very few exceptions. Mainwood, writing 35 years ago with perhaps a touch of hyperbole commented:

> Perhaps the most significant development in the post-war years in Britain has been the extension of school library provision to pupils of all ranges of age and ability. Where, hitherto, only the senior pupils pursuing academic courses in grammar schools had access to reasonable library facilities in their schools – and even these facilities tended to range from large and comprehensive collections in well-endowed schools, to the woefully inadequate – we can now expect to find attractive and well produced books suitably displayed and accessible to children from the age when they first attend school, and providing for all types of interest and ability.
>
> (Mainwood, 1972)

In the USA an event of particular importance was the issuing in 1961 of a policy statement by the chief officers of school districts, recognizing school libraries as 'intrinsic to the purposes of the school and . . . a basic service for which the board of education is responsible' (Council of Chief State School Officers, 1961). From this period there emerged a consensus on the importance of school libraries, and a series of standards and guidelines was issued. By the early 1970s, Gaver (1972) was reporting:

> the present situation, however, is quite different from the time a generation ago when only the exceptional school had a library with a qualified staff, an excellent collection of materials, and an effective program of services. Today, in American schools and communities, it is the generally accepted goal to provide both public library and school library service, although the achievement of that goal may not yet be universally recognized.

The reasons for this success were various – Mainwood (1972) lists them as:

> the shift of emphasis from 'teaching' to 'learning', from class instruction to individual exploration, from the uniformity of sets of textbooks to the diversity of many different books of interest and information.

Much, however, remained to be done:

> In the past, the school library has tended to be the special . . . concern of the English department. . . . there is considerable need for the use of the resources of the library to form a normal part of the teaching of other subjects. Closely linked with this . . . is the whole range of possibilities which are being opened up by the current interest in educational technology, group teaching, curriculum development projects, and new teaching methods.

After another 20 years had elapsed it had become clear that this central, cross-curricular place was broadly recognized and indeed was being widened beyond the curriculum itself. In 1986 an official UK report proclaimed that the school library should be the 'foundation of the curriculum' (Library and Information Services Council, 1986) and in the UK The Library Association's *Guidelines for School Libraries* (Kinnell, 1992) the purpose of school libraries is described as 'wide-ranging. . . . They have a central place in providing a range of information resources in support of the curriculum and of pupils' personal and social development'. Furthermore, 'school library resource centres have been recognized as part of the national information network'. More fundamentally still, 'the purpose of the school library is to facilitate teaching and learning . . . the emphasis on learning to learn, and learning to handle information, so evident in modern curricula, brings library and information services into the centre of the learning process'.

So, a more modern view would be that the school library is:

> not just a physical space in which various media are stored; it is a concept, a tangible expression of the school's ethos and values, its approaches to equality of opportunity, the moral and spiritual development of children and young people and its educational purposes. It has the potential to introduce young people to the world of literature and information and to enable them to develop skills which will enhance their lives as adults.
>
> (Tilke, 1998)

This kind of consideration led to the setting up of an investigation into the kinds of library services which children and young people need in the modern age. *Start with the Child* was published in 2002 based on the deliberations of a Chartered Institute of Library and Information Professionals (CILIP) working group and stated:

> Libraries are a hugely important part of children's and young people's lives because they bring books and children together, they provide reading opportunities free of charge, and so they encourage experimentation and learning. They represent a non-judgmental place for children to feel safe and empowered to make their own choices. The library ethos emphasises individual rights, voluntary involvement and exposure to minority interests and challenging ideas, through print based or other media.
>
> (CILIP, 2002)

This influential report led to the development of new school library guidelines. Thus, those for secondary schools 'aim to establish the school librarian firmly as a co-educator and the school library as central to learning' (Barratt, 2004). As in the academic sector there is a very noticeable emphasis on the development of information literacy and its effects: 'information literacy changes the role of the librarian and demands a high level of collaboration with teachers. It requires an understanding of teaching and learning and the ability to apply this in working with teachers' (ibid.)

What must not be forgotten is that information skills can only be built on the foundation of reading skills: that the child who not only *can* read but *enjoys* reading, the child who is a *voracious* reader, has an enormous head-start on others regardless of the medium in which information appears. McGonagle (1998) wrote:

> For our children to take their place in today's world, being technically literate is not enough. They need to develop an enthusiasm for books, reading and acquiring information. Children need to learn to make fully informed decisions, so that they can influence their own destinies. The most effective way that this can be achieved is by having a central resource of books and other information material, so that all children and staff can have access to it – in other words, a school library.

Royce (1998) goes further:

> Able users of information develop strategies for finding, choosing and using information. Their strategies are built on three skills areas: reading, information-handling, and technical. The skills are interdependent and often practiced simultaneously; their boundaries merge and overlap. . . . It all comes back to reading, and thus to the twin needs of getting readers hooked early in life, and that of providing plenty of practice, reading for information as well as reading for pleasure. You *can* survive in today's world, even if you can type with only one or two fingers. You *can* survive without ever using keyboard shortcuts or realizing the full potential of your software. But even in a world of pictograms and icons, of sounds and pictures and Internet and intranets, you are going to find survival both difficult and expensive if your reading skills are poorly developed.
>
> [*Original emphasis*]

The school library, then, even when renamed and clearly embedded within a 'whole school' paradigm, needs to retain a core emphasis on skills, a role valued by pupils as well as teachers. It is also noticeable that one reason that the library has become known as a learning resource centre in many schools is that it is the locus of choice for IT access, whether or not this is physically distributed. This opens up the possibility of delivering IT-based services across the curriculum, provided – as already mentioned – that the library can position itself to deliver within the electronic learning environments becoming more and more commonplace.

The view from the sectors 5: workplace libraries

Generalizing about workplace (or, as they used to be known, 'special') libraries is fraught with difficulties. The sector covered is immense – everything from information services in high-technology industries through libraries serving the health service to advisory services in the voluntary sector. They differ enormously in scope and size – from the one-person band to multinational services employing hundreds. The terminology itself is difficult. 'Special' has survived for many years when it really meant, if anything, 'specialized'. 'Workplace' seems rather insulting to the other sectors (are they not also 'workplaces'?), while many object to the term 'library' on the basis that they operate an information service regardless of physical location and without physical objects such as books.

Again, it is useful to look at the way these services have developed over time. Although the origins of the workplace library can be traced back a very long way (perhaps the medieval alchemist poring over his secret tomes might form an appropriate genesis) it was only during the 20th century that a recognizable sector developed. The creation in the UK of Aslib (then an acronym for the Association of Special Libraries and Information Bureaux) in the 1920s drew on American experience, where a Special Libraries Association had been founded even earlier, and proved a seminal event. Hutton (1945), one of the founders, commented:

> We had all for long been interested in the improvement of provincial technical library resources and had been impressed by special library developments in the United States . . . we had prominently in mind two vital problems which faced industrial research associations . . . how to make as complete as possible a survey of information on some special subject from world-wide sources, and how to bring the more important results of the survey to the attention of members of the organization.

From this comment it can be seen that special libraries concerned themselves not only with collecting information objects and organizing them but saw part of their role as analysing the information, creating digests of key information and disseminating these to their clientele. These concerns have continued, but it is worth also reflecting on two trends which have greatly affected workplace libraries in recent years. From the health sector the demand is for 'evidence-based practice' and from the commercial sector the emphasis is on 'knowledge management'. Both have significant implications for library services.

Evidence-based practice

Evidence-based medicine is one of those issues which, with hindsight, appears glaringly obvious – the idea that before embarking on a medical procedure or other course of treatment, a doctor should have weighed all the available evidence and, if challenged, should be able to demonstrate why one procedure is preferred over other possibilities. The issue has been brought into sharp focus by allegations of malpractice or ill-informed practice. The size of awards where liability is proved provides a particularly strong motivation for health professionals to take evidence-gathering seriously.

Evidence may be acquired from a number of sources, but the medical library clearly has an important role to play. It is telling, for example, that one of the key services offered by the UK's National Library for Health (NLH) is The Cochrane Library, part of an international collaboration to identify significant published information on health care, to arrange for its expert appraisal and to produce reviews and summaries which can be used by clinical practitioners. The need for services like Cochrane were demonstrated by observation of the difficulties encountered in the health field where:

- even expert searching of well-designed databases like Medline cannot guarantee to find all the relevant information
- it is not immediately clear how much reliance can be placed on many of the research studies reported, which may, for example, be based on small sample sizes
- there is difficulty in determining whether reported results are suffering from bias, since so much funding of medical research originates with pharmaceutical companies
- the practitioner is often faced with information overload and has no easy way to sift out the relevant from the irrelevant.

Each of these issues is familiar to librarians, but their identification in the health library context provides some idea of why librarians' roles, at least in this sector, are developing. For example, what health practitioners clearly need are:

- better and more reliable search tools
- expert evaluation of published work, going beyond standard peer review (which merely states an opinion that it is worth publishing)
- additional information on the source and background to any published report
- help to handle large volumes of data.

These issues are, of course, not confined to health practitioners even though they became prominent in that context. The *British Medical Journal*'s definition of evidence-based medicine is capable of much wider application: 'the conscientious, explicit, and judicious use of current best evidence in making decisions . . .' (*British Medical Journal*, 1996). Such widening is exemplified by librarianship itself which has espoused the concept of 'evidence-based librarianship' and 'evidence-based information practice':

> Evidence-Based Librarianship (EBL) seeks to improve library practice by utilizing the best available evidence in conjunction with a pragmatic perspective developed from working experiences in librarianship. The best available evidence might be produced from quantitative or qualitative research designs, although EBL encourages more rigorous forms over less rigorous forms of evidence when making decisions.
>
> (Eldredge, 2002)

Booth emphasizes that a focus on clients and their particular needs is important:

> Evidence-based librarianship (EBL) is an approach to information science that promotes the collection, interpretation and integration of valid, important and applicable user-reported, librarian observed, and research-derived evidence. The best available evidence, moderated by user needs and preferences, is applied to improve the quality of professional judgements.
>
> (Booth, 2003)

The idea that understanding of the end-user experience is critical has led to interest in the broadening of the evidence base to include qualitative sources and to the use of narrative both as evidence in itself and as a way of communicating meaningfully:

> [I]n order to improve our management practices and the delivery of services to our clients, we need to take much more seriously the role of narrative and to find ways to capture narrative systematically as part of our evidence base. We need to acknowledge explicitly that, in fact, good managers have always relied on story – the anecdote shared in the corridor or the 'war stories' swapped over a drink in the conference bar. But sharing anecdotes in a haphazard and random fashion is by no means an adequate response to the challenge of professional practice in the modern world. Rather we need to develop new ways of capturing, sharing and using narrative as a systematic part of service delivery and management. We need to develop narrative-based practice.
>
> (Brophy, 2007)

Knowledge management

A linked development which has emerged from workplace libraries, although it also has roots in business management, is that of knowledge management (KM). It thus provides an interesting example of convergence between library and information services and broader business practices. An increasing number of businesses are based on the exploitation of knowledge. Examples include management consultancies where work on one contract needs to draw on experience gained in earlier, similar work, and many dot.com companies where knowledge of customer preferences and previous transactions provides the key to future sales.

The essence of knowledge management lies in the capture and exploitation of learning, expertise and understanding as well as information. Thus a company which has learned from the experience of advising a client in, say, bringing an e-commerce company to market can gain competitive edge if it can exploit the knowledge gained to the full in the next similar contract. The knowledge which is captured and used consists not just of formal reports, but best practice digests, diaries and other narratives (including those describing failures) and interpreted statistical data. Subjects may include such matters as the impact of outsourcing, how production times were speeded up, improved error handling and customer relations. It is interesting that the focus during the 1980s on expert systems – software which would solve problems using the distilled experience of human experts – has given way to this new emphasis.

An issue of great importance is that knowledge management is not primarily about building IT-based knowledge systems, although many companies are benefiting from systems that permit online access to the corporate knowledge resources. However, the following comment from a Japanese perspective is pertinent (Takeuchi, 1998):

> Many American companies equate 'knowledge creation' with setting up computer databases. Professor Nonaka [Takeuchi's co-author of *The Knowledge-Creating Company*] argues that much of a company's knowledge bank has nothing to do with data, but is based on informal 'on the job' knowledge – everything from the name of a customer's secretary to the best way to deal with a truculent supplier. Many of these tidbits are stored in the brains of middle managers – exactly the people who re-engineering has replaced with computers.

An important insight from this viewpoint is that knowledge is, in essence, socially located, being invested in individuals and in groups. Because much of knowledge is tacit it is difficult to capture, store and transfer. In this view, knowledge management may be better thought of as the process of engineering conditions under which knowledge transfer and utilization happen. It could be argued, for example, that the library which creates attractive social spaces in which users chat and exchange ideas is engaging in knowledge management.

Oxbrow and Abell (1998) emphasized this idea when they argued that knowledge management is not simply a matter of identifying and codifying knowledge, but just as much concerned with its effective use:

> The ultimate corporate resource has become information – the ultimate competitive advantage is the ability to use it – the sum of the two is knowledge management. . . . the essence of KM is connection. The connection of people with people – enabling people to share and build on what they know, to collect information of value and make it easily and appropriately available, to ensure that people understand the value and potential of what they know.

Bellinger (2004) puts it this way:

> [T]he value of Knowledge Management relates directly to the effectiveness with which the managed knowledge enables the members of the organization to deal with today's situations and effectively envision and create their future. Without on-demand access to managed knowledge, every situation is addressed based on what the individual or group brings to the situation with them. With on-demand access to managed knowledge, every situation is addressed with the sum total of everything anyone in the organization has ever learned about a situation of a similar nature.

These analyses lead naturally to the idea of the 'intelligent enterprise' which is able to exploit knowledge both to deal with current challenges and to be effective in achieving its future strategy. Knowledge is seen as the underpinning resource which enables organizations to act intelligently, and this in turn leads to a view that at the heart of the successful organization is the ability to build relationships. These are not just supplier–customer, contractual arrangements but suggest that the organization should view itself as part of a wider social system, paying due regard to the needs, views, knowledge and intelligence of all its stakeholders – customers, suppliers, employees, members of the local community, local and national government, voluntary organizations and others.

Of course, managing knowledge and enabling intelligence at the organizational level is not without its pitfalls. Many employees are reluctant to reveal or share their knowledge – after all it may represent their real value to the company. Much knowledge may be too specialized, when the issue is how to draw general conclusions from it. Knowledge may be used as a weapon instead of an asset. There are few rewards for being a good knowledge manager and thus helping others to improved performance. And, as noted above, knowledge management easily becomes subverted into IT systems development.

Abram (1998) draws some interesting, and perhaps controversial, conclusions about the implications of knowledge management for workplace libraries:

> [S]pecial librarians made a potentially disastrous error, those many years ago when we decided to position ourselves in the 'information business'. Information businesses are marked by their ability to create information, and disseminate it widely – often for a profit. Generally, special librarians do not, as part of our core mandate, create information. While we do create information about information (metadata), I believe this is a higher level calling in the knowledge continuum. . . . The plain fact is that knowledge, per se, *cannot* be managed. In fact, capturing knowledge in any form other than into a human being's brain, reduces it to mere information, or worse, data. Only the knowledge environment can be managed.

He suggests a four-fold strategy. Firstly, focusing effort where libraries can add value by transforming their resources, whether traditional information or knowledge based, by organizing them for users. Secondly, placing emphasis on the idea of the learning organization (discussed further in Chapter 6). Thirdly, providing guidance and navigation tools which enable people to put knowledge to work. Finally, taking a broad view of 'transformational librarianship' which sees the key resource as the people who adopt technology and other tools and use them to enable improved knowledge creation and management.

While it is difficult to extract generic lessons from across the whole workplace sector, the examples described above suggest that the most dynamic services are those which have succeeded in embedding the 'library' – often under a different name – in the core strategic concerns of the organization and in the workflow of its employees. In the best examples, libraries have recognized the implications of an information-based economy and taken their place at the heart of the enterprise. It must also be admitted, however, that others have failed to secure this position and new information and knowledge structures have emerged which have sidelined the library or made it irrelevant.

Conclusion

Libraries across most sectors have proved remarkably resilient during the last decade. Each sector can contribute strengths and demonstrate signs of the regard in which it is held – whether it is the new buildings which so many national libraries have achieved, the continuing collection strengths and co-operative endeavours of research libraries, the modernization of leading public libraries or the innovative practices and paradigms characterizing workplace libraries. In mapping the library of the future each sector offers intriguing and useful insights into ways forward.

What is more difficult to gauge is what is happening beneath the surface of these 'fanfare' stories. Yes, national libraries have impressive new buildings but are they providing national information policy leadership suitable for an e-world? Are academic libraries as a whole really positioning themselves to operate within new models of scholarly communication and to integrate resources in learning? Are school libraries doing more than becoming IT access centres providing a glitzy entrée to impoverished resources? Are workplace libraries demonstrating a capability in information and knowledge handling, as it enters mainstream business practice, proving that such entities are still needed? Are the majority of public libraries, the branches in suburbs and villages, really succeeding in community engagement, becoming the 'hearts of these communities'? These are the questions which challenge library professionals across the sectors.

3

What is a library? Cross-sectoral models

> Nobody will say what precisely libraries are supposed to be doing.
>
> (Hawgood and Morley, 1969)

Introduction

In this chapter attention turns from the issues raised by consideration of libraries in their various sectoral settings to more general approaches which have validity across all sectors. Theoretical models of this type are intended to be simplified representations of reality which, because they do not describe particular cases, allow general conclusions to be drawn and principles elucidated. They can be used to shed light on purposes, functions and structures, to identify meaningful interactions between sub-systems and the broader environment and to enable the whole to be seen as greater than the sum of its parts. They also help in the identification and exploration of commonalities between practical implications, which on the surface may seem very different. In short, to quote Underwood (1996), 'a model . . . stands in place of reality in order that we can think, negotiate, play or experiment'.

When thinking of libraries people have many different images in front of them. By stepping back from individual cases and examining the context in which library services are provided, and the trends which are likely to affect them in the future, it is possible to arrive at some conclusions about how libraries' roles are likely to develop and to start to answer the central questions posed in Chapter 1: do libraries have a central role to play, or are they in fact simply anachronisms?

Four models are identified here, drawing on the descriptions of sectoral roles, purposes and functions from Chapter 2. These are: the library as collection; the library as organizer of resource sharing; the library as provider of access; and the embedded or immersive library.

Before moving to the models themselves it is worth reflecting on how information and knowledge, the 'stuff' of libraries, is used within our user communities. Human activity is, of course, almost always a social process. We do not act, make decisions or learn in isolation but within a process of interplay between individuals collaborating or competing. This suggests that library services need to be designed in the context of their users' social engagement. Taking academic users as an example (although the argument applies equally in other contexts) and thinking about their use of information, an observer would note that users converse routinely with their peers in other communities, in the case of academic scholars, across the world. To do this, they have become steeped in the sometimes arcane and always developing vocabularies of their disciplines. They are communities of practice with all kinds of unspoken assumptions. What underlies the discourse of any of these disciplines, however, is a shared search for knowledge and for meaning – and, again, the same would be true of users of a school or a legal or an industrial library. However, here there is a discontinuity between what we usually see as the library's role and the *modus operandi* of academic disciplines. It is as if the library stands outside the discipline, occasionally offering resources to help in the search but unsure whether it has a role to play.

The development of knowledge management, as described in Chapter 2, is one way in which libraries have sought to move forward and enter into the discourse. What immediately becomes apparent, however, is that as the emphasis shifts towards the management of knowledge, the librarian has to be able to participate in the discourse, has to acquire deep understanding of the ways in which language is used to express meaning within each community. Exactly the same is true of the public librarian seeking to work with a disadvantaged group; unless there is real familiarity with the way that language is used, which means avoidance of superficiality and condescension, there can be no real engagement with the users. Thus 'a key element of the librarian's skill is being able to grasp those deeper tacit understandings from what is in fact made explicit to them by the user' (Sotiriou and Gilroy, 2004).

Wittgenstein focused his attention on this problem in his later philosophical writings. He used a simple example in *Philosophical Investigations* to illustrate it:

> Let us imagine a language . . . The language is meant to serve for communication between a builder A and an assistant B. A is building with building-stones; there are blocks, pillars, slabs and beams. B has to pass the stones, and that in the order in which A needs them. For this purpose they use a language consisting of the words 'block', 'pillar', 'slab', 'beam'. A calls them out; – B brings the stone which

> he has learnt to bring at such-and-such a call. – Conceive of this as a complete primitive language.
>
> (Wittgenstein, 1953)

The problem to which Wittgenstein is drawing attention is that in order to elicit meaningful dialogue we have to assure ourselves that we share the meaning of the words we use – language is again a social process. Externally defined meanings have limited value – real meaning exists in the sharing of concepts and ways of acting. This again creates a huge problem for libraries: the stuff we deal in rather supposes that meaning can be captured, stored and retrieved outside its social setting. Wittgenstein characterized the process by which our users operate within a social setting as a 'language game': 'meaning is embedded within a social context and so finds expression through the use made of particular terms'. Just as a game has to have rules – though not all of them may be written down – so any social context has its rules, both explicit and implicit. Without acquiring enough understanding of the rules to play the game, we cannot participate in sharing and developing meaning.

However, the rules of these language games are ever changing and it therefore follows that unless we immerse ourselves in their social spaces we lose whatever familiarity we once had with their practitioners. What T. S. Eliot referred to in *East Coker* as 'the intolerable wrestle with words and meanings' is the inevitable price of joining the game. Bearing all this in mind, we can turn to the dominant models of libraries.

Alexandria: the enduring collection

The library as a collection of books provides perhaps the most enduring model and the one which is probably most common in the popular mind. It is represented by the image of lofty rooms lined with book shelves on which books are carefully arranged in long rows, and its essence is the physical collection in its own, dedicated building. The great library of Alexandria, described briefly in Chapter 1, is the archetype. The collection of such a library, whether it consists of clay tablets, papyrus scrolls, wooden blocks, parchment codices, bound paper, microform or even digital media, is representative of the recorded knowledge of humankind. As George Dawson is reported to have said at the opening of the Birmingham Free Library in 1866, 'a great library contains the diary of the human race' (Taylor, 1993). Its ideal lies in its comprehensiveness – if possible it would possess a copy of everything ever published, although realism acknowledges that this is in fact unattainable. This impossibility may turn out to be beneficial as selection can also be a form of quality assurance, added to the existing information chain processes from peer review to publishing houses' market research.

Comprehensiveness of collection persists as a target even when the scope is limited. For example, as described in Chapter 2, a national library pursues the Alexandrian model, usually limiting its 'comprehensive collection' to its own nation's output, using legal deposit as a mechanism to acquire a copy of each item in the national bibliography. The public library pursues comprehensiveness of its local history collection. The academic library pursues the model in relation to its parent university's areas of research excellence. In each sector there is still an unconscious equivalence drawn between size of collection and excellence of the library, a point which will be examined in more detail in Chapter 6. The Conspectus methodology, originating in the USA in 1979, although no longer as widely used as it once was, enabled collection strength to be described in terms of both comprehensiveness and currency. Behind this ideal lies the concept of the research library, sometimes described as the scholar's laboratory, allowing researchers to explore a large collection of material brought together in one place. This perspective also draws attention to the function of libraries in selecting, describing and organizing their collections. They are not merely warehouses of books heaped anyhow on their shelves; each item that is judged suitable for addition to the collection is carefully described and placed where it can with certainty be retrieved. Organization is thus of the essence of the library as collection. Greenberg (1998) notes: 'the modern research library is a marvel of the human genius for organization, structure, and order, as well as for creating the tools through which that order can be understood and navigated'.

The importance of description in the development of library collections can hardly be over-emphasized and, as already noted on page 23 it was one of Panizzi's seminal contributions to the field. The library catalogue was developed to fulfil a number of functions:

- It forms a record of ownership of each item in the collection, and as such has to identify each copy uniquely.
- It enables the collection to be searched by a variety of descriptors (e.g. author, title, subject) to check whether a known item is present. In passing it is worth noting that users' criteria do not always seem to have had much influence on the choice of descriptors, witness the lack of title catalogues in the pre-automation era.

- It enables exploration for items which fit more general criteria – such as works by a particular author, or on a particular subject.
- It may enable comparison between seemingly similar items as, for example, when it differentiates between editions or when pagination differs within the same apparent edition.
- It is constructed to collocate works which are intellectually similar or equivalent, for example, by enforcing the use of standard forms of headings.
- It simplifies the description of items by selecting elements which will aid unique identification – so, for example, it will always include title but rarely the colour of the binding (even though, again, some library users prefer the latter description!).

The world would be greatly impoverished were it to lose collection-based libraries modelled on that at Alexandria. They have been and remain responsible for preserving some of the greatest artefacts of civilization, and it is idle to pretend that new technologies could make this function redundant. Scholars will always want to be able to examine the original, not merely its electronic surrogate. Yet the model has its limitations. Its emphasis on acquisition and preservation can make actual use a secondary consideration and the scholar's laboratory has certainly shifted its focus towards electronic networks. Perhaps more seriously, the model has yet to demonstrate that it is capable of adjusting itself quickly enough to the era of electronic publication. Already a large part of the electronic memory has been lost. Finally, while the embodiment of the Alexandrian model in the national library context may (just) be sustainable, it can no longer provide the basis for university and research libraries. Even the University of California, one of the largest universities in the world, had to conclude that 'the building of . . . comprehensive research collections . . . cannot be sustained' (Ober, 1999). So, while the building, organization and maintenance of a large collection remains a function of some libraries, it is no longer adequate as a generic model for the library of the future. The concept of the physical collection, and more specifically of the organization of knowledge which it represents, does however make an enduring contribution to understanding some part of the future role. Furthermore, the experience of selecting items for addition to collections has provided libraries with unparalleled expertise in the art of quality assurance, while ensuring that individual items are retrievable has generated a high level of skill in the science of information description. These professional assets should not be neglected.

Before leaving the 'collection' model it is worth adding an observation that in practice nearly all of these libraries organize their resources as 'collections' rather than as 'a collection'; this was particularly marked during the latter half of the 20th century. Books generally form the core of the collection, closely followed by journals – housed separately and often listed in a quite separate catalogue. There may also be collections of images, perhaps with slides, prints and other forms organized separately, secondary publications such as printed abstracts and indexes, report series and so on. Sub-collections may be provided for particular users, as with undergraduate libraries and short-loan collections in academic libraries. In addition, many libraries perform an explicit and separate archival function with 'special collections' of different types, each divided into its own sub-collections by form or other criterion.

One final observation: as noted in the last chapter, there is something of a paradox in the way government has brought libraries together at the policy level with museums and archives, which remain collection focused, for example, with the formation of a single Museums, Libraries and Archives Council (MLA), at the very time that libraries themselves have moved away from the collections model. Does this perhaps indicate a discontinuity between government perceptions and the reality of library services? After all, there are very few examples of integrated library, museum and archive services, which, if the combination has real substance, one might have expected to occur with increasing frequency.

The resource-sharing model

Libraries have engaged in resource sharing for a very long time. Substantial interlending services, based on regional bureaux, were developed in the UK in the first half of the 20th century and were followed in the period after World War 2 by the innovatory National Lending Library for Science and Technology (NLLST) at Boston Spa, later to become part of the British Library. However, by and large these services were a relatively small addition to individual libraries' services.

It was the expansion of publishing and of higher education in the 1960s and 1970s, when coupled with the mid-1970s oil crisis, that brought home to academic librarians in particular the impossibility of any semblance of self-sufficiency. Not only were budgets insufficient to keep up with increasing quantities of ever more expensive books and journals, but there was little hope that buildings would be expanded to create the space needed to house such collections. Clearly something had to give.

The defining moment for academic libraries in the UK was the publication of the Atkinson Report (University Grants Committee, 1976). In 1975 the University Grants Committee (UGC) had set up a Working Party on *Capital*

Provision for University Libraries with a brief to consider how best to cope with the situation where demands for enhancements to library space and for new library buildings simply could not be met. The Working Party reiterated that 'the library is the core of a university', but went on to propose the idea of 'a "self-renewing" library in which new accessions would be relieved by the withdrawal of obsolete or unconsulted material to other stores'. University librarians did not let go of the comprehensive collections model lightly, however, as this comment from Norman Higham, then University Librarian at Bristol, indicates:

> If the library is full, and the space limit of those who set the rules [the UGC in Britain] . . . has been reached, it is one book out for every book in, new books for old. . . . Not only the reserve store, but the library itself would be a transit camp between acquisition and obsolescence. Consumer durables may have a predictable obsolescence but books do not, and we should find ourselves discarding books which we wanted to keep.
>
> (Higham, 1980)

However, a combination of tightening budgets and growing use of access to remote electronic databases, albeit initially moderated by library staff, meant that the resource-sharing model became widely accepted and very few librarians, even in the academic sector, would now argue that it did not lie at, or near, the heart of their provision.

To make resource sharing effective the first requirement is the sharing of information about one another's collections. The union catalogue has a long history, and remains as a common means of making the contents of collections known widely. Many regional and national consortia, such as the Consortium of Research Libraries (CURL), have the union catalogue as one of their core resources. Member libraries contribute copies of their bibliographic records (and hopefully remember to inform the consortium when an item is withdrawn) so that all may benefit from the broader collection strength. Of course the catalogue itself is of little use without some kind of access arrangement, whether through formal interlibrary loan, an agreement to allow reciprocal access for members of the constituent libraries or some other arrangement. The problem remains of checking availability – it is more difficult to attach holdings and status data to union catalogues than to those of individual libraries which can integrate their circulation systems far more easily. As a result delays can occur while a location with an available copy is found. There is an ongoing debate (referred to in greater detail in

Chapter 10) as to the place of the union catalogue in networked environments where each library's own catalogue is available online.

Of course, a vital issue is the contents of the different catalogues. It is interesting and of considerable significance that while libraries have developed the description of books into a fine art, in general they have left the description of journal articles to other agencies, limiting themselves to the description of journal titles, rarely of sufficient granularity for the user. The difficulty of creating comprehensive union catalogues for journal collections is compounded by the problem of knowing exactly which runs a particular library holds. This is a critical challenge for the shift to electronic services, as evidenced by the work undertaken to establish the UK Serials Union Catalogue (SUNCAT). Burnhill and Law (2005) note 'the importance of the serial article, rather than the serial title, as the ultimate object of desire for the researcher . . . SUNCAT must also be sympathetic to onward linkage, for the researcher, or those who act for the researcher, to "request" and "access" facilities for access to that article of desire, including services for document supply'.

A union catalogue, or even access to another library's catalogue, is by no means essential for interlibrary lending, which is probably the best example of the resource-sharing model. For most libraries, of course, interlibrary borrowing – and still more, interlibrary lending – forms a very small part of their operations if counted by volume of transactions. It does, however, form a vital service for users, since it in effect places the local library at the centre of a regional, national and international network of resources. The library may then be seen as not so much concerned with developing its collections, or with acquiring items on the basis of an assessment of likely access requirements and then later discarding them, but as a node in the international recorded memory, the local library's own resources being, for these purposes, irrelevant. The legal environment of most countries recognizes this situation by making provision for library privileges within its copyright legislation.

In most countries there are some regional or national arrangements which, having evolved over time, offer particularly well-developed interlending service support. The UK has perhaps the most centralized of these services, with the British Library's Document Supply Centre (based on the former NLLST) being used as a matter of automatic choice for interlending requests by many libraries. In the USA the existence of the Online Computer Library Center (OCLC) database provides a major resource for interlending, although requests are referred to the participating libraries rather than to a centralized national supply service.

It is worth adding, when considering this model, that commercial document delivery or individual article supply companies fit well with the resource-sharing approach. Non-library players, like ingenta and Emerald, provide an alternative to library supply. Although their charges for individual article supply are generally higher than library-to-library prices, they are in effect members of the library resource-sharing network. Viewed in this light they make a valuable contribution to the concept of the library as a shared resource.

One final point worth making about the resource-sharing model relates to the *internal* sharing of resources in an organization. The essence of a library can be seen in its role as neutral umpire between different resource demands in an institution, ensuring fair distribution. For example, the whole point of lending books for a fixed period of time, rather than giving them away to whomever first asks for them, is to ensure that the resource, in this case the opportunity to read the book, is shared between users. Fairness is expressed in having the same loan period for all. There is, incidentally, an interesting issue in academic institutions regarding the differential loan periods offered to students and academic staff, which may be interpreted as an indication of what the institution (or at least the librarian) regards as equitable. This role can also be seen in extending opportunities to individuals which would otherwise be unavailable. So, for example, very few individuals would be able to justify purchasing an expensive reference book for themselves, but they can justify their share of the cost when they are but one of thousands of users gaining access through the resource-sharing arrangement that is the library, especially when it is raised indirectly through taxation or a general membership fee. In this view, libraries are in practice co-operatives. This brings us to the next model.

The access model

The idea that the library's *primary* role is to provide access to books, journals and other sources of information is relatively modern, although access as *part* of the role is of course ancient in origin. After all, there was never much point in developing collections unless someone at some time was going to use them. In medieval times, access was carefully regulated and chained libraries bear witness to some of the problems it presented. Nevertheless, arrangements were always made for those with sufficient reason and warrant to gain access.

The move of access to centre-stage can be seen in a number of different developments in different sectors and more recently in the massive shifts taking place in the environments in which libraries operate. Early entrants in the access approach can be found among public and subscription libraries, where, by the early

20th century, members were allowed to browse freely among the shelves. Academic libraries followed, mainly in the second half of the 20th century, with closed access giving way to open collections.

A number of trends accelerated the move towards access as the central tenet of librarianship, not the least being the influence which Ranganathan's ideas had on a generation of librarians. Ranganathan's *Laws of Library Science* (1931) represent an early 20th-century attempt to express the role of the library and significantly turn away from collections per se, and even from organization as a primary objective:

- books are for use
- every reader his book
- every book its reader
- save the time of the reader
- a library is a growing organism.

While some of these statements have dated – the last in particular must be questionable, unless it is taken to refer to the world wide web! – it is interesting to note that the emphasis in these 'laws' is very much on the library user, rather than the collection itself, and very much about access.

The great 'access v holdings' debates which occupied professional librarians for much of the 1970s and 1980s served a useful purpose, but the issue no longer engenders much controversy. Access is so much the experience of users of electronic systems, and so embedded in the prevailing social norms, that it now seems odd that so much heat was once generated by the issue. The concept of the library as one contributor to the user's whole experience of accessing resources, whether through Google, YouTube or e-government websites, now dominates the literature. For example, Spencer (2006) comments that by the end of the 1990s 'students and faculty had new and attractive options for accessing information – options that did not include a trip to the library or queuing up to ask questions at a service desk'. Thus even as access as a driving model for library development took hold, the challenges intensified because the whole environment in which users operated, became dominated, not just by the availability of access, but by the ease with which that access could be obtained. As the new millennium took hold it was time to move on.

The immersive library

'Instead of pulling people in, librarians need to reach outward to become an integral part of the routine interactions of faculty and students' (Ramsay and Kinnie, 2006). Here the argument comes full circle to the discussion of disciplinary language in the introductory part of this chapter. The challenge now is to realize a new model, finding ways to envisage, develop and deliver services which are not just embedded in user environments but an integrated part of those environments. To borrow a term from computer games, this could be called 'the immersive library', noting that it is immersed in the real as well as the virtual environment. 'Immersive' as an adjective comes, of course, from the noun 'immersion'. The *Oxford English Dictionary* gives a primary definition: 'Immersion: Dipping or plunging into water or other liquid' (2007). Libraries need to dip, plunge and immerse themselves into real and cyberspacial discipline-based environments.

The most obvious of these are the virtual learning environments (VLEs) which have been implemented by most educational institutions during the last decade. Because these offer a self-contained view of the course unit being studied there is a tendency for students to focus on the resources presented there. A simple link to the library website is commonly provided but this takes the user away from the learning environment. Facilities to enable tutors to import resources from the library simply and easily are available but there remains a danger that the exploration of the full depth of library resources will be neglected. Furthermore, the critical issue of how library staff become significant players within such environments remains unanswered by such tools.

A more convincing example of academic libraries' attempts to immerse themselves in the users' environment is provided by work on information skills and information literacy. This will be discussed in Chapter 9 but its importance lies in the way in which it seeks to enter the students' and tutors' worlds and work from within by helping the development of skills appropriate to coursework. The same trend can be seen in some school libraries, where it may be observed alongside a 'whole school' approach which puts library services within the delivery of the curriculum. Knowledge management, where it occurs within the workflow, is the obvious example from workplace libraries. For public libraries, straws in the wind would be the increasing emphasis on learning, though with the caveat that few learners yet see the library as the obvious locus for learning, and on delivering the service within disadvantaged communities. On a more general level, work to make library services accessible to people with disabilities demonstrates that the idea of immersion in user environments can cut across all sectors:

> Library researchers have been prominent in exploring ways of improving Web accessibility for the last decade. They have brought to the field an overriding concern for a user-centered approach, which has led to a series of user-focused studies showing precisely where common approaches to Web design have been failing those with disabilities. . . . Over this period of time, libraries throughout the UK and elsewhere have been encouraged to mainstream accessibility, and, partly as a result of new legislation, to maintain the issue high among their priorities.
>
> (Brophy and Craven, 2007)

This is, of course, a particular way of interpreting the need to speak the users' language, yet it illustrates the principle behind immersive services.

Conclusion

The dominant view through most of history has been that libraries were places where written, including eventually printed, materials were held together both for security and to create a collection organized for use. The enforcement of legal deposit by Panizzi in the 19th century can be seen as the clear outcome of such a view. The collection was paramount and steps had to be taken to secure its development and representativeness. Besides the collection, resource organization became of ever increasing importance, and the outcome of this view can be seen in the work of pioneers of library cataloguing and classification, such as Melvil Dewey and Charles Cutter.

Alongside the concepts of the collection, the organization of access to knowledge and the needs of the user as an individual, a view developed – expressed most clearly by the early public library pioneers – that the library was a social institution which played a role in the organization of society. While some saw this as social control, others took a more liberal and progressive view, seeing in the public library a means to spread literacy and a love of learning.

Sack has suggested that 'instead of the traditional "Ptolemaic" view of the library world with the library at the centre and users at the periphery we now have a "Copernican" view with the user at the centre and a variety of services and people surrounding and supporting the user' (Steele, 1995). This echoes a comment made ten years earlier by Surridge (1984) when he remarked of the emergence of community librarianship that it represented 'a move from the subject materials orientation of yesteryear, to the orientation to users and their needs'. However, these ideas now appear dated, as the need to engage the users within their own environments starts to emerge.

What is notable from each of the sectors is the very clear focus on user needs that emerged during the second half of the 20th century. Collections remain important, and there is an almost non-stop debate on the role of ICTs, yet each sector has focused itself on its users – the public, students, researchers, pupils or employees. The conclusions of a 1991 study of academic library mission statements could almost certainly be broadened to the other sectors: 'the most frequently cited purpose of the . . . library is "to serve the needs of the users" or "to provide services to the library's users"' (Brophy, 1991). Although often unstated, the needs which are being referred to are those related to information, knowledge, understanding and learning so that, in their different ways, the sectors have refocused on the purposes of information use. What remains unanswered is the question as to whether the library can go beyond an interest in users' needs to become a vital component within the users' environments, immersed in their day-to-day activities.

4

What is a library? The profession's view

> The library as a *total* system, and the social *context* within which it operates, must first be analysed, and in the light of the analysis an appropriately designed system developed.
>
> (McClellan, 1973)

Introduction

Given that librarianship forms a well-established profession it is useful to explore the views of professionals on the role that libraries play. They, after all, have been trained to provide library services, have experience of doing so and are, presumably, at the forefront of developments in their profession. Taking this approach, this chapter examines four arenas in which the role of the library, or that of the library/information science professional, is exposed. These are:

- various published statements and a list of the professional issues with which the UK Chartered Institute of Library and Information Professionals (CILIP) is concerned
- the 'Benchmark Statement' for academic librarianship and information management courses, initially issued by the UK Quality Assurance Agency in January 2000 and revised in mid-2007
- the American Library Association's published *Key Action Areas* and *Library Bill of Rights*
- statements and documents issued by some of the major sectoral professional bodies.

Before turning to these statements and position papers, however, it is interesting to observe the profession's first faltering attempts to define its underlying philosophy. In 1887, Melvil Dewey, then Professor in the School of Library Economy

(SLE) as well as Library Director at Columbia University, launched the first formal 'library school' class. Wiegan (1999) records its underlying character:

> The job . . . was to acquaint SLE students with how best to function as librarians – how to run the institution and what expertise was necessary to select its information resources and exploit them most efficiently for the benefit of the public. They were also expected to inculcate the library 'spirit', an attitude about library use and access to collections that distinguished Dewey's from previous generations of librarians who were more concerned with security and preservation. . . . They firmly believed that by providing the masses with access to quality literature and information resources they would benefit society and make America a better place to live for all.

CILIP's view of the profession

The first purpose of CILIP is, according to its *Royal Charter*, 'to foster and promote education, training, invention and research in matters connected with information science and libraries and information services and to collect, collate and publish information, ideas, data and research relating thereto' (CILIP, 2004a). Its mission is more a declaration of principle than a purposive statement but it does, in its second clause, focus on access:

- set, maintain, monitor and promote standards of excellence in the creation, management, exploitation and sharing of information and knowledge resources
- support the principle of equality of access to information, ideas and works of the imagination which it affirms is fundamental to a thriving economy, democracy, culture and civilization
- enable its Members to achieve and maintain the highest professional standards in all aspects of delivering an information service, both for the professional and the public good.

(CILIP, 2004b)

To understand what CILIP regards as the core of these 'library and information services' of which it speaks it is necessary, however, to dig somewhat deeper. One way to do this is to look at the issues listed on its website under 'Professional guidance, policy and research'. In early 2007, and leaving aside issues focused more on employment matters, etc., these were listed in the left-hand column of

Table 4.1 below (CILIP, 2007). On the right are the issues which were listed seven years earlier by the then Library Association, recorded in the first edition of this book (Brophy, 2000b). Note that the lists have been reordered from the originals to show where similarities occur between the two.

Table 4.1 A comparison of the key issues of CILIP, 2007, and The Library Association, 2000

CILIP 2007	The Library Association 2000
Copyright	Copyright
Equal opportunities	Equal opportunities and the implementation of the 1995 Disability Discrimination Act
Freedom of information	Access to information, including impending Freedom of Information legislation
CILIP in the knowledge economy	Knowledge management
Lifelong learning	Lifelong learning and libraries
Library management systems	ICT futures
Research	The research agenda in the field
Social inclusion	Public libraries, including their role in social inclusion, charging for services and internet filtering
Information literacy	
Library and information services in the UK	
Preservation and conservation	
Professional ethics	
Reader development	
Rights of access to confidential information	
Terrorism Act	
Workforce development	
	Archives, including issues raised by electronic documents
	Funding of libraries
	Legal deposit
	Regionalism and its impact on libraries
	School libraries, including funding issues and the impact of various homework initiatives
	A statement on the sale of rare books by libraries
	The strategic review of the British Library
	Theft of books from libraries and resulting security issues
	Unification between The Library Association and the Institute of Information Scientists (to form CILIP)

Considerable care has to be exercised in treating these lists as representative of the profession's overall concerns, since it is noticeable that very many of the 'professional issues' listed are actually generated as responses to government discussion documents, green papers and white papers, so that in part the lists are reactive rather than proactive. Care also needs to be exercised in interpreting what is meant by the headlines – a case in point is that 'CILIP in the knowledge economy' is not really the same issue as 'knowledge management' which, surprisingly, is mentioned only once in the statement referred to by the 2007 website. Nevertheless, there is some significance both in the current list of concerns and in the changes that have occurred in seven years. There is also significance in the entries at the foot of the table showing concerns which have no equivalence in the alternative list. It is noteworthy that there is very little reference to ICTs, either in terms of strategic development or of a research and development agenda, which appears odd given their prominence in the literature of librarianship.

The American Library Association's *Library Bill of Rights*

The American Library Association (ALA) publishes a number of documents which define its interests and concerns. Central to these statements is the ALA's *Library Bill of Rights* which states:

> [T]he American Library Association affirms that all libraries are forums for information and ideas, and that the following basic policies should guide their services.
>
> I. Books and other library resources should be provided for the interest, information, and enlightenment of all people of the community the library serves. Materials should not be excluded because of the origin, background, or views of those contributing to their creation.
> II. Libraries should provide materials and information presenting all points of view on current and historical issues. Materials should not be proscribed or removed because of partisan or doctrinal disapproval.
> III. Libraries should challenge censorship in the fulfilment of their responsibility to provide information and enlightenment.
> IV. Libraries should cooperate with all persons and groups concerned with resisting abridgment of free expression and free access to ideas.
> V. A person's right to use a library should not be denied or abridged because of origin, age, background, or views.
> VI. Libraries which make exhibit spaces and meeting rooms available to the

> public they serve should make such facilities available on an equitable basis, regardless of the beliefs or affiliations of individuals or groups requesting their use.
>
> (American Library Association, 1996)

The interpretation of this document occupies considerable space on the ALA website and there is a separate office (and website) concerned with intellectual freedom. The interpretation of the document reveals a considerable amount about what the ALA regards as its priorities (American Library Association, 2007a). There is recognition of the first three models described in the last chapter, *the collection*, *resource sharing* and *access*, for example, in an interpretation entitled *Diversity in Collection Development* (American Library Association, 2007b), which states:

> Librarians have a professional responsibility to be inclusive, not exclusive, in collection development and in the provision of interlibrary loan. Access to all materials legally obtainable should be assured to the user, and policies should not unjustly exclude materials even if they are offensive to the librarian or the user.

Another example, a document on *Evaluating Library Collections* (American Library Association, 2007c), talks in terms of the continuous review of the library collection and warns that this process 'is not to be used as a convenient means to remove materials presumed to be controversial or disapproved of by segments of the community. Such abuse of the evaluation function violates the principles of intellectual freedom and is in opposition to the Preamble and Articles 1 and 2 of the Library Bill of Rights'.

The ALA has, of course, also been involved in the issue of access to library resources, in both traditional and electronic formats, for many years and has led opposition to internet filtering. In the USA, the First Amendment to the Constitution guarantees freedom of expression and this has been upheld in the courts as requiring libraries which provide internet access to do so without filtering on at least some workstations provided for adult use. The celebrated (or infamous) *Loudon County* library case, in which a US District Judge ruled that the installation of *X-Stop* filtering software on public library internet terminals 'offends the guarantee of free speech in the First Amendment' (McCullagh, 1998), was a *cause célèbre* for the ALA. In 2002, however, the Supreme Court ruled definitively that filters to prevent young people accessing pornography were lawful. In Britain, it is general practice for public libraries to employ filtering, although McMenemy and Burton (2005), in a volume aimed at public library managers, note that 'filtering of internet content is quite simply a form of censorship. It is an acceptable form of censorship for many organizations, but it is in the raw definition of the word, censorship. Indeed filtering is perhaps the most controversial of all management decisions that are made when it comes to providing internet access . . .' before going on to remark that both the ALA and CILIP 'take a pragmatic approach . . . suggesting that in an ideal world we should never censor information we supply to customers, but [acknowledging] the unique dimension the internet offers for providing easy access to inappropriate material'.

The Society of College, National and University Libraries

The Society of College, National and University Libraries (SCONUL)'s recent strategy statements place emphasis on the role of the academic library in providing access:

> [A]cademic and national libraries support academic and research excellence and development through the provision of intellectual, physical and electronic access to knowledge, information sources, ideas and services that sustain our diverse user communities. Our members also support users in the development of the information skills and information management competencies required to support their research, teaching and lifelong learning.
>
> (SCONUL, 2006a)

SCONUL was of course heavily involved in the earlier access v holdings debates and it is not surprising to find this emphasis in current statements.

SCONUL regularly debates the key issues for academic libraries and posts a list of 'hot topics' on its website (www.sconul.ac.uk/hot_topics). In early 2007 these were:

- e-learning
- e-research
- information literacy
- performance improvement
- scholarly communication
- space planning.

These topics relate very clearly to the issues identified above, but also reflect some of the changes which have taken place in UK academic institutions in recent years. These include:

1 A marked shift in the relationships between students and universities. This has arisen partly because of the introduction of fees – already common almost everywhere else in the world – and partly because uncertainties in the job market have made students more aware of the need to obtain good qualifications. For libraries this change in relationship could be highly significant as students, seeing themselves as paying customers, demand services delivered to the highest standards.
2 Encouragement for institutions to explore the use of ICTs in learning and teaching more vigorously.
3 An insistence that teachers in higher education should be qualified to teach, which should include clearer understanding of pedagogical issues and a commitment to excellence in delivering learning.
4 Emphasis on quality assurance of learning, teaching and research.

It is also noticeable that SCONUL has placed considerable emphasis on building design, and shown its commitment to excellence in this area through its own Design Award. Among recent trends has been stress on supporting multiple roles, with concern to provide appropriate spaces for both research and learning. New buildings, like the Saltire Centre at Glasgow Caledonian University, are deliberately user rather than collection focused. As the University's Pro-Vice Chancellor put it:

> [W]e needed to put people, and their learning – both in groups and as individuals – first. This aligns with current thinking in much of the library world where many are seeking to move the focus to people and learning. We were also aware that we had to accommodate our significant, and important, legacy of paperbased materials and at the same time develop and promote our increasing stock of electronic resources.
>
> (Watson, 2006)

This 'information commons' approach sees the future in shared spaces where students and staff of an academic institution are encouraged to interact, study, discuss and obtain help and support, whether with learning or technology. It moves towards the idea of the immersive library.

The Society of Chief Librarians

The Society of Chief Librarians (SCL) brings together the chief library officers of all the English and Welsh local authorities and acts as a forum and lobbying group. It is generally involved at a policy level in emerging and ongoing initiatives, such as the implementation of *Framework for the Future*. There is some sense of public libraries being bombarded with government initiatives of one kind and another. A recent guidance note suggests that 'the main focus should be on activities with children and young people, and on activities to support literacy where resources are stretched and help is required in determining priorities between competing initiatives' (Society of Chief Librarians, 2006a).

The SCL's concerns focus very much on community engagement, learning, literacy and reading. A recent consultation paper on the definition of a 21st-century reading service suggested that, inter alia, it would include:

- Reading service designed through community profiling/involvement
- Great building, inside and out – layout giving immediate ways into books
- Long opening hours, including Sundays
- Excellent stock range and depth – book expenditure higher than national average of 9%
- Powerful, interactive reader development programme making the library a community hub for reading
- Outreach work with segmented audiences, including socially excluded
- Harnessing of new nationally brokered partnerships.

(Society of Chief Librarians, 2006b)

This analysis is quite revealing of the ways in which public libraries see their futures. It again stresses the importance of supporting reading. It lays stress both on the excellence of the building and on outreach into the community, although the latter is still seen largely as a way of engaging excluded communities rather than a broader attempt to integrate library services into all relevant community services. The opening hours statement recognizes that libraries need to be available when people are free to use them, while the emphasis on 'excellent stock range and depth' has resonance with the former concept of the centrality of the collection from which services are delivered. While this particular paper was specifically concerned with reading, that in itself shows a current concern for what is the basis of all literacy and virtually all learning activities.

Benchmarking librarianship

Following work by a distinguished group of library and information management academics during 1999, a 'benchmark statement' was published by the UK Quality Assurance Agency, the body charged with assessing quality standards in all subjects in UK universities (Quality Assurance Agency for Higher Education, 2000). In 2007 another group of senior professionals undertook its revision (Quality Assurance Agency for Higher Education, 2007). These statements cover both the specific subject knowledge and skills which it is expected that a graduate at honours level will have acquired and their generic, transferable skills – among them generic skills related to knowledge acquisition and understanding, the ability to manage and reflect on their own learning, management skills, communication and interpersonal skills and competence in the use of ICTs.

The more specific knowledge and skills expected of graduates of librarianship and information management are based upon the following definition of the discipline:

> Librarianship and Information Management are closely related disciplinary fields which together encompass the principles and practice of knowledge representation, organization and communication in society, articulated by the generation, dissemination, exploitation and evaluation of information.
>
> (Quality Assurance Agency for Higher Education, 2007)

The core areas of the discipline are then defined in the following terms:

- Information resources and collection management.
- Information retrieval and knowledge organisation.
- Information literacy and user support.
- Information services and intermediary roles.
- Information agencies and professional institutions.
- Information environment and policy context.

(ibid.)

Following this, the benchmark statement goes on to describe the more specific subject knowledge and skills required, such as regulatory frameworks, information literacy and classification and indexing. It is the twin emphases on information content, and the techniques for exploiting it, and on users, including societal and organizational dimensions, which is perhaps most striking.

Conclusion

The professional and allied statements which have been summarized in this chapter reveal both similarities and differences of approach to libraries. It is noticeable that there is an increasing emphasis on the library as an agent of learning and that the access model (as described in Chapter 3) is prominent. At the same time there seem to be differing views on the importance of the library's collection, its organization and exploitation, although something of a renaissance of interest in developing appropriate collections on which to base services. The ethical concerns of librarians are prominent, as is the desire to engage closely with the user communities. All of the professional bodies give prominence to examples of good practice, from which emerges an impression of vitality at the local level – although it is difficult to judge how widespread this is.

The benchmark statement offers a more theoretical overview, but seems to confirm the validity of the overview of the different sectors presented in Chapter 2 and the models identified in Chapter 3.

5

What is a library? Digital libraries

> The cost of data storage is coming down rapidly . . . so for the money we can store more data. But all that we will then have is cheaper garbage.
>
> (Shank, 1983)

> Conceptions of the role of Digital Libraries have shifted from static storage and retrieval of information to facilitation of communication, collaboration, and other forms of dynamic interaction among scientists, researchers, or the general public on themes that are pertinent to the information stored in the Digital Library.
>
> (Candela et al., 2007)

Introduction

Many studies of libraries and librarianship at the present time are dominated by concerns with the effects of information and communications technologies (ICTs). In the preceding chapters it is clear that whether the view taken is sectoral, theoretical or professional, ICTs have become of almost over-riding importance to nearly all in the library and information management profession. In later chapters aspects of the technological underpinning of future libraries will be examined in more detail, but first it is useful to examine some of the approaches being taken to designing new types of library on technological foundations. While terminology is unsettled – with digital library, electronic library and virtual library vying for prominence – the first of these is preferred here because it appears to encompass the widest scope. However, it is important to acknowledge that the concept of the *hybrid library*, a blend of the traditional and the digital, represents the reality for most libraries at the present time.

Perspectives of digital library developers and commentators tend to be driven by their backgrounds in librarianship, information science, computer science, systems development, education or other disciplines. The discussion focuses most often on the technology, but also encompasses the development of new economic models, legal frameworks, user perspectives and social impacts. A small selection of approaches is discussed here in order to paint in the historical background and shed light both on the concept itself and on what it has to contribute to the development and shaping of future libraries. Lengthier discussion of digital library research can be found in Arms (2000, 2005), Deegan and Tanner (2002), Chowdhury and Chowdhury (2002), Dahl, Banerjee and Spalti (2006) and Candela et al. (2007). Online sources, such as *D-Lib Magazine* (www.dlib.org) and *Ariadne* (www.ariadne.ac.uk) contain important contributions to the debate. The overall issue is how libraries can offer enhanced service by utilizing electronic sources. Or, as Arms (2005) put it, 'the fundamental reason for building digital libraries is a belief that they will provide better delivery of information than was possible in the past. Traditional libraries are a fundamental part of society, but they are not perfect. Can we do better?'

Knowledge mediators

The European Commission was early on the scene with its *Telematics for Libraries Programme*. A supporting study within the programme, undertaken by Owen and Wiercx of NBBI in the Netherlands, developed what were called 'knowledge models for networked library services': 'libraries, as a component of the information chain, act as a link between knowledge sources and users' (1996). The authors suggested that they can therefore best be understood as *knowledge mediators*: 'the process whereby libraries provide users insight into the existing body of knowledge and assist users in acquiring resources referring to or containing such knowledge' (Owen and Wiercx, 1996).

In the context of networked information retrieval, libraries would no longer be 'restricted to the catalogue' but would make use of a wider range of tools in fulfilling this function. Three fundamental functions of the digital library were defined in this work:

- Making available various types of knowledge resources
- Providing resource discovery mechanisms which allow users to identify relevant or requested resources and their locations
- Providing mechanisms for delivery of specific resources to the user; delivery includes both obtaining a resource when it is not already available in the library, and passing it on to the user in a suitable way.

(Owen and Wiercx, 1996)

The process of acquiring information, or *resource discovery* in the authors' terminology, was shown in this model to involve three processes: *resource location*, through which the user discovers the existence of an item and a location for it; *resource provision*, involving the provision or acquisition of the resource to the library; and *resource delivery*, which involves such processes as on-site consultation, photocopying and downloading. The resource discovery system itself contains document descriptions, pointers to locations, searching or browsing mechanisms and, sometimes, abstracts or full text. Owen and Wiercx pointed out that the choice of resource discovery mechanism restricts the set of resources that the user can access – most obviously, the library catalogue usually restricts the set to those publications held by that library.

Owen and Wiercx developed their model further by examining parallels with traditional library functions (such as user support) and then developed a series of 'application models' to assist libraries to incorporate networked resources alongside traditional services. One of the main issues for libraries which they identified was the management of user expectations, which they recognized as being raised by the ease with which networked resources could be accessed directly: 'This creates an unfavourable situation for both sides: the user has to cope without the support and quality mechanisms of the modern networked library, and the library loses part of its user base'. This finding echoes earlier theoretical work by Buckland (1988). Other issues include staff awareness and skills, and the availability of adequate financial resources needed to migrate to networked services.

MOving to Distributed Environments for Library Services

A second major programme of research and development occurred in the UK in the mid to late 1990s. As described in Chapter 2, the Electronic Libraries Programme (eLib) funded a large number of experimental projects and a series of sometimes influential supporting studies. The eLib *MOving to Distributed Environments for Library Services*, or MODELS study, developed a 'MODELS Information Architecture' (MIA) as a way of describing systems which unify access to service providers through an intermediary while providing flexibility of data presentation to the user – and where the 'user' may in fact be software which processes, analyses and possibly re-uses results in some way on behalf of the human end-user(s). The MIA was described as both 'a conceptual, heuristic tool for the library community' and 'a tool to assist developers as they think about future systems work' (Dempsey, Russell and Murray, 1999).

In brief, the MIA characterized libraries as 'brokers' which both hide the complexities and differences of underlying resource discovery services from their users and facilitate data flows so as to enable processes to be automated. In this conception the broker is a *trading place*, 'where service requests and service providers come together' (Dempsey, Russell and Murray, 1999). A generalized description of such services includes the provision of:

- *user access*, including the presentation of an 'information landscape' and support for user profiles
- *an applications framework* consisting of software and data needed to manage the services, passing data between functions
- *distributed service interfaces*, which determine and control how requests are presented to underlying services
- *access control*, including the authentication of users and commercial transactions such as payments.

New or revised underlying services are handled by the applications framework and distributed service interfaces without requiring changes to the user access layer, since the service must operate in an environment of rapidly changing target services. Thus, adding a new service should be cost-effective (and the library both scalable and sustainable) since it does not require a new user interface to be built.

The applications framework was defined in terms of four key functions (similar to Owen and Wiercx's analysis described above): resource discovery, location, request and delivery. These require descriptions of the underlying services, including collection descriptions and interface descriptions (i.e. what information is available and the protocols needed to access it) and profiles of users which enable the system to determine access rights, preferences and so on. The MIA provided an underlying theoretical framework for the JISC's Information Environment – described below – and was of considerable significance for both digital and hybrid library developments worldwide.

Objects, handles and repositories

A series of papers produced as part of the US Computer Science Technical Reports Project, associated with the Library of Congress's National Digital Library Program (NDLP), and its precursor programme, *American Memory*, suggested a basic architecture for digital library services (Kahn and Wilenski (1995); W. Y. Arms (1995); C. R. Arms (1996); Arms, Blanchi and Overly (1997)). In essence the digital library was seen as constituted from digital objects, 'handles' or unique object identifiers, and repositories. One of the early implementations of this architecture occurred in the digitization of the Library of Congress's historic collections.

The development of the 'handle' system was central to the implementation of the concept in real-life systems, and it has evolved over recent years into an internationally significant service to the networked information community as a whole. Its essence lies in the development of persistent identifiers for digital objects which are independent of the current location or other 'state' of the resource, but which can be resolved into a location by a resolution service. The handle system has been developed by the Corporation for National Research Initiatives (CNRI), which is also the publisher of the influential *D-Lib Magazine*. It is the basis of work on Digital Object Identifiers (DOIs) – see www.doi.org and www.handle.net. This work is discussed in more detail in Chapter 10.

Core digital library services

Related to the NDLP described above, work at Cornell University explored issues associated with the development of distributed digital libraries. The Cornell Reference Architecture for Distributed Digital Libraries (CRADDL) was developed at much the same time as the MODELS work referred to above and defined a number of core services of the digital library (Lagoze and Fielding, 1998). These included:

- *a repository service* where digital objects can be deposited and stored, and to which the digital library provides access
- *a naming service* which ensures that each digital object has a globally unique name and that this can be resolved into at least one physical location
- *an index service* which enables sets of digital objects to be described and queries to be resolved into result sets containing unique names
- *a collection service* which performs selection against defined criteria, tailored and specialized catalogues or other resource discovery aids, and administrative processes.

CRADDL emphasized that without effective *naming* conventions and systems effective retrieval is impossible: in the CRADDL model this element consists of the application of Universal Resource Names (URNs) to digital objects, coupled with the provision of a *naming service* which links the URN to physical locations

– implemented using the handle system described above. It thus takes on the traditional library's catalogue-as-finding-tool role, but within a distributed environment. Again it is important to note that the architecture separates *naming* from *location*, which tend to be concatenated in the traditional library catalogue.

CRADDL also defined the *collection* as 'a set of criteria for selecting resources from the broader information space' (Lagoze and Fielding, 1998). This is a very important approach because it removes the concept of 'collection' from that of 'physical location' (whether physical artefacts or electronic entities on a particular server) back to the idea of the creation of collections by selection from the universe of information objects available. In the CRADDL model the collection needed to have no existence beyond the criteria for its selection: items could be selected for the collection dynamically from a wide range of sources as they are needed. Furthermore, the 'collection' might, through a carefully crafted set of criteria, grow or shrink with the development of its subject. Lagoze and Fielding suggested that this provides three key advantages: location and administrative independence, dynamic information object membership and extensibility.

The JISC Information Architecture

Drawing together much of the earlier work, and especially that emerging from the MODELS process within eLib, the JISC put considerable resources into articulating and implementing its Information Environment (IE), designed to 'provide a range of services, tools and mechanisms for [UK] colleges and universities to exploit fully the value of online resources and services. It will enable presentation, delivery and use of online resources in ways tailored to support individual and institutional requirements in learning, teaching and research' (JISC, 2003). The underlying basis for this development was the JISC Information Architecture, which provided a functional view of the design together with definition of appropriate standards and protocols to achieve interoperability between components. Powell and Lyon (2005) provided a series of use cases to illustrate how the functionality was derived from a series of scenarios and identified the processes of 'enter', 'discover', 'detail', 'useRecord' (i.e. the metadata record), 'request', 'access' and 'useResource' (i.e. the information object itself).

The model developed by JISC consists of four 'layers' together with a series of services which facilitate communication across the layers. A simplified diagram of this architecture is shown in Figure 5.1.

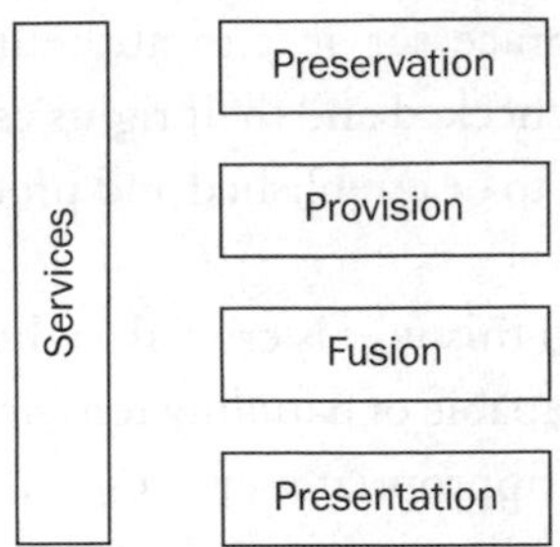

Figure 5.1 Simplified view of the JISC Information Architecture

The 'provision' layer contains the raw data services that provide the basic digital objects containing information which the library needs to be able to deliver to its customers. These are not simply databases on the familiar pattern, but a wide range of services including repositories of various kinds, many focused on different sectors, of which a learning object repository would be a good example.

The layer schematically above is labelled 'preservation' and is concerned with the long-term availability of resources – to future generations as well as today's users. It is important to distinguish between storage for preservation and storage for access, which have very different requirements in many respects, including physical storage, security and metadata. However, there also needs to be dynamic interchange between resources created primarily with access in mind and those held for long-term preservation purposes.

The 'fusion' layer contains a wide variety of services which bring together information on what is available. Obvious examples would be library catalogues, including union catalogues, indexing and abstracting services. They draw on the provision layer and make it more accessible through description, clustering and other approaches.

The bottom 'presentation' layer is the part which interacts with the end-user and is thus concerned with making use of intelligence on the user's precise needs and later transforming retrieved data into meaningful presentation. In essence it receives requests from a user interface and 'intelligently' transforms them into requests for transmission to services in the fusion or provision layer, or both. It may include various types of portal, although there is increasing use of a variety of plug-ins and Web 2.0 'mashups' to enable clients, including those hosted on mobile devices, to be multipurposed.

The services are concerned with providing the 'glue' which helps all of the independent components to work together. For example, they include terminology services to allow the user's language to be interpreted in respect of different services in the provision layer. They also embrace services to authenticate and authorize users, so that their identities can be checked and their rights established. They enable intellectual property rights (IPR) to be established and protected and the necessary transactions to be negotiated.

Separating the different types of services in this way is crucial to the development of integrated digital libraries which are capable of handling tens or hundreds of thousands of sources, identifying the most appropriate services to provide the intelligence which enables them to fulfil each user request and then to deliver an integrated product to the end-user. Most important of all, separation into service components breaks down the 'silo' effect of much early digital library development and opens up the possibility of any end-user service accessing any data provider, with strict adherence to standards and protocols enabling programmatic interpretation of result sets for integrated delivery to the end user.

The Digital Library Federation

In parallel with the JISC work, major research libraries in the USA have collaborated within the Digital Library Federation (DLF). The focus of the DLF has been on elucidating a 'discovery to delivery' (sometimes termed 'd2d') library business model, which is clearly related to the knowledge mediators, MODELS and other work described above. It 'creates and promotes standards and strategies that will lead to an extensive, open, distributed digital library with coherent pathways for scholars to discover, access, and use meaningful content' (Brogan, 2006). Not surprisingly, DLF has been particularly concerned with issues related to the development and exploitation of large collections. It has been particularly prominent in recent years in the development of standards-compliant repositories based on the Open Archives Initiative (OAI) framework and on the exploitation of the Open Archives Initiative Protocol for Metadata Harvesting (OAI-PMH).

User workflow and the digital repository

An emphasis that has emerged in recent years – which is not to say that it was wholly absent formerly – is that of the digital library as part of the workspace of the user. This has been particularly noticeable in the academic community where it is now common to talk of the library as a contributor to the scholarly communication process, rather than as an organization in its own right, offering services which fit into the user's workflow. Various influential studies have been published with this emphasis (see, for example, Lyon, 2003; Dempsey 2006a). There is a strong emphasis on the need to revisit library processes and services to determine how they can effectively deliver service into the natural working – or for that matter, leisure – environment of the user. For example, speaking of scholarly research, Clifford Lynch, Executive Director of the Coalition for Networked Information (CNI), has been reported as saying 'new practices, products, and modes of documenting and communicating research will have far-reaching implications for all organizations involved in managing the scholarly record and supporting the ongoing enterprise of scholarship, and that libraries in particular are in a central role due to their perspectives of managing the record across time and across disciplines'. He continued, 'these changes in scholarly practice will create profound changes throughout the entire system of scholarly communication, and a failure to put into place effective new support structures in response to these changes would pose tremendous risk to the enterprise of research and scholarship' (Goldenburg-Hart, 2004).

The concept of the digital repository has emerged as central to debates about changes in scholarly communication, with institutional repositories emerging as an essential part of universities' infrastructure. The repository has been defined in many different ways but derives from the idea that information objects will be placed in some kind of organized datastore, with associated metadata (though the metadata is of course not necessarily held alongside the objects themselves) from which they can be retrieved and served up to the user on request. Instead of giving their intellectual property away to journal publishers, universities will be able to make those results available worldwide, thus freeing the scholarly literature from current constraints. The arguments are rehearsed in a paper prepared for the UK Research Councils (Berners-Lee et al., 2005) and discussed further in Chapter 10.

Summary of digital library concepts

There are many approaches to modelling the digital library, but a number of common features emerge from the research and development which has taken place in recent years. These are:

- recognition that in the real world the information of interest to digital library users is to be found in a vast range of heterogeneous databases and collections, physically distributed but connected by electronic networks and containing objects of many different types

- distributed ownership and rights, including complex intellectual property rights
- a need to provide organization, provenance and authority for items and collections
- a wide range of users with a variety of client systems operating within a broad selection of environments and pursuing many different purposes
- a business need to control access to resources although the models, and especially the economic models, are far from clear
- a role, variously defined, for a broker or other intermediary which connects the users to the resources of interest to them
- a range of standards and protocols, for describing resources, for encoding them and for delivering them, including for searching and retrieval so as to achieve full interoperability between services.

It has already been noted that the term 'digital library' is used quite loosely in the literature. The European DELOS Network of Excellence has argued that it is helpful to differentiate clearly between the digital library itself, the digital library system and the digital library management system. It defines these as follows:

> **Digital Library (DL)**
> A (potentially virtual) organization that comprehensively collects, manages, and preserves for the long term rich **digital content** and offers to its **user** communities specialized **functionality** on that content, of measurable **quality**, and according to prescribed **policies**.
>
> **Digital Library System (DLS)**
> A software system that is based on a (potentially distributed) **architecture** and provides all functionality that is required by a particular Digital Library. Users interact with a Digital Library through the corresponding Digital Library System.
>
> **Digital Library Management System (DLMS)**
> A generic software system that provides the appropriate software infrastructure to both (i) produce and administer a Digital Library System that incorporates all functionality that is considered foundational for Digital Libraries and (ii) integrate additional software offering more refined, specialized, or advanced functionality.
>
> (Candela et al., 2007, *original emphasis*)

The DLMS has been likened to the system software or operating system of a PC.

The DELOS team has argued that one of the reasons for the slow development of sustainable digital libraries is the lack of this common underpinning infrastructure, leading to most DLSs being developed from scratch. Thus one strand of development which is likely to occur over the coming years is towards a small number of DLMSs on which services can be built which themselves are instantiated within particular digital libraries.

The real-world library

In the first edition of this book, published in 2000, I wrote that:

> a pragmatic view of the future of libraries would suggest that it is likely that most libraries will for the foreseeable future – which after all is not all that long – base their services on a mix of physical objects (books, paper-based journals, videotapes and the like) and electronic 'stuff' (web pages, remote data services, CD-ROMs etc.). For this reason, approaches which stress the management and delivery of 'hybrid library' services would appear to be the most useful.

There seems little reason to change that view, although the term 'hybrid library' is no longer as widely used as it once was. Nevertheless, the summary below, written nearly ten years ago, remains valid:

> Most users will continue to be offered a mix of formats via a mix of delivery systems. The challenge for library managers is to create integrated services which provide a 'seamless' service to the user. The user should be able to access services through consistent interfaces which provide compatible features (so that, for example, the user does not have to adjust her search strategy and syntax each time she wishes to use a different source). The hybrid library should not, however, be homogeneous: it should be able to adjust its services to the needs and rights of each user.
>
> (Brophy and Fisher, 1998)

What has changed in the last ten years is that virtually every library service is now 'hybrid' in the sense referred to above.

Conclusion

The digital library concept has been hugely influential in the development of real-world library services over the past decade. Very few libraries in any sector remain unaffected, and the underlying architectures are driving the development of all the systems which libraries exploit. They are of supreme importance to future development.

6

What is a good library?

> Librarianship is a curious profession in which we select materials we don't know will be wanted, which we can only imperfectly assess, against criteria which cannot be precisely defined, for people we've usually never met and if anything important happens as a result we shall probably never know, often because the user doesn't realize it himself.
>
> (Charlton *in* Revill, 1985, 132)

Introduction

A useful way to explore the essence of libraries is to examine how researchers and practitioners view 'goodness' in the library context. What is it that makes a 'good' library? The question was formalized some decades ago, most notably in a seminal paper by Orr (1973) entitled 'Measuring the Goodness of Library Services'. He suggested that in fact two questions need to be asked: 'How good is this library?' and 'How much good does this library do?'. Today we might be more likely to label these as the *effectiveness/efficiency/economy* and *impact* questions. The first is, in essence, concerned with measuring and assessing the performance of the library against some agreed criteria, as when the number of books issued per head of population is compared with the national average. The second, much harder to measure, is whether the library made a difference, for example, to the student studying for a degree.

During the last 50 years, a great deal of work has been done on the assessment of library performance. Initially much of this effort was based on the systems view of the library, examining questions of inputs, processes and outputs. Somewhat later, the emphasis shifted towards the application of quality management concepts to libraries, with questions such as the service's fitness for purpose. Still more recently, the emphasis has been on the assessment of impact. A more extended consideration of this field than can be attempted in this chapter will be found in Brophy (2006).

The library as a system

The term 'system' can become a catch-all, and is particularly dangerous in an ICT-intensive world where it too often is assumed to have technological meaning. But it has a long history in management and organizational theory, and is helpful in defining libraries, because, as earlier chapters have indicated, they are concerned with systematic *processes* in their particular context of information and its use.

The essence of the systems approach lies in the view of the library as an organization operating within an external environment and interacting with that environment in terms of inputs and outputs. The organization itself is concerned with processing inputs to create outputs. At its narrowest, the systems approach can lead to a rather blinkered view of the library – as though outputs (such as book issues) have outcomes (such as well-read students) that are not seen to be the concern of the librarian. This is, of course, a dangerous state of affairs, since users can find other ways to satisfy their reading needs – or not bother! The simple closed system model is clearly inappropriate.

Libraries are better thought of as open systems, where the influence of the system on the environment and the environment's influence on the system are explicitly considered. At one level this is a question of survival – Childers and Van House (1989) commented, in terms of inputs: 'To survive, the organization must acquire resources, which are controlled by various external groups. Therefore the effective organization is one that responds to the demands of its environment according to its dependence upon the various components of the environment for resources.'

The simplest view of a system is that shown in Figure 6.1, where an example of an output would be a book lent to a library user.

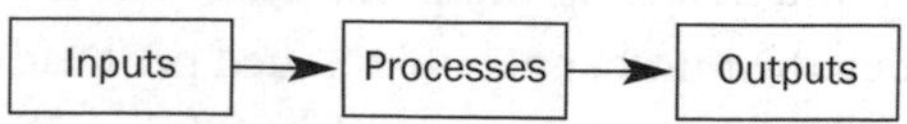

Figure 6.1 Simple systems diagram

The question of value, and the recognition that real-life systems are open leads to the inclusion of outcomes, which may be thought of as short-term effects, such as books being read, giving Figure 6.2.

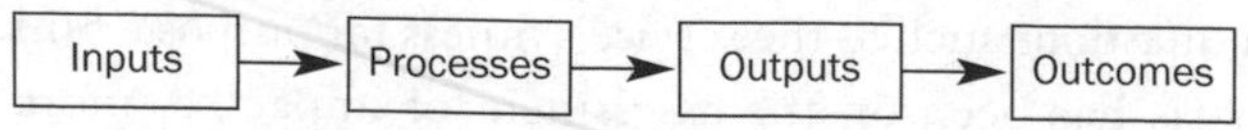

Figure 6.2 Systems view including outcomes

Impact takes this a stage further by asking what happened as a result of the outcome. For example, did reading Sir Ernest Gowers' *The Complete Plain Words*, published in 1954, lead to improved use of English? Or did *Das Kapital*, published in 1864, lead to a revolution? Both would be 'impacts' (Figure 6.3).

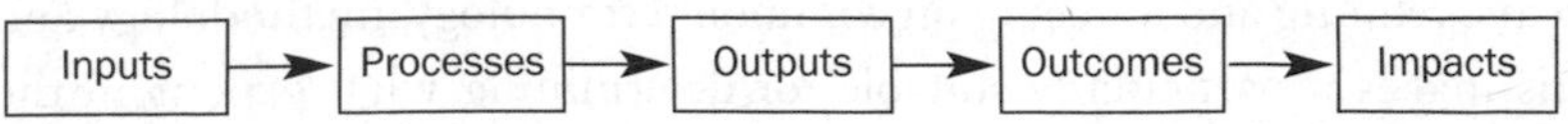

Figure 6.3 Systems view including impacts

Management of the system assumes that outputs, outcomes and impacts generate feedback which is used to control inputs and processes as in Figure 6.4.

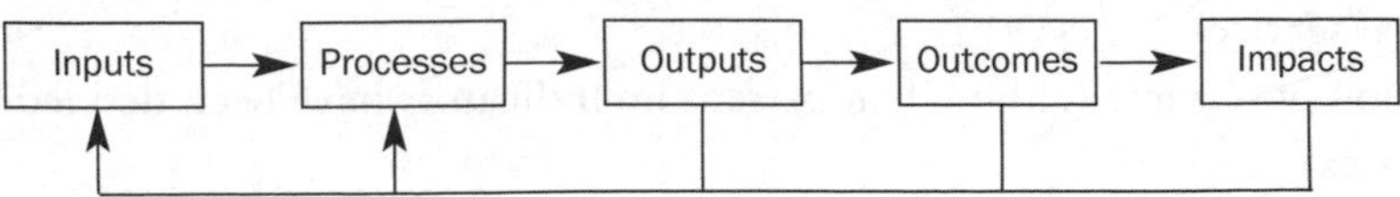

Figure 6.4 Systems view with feedback

The question of goodness can then be related not only to the efficiency and effectiveness of the *processes*, and not only to actual outputs and outcomes, but also to the adaptability and responsiveness of the library to its environment. This model underpins many of the studies of library performance and library quality which have been published in the past.

International standards

The International Organization for Standardization (ISO) has published both a standard on library statistics, ISO 2789 (International Organization for Standardization, 2003a) and a standard set of performance indicators for libraries, ISO 11620 (International Organization for Standardization, 1998). The latter has been supplemented by a technical report, ISO/TR 20983 (International Organization for Standardization, 2003b) on indicators for electronic services.

For the purposes of this discussion, namely to explore what performance measurement standards reveal about the key aspects of library services, ISO 11620 and ISO/TR 20983 are the critical documents. ISO 11620 is intended to be applicable to all types of library in all parts of the world. However, it explicitly states that it does not include 'indicators for the evaluation of the impact of libraries either on individuals or on society', so assumptions must not be made that this omission is significant.

The Standard begins with definitions of terms: a 'user', for example, is simply a 'recipient of library services'. It then sets out the criteria for inclusion of an indicator in the Standard: it has to be 'thoroughly tested, validated and (preferably) documented in the literature'. In other words the Standard is effectively a drawing together of work which has been undertaken by libraries and research centres over the years, refining and agreeing on common terminology, methodology and usage. This makes it particularly suitable for determining what experts in the field feel has been noteworthy.

There are five categories of indicator:

- user perception
- public services (by far the largest section)
- technical services
- promotion of services (although at present no indicators have been defined in this area)
- user services.

User perception is to be measured by satisfaction with services. Public services include:

- the percentage of the target population reached
- library visits per capita
- percentage of required titles in the collection
- in-library use per capita
- shelving accuracy
- time to retrieve a document from closed stacks
- loans per capita
- seat occupancy rate.

Technical services indicators are concerned with such matters as the time taken to acquire and process documents, while user services measures are focused on numbers of staff.

It is perhaps not surprising to find that these performance indicators describe a fairly traditional library, with the emphasis on the building and use of collections of physical artefacts. Turning to electronic services, ISO/TR 20983 complements ISO 11620, in some cases simply confirming the earlier indicators, such as user satisfaction. It draws heavily on work undertaken in the EC-funded EQUINOX project (Brophy, 2001a) which involved a wide range of European libraries. A pertinent observation is that it is by no means obvious what units should be chosen for measurement. As Brophy and Wynne (1997) remarked:

> In the electronic environment it is necessary to find new, reliable indicators of 'service provided'. There is thus a basic issue here concerning the most appropriate indicators to use: for example, use of electronic services could be measured by reference to *connect time*, *number of sessions*, *number of concurrent sessions*, *number of hits*, *cost*, *number of active users* or a variety of other factors. Care has to be taken with each of these possibilities, since it is possible that each could be affected by irrelevant and indeed uncontrollable variables. For example, *connect time* may well depend on network response times outside the control of the individual library, while number of hits could be drastically curtailed if a cache came into use.

Work undertaken in the USA at much the same time as that paper was published explored some of these issues in more depth. The influential *Developing Statistics and Performance Measures for the Networked Environment* (Bertot, McClure and Ryan, 2000) built on a key precursor report – McClure and Lopata (1996). This work sheds some interesting light on the underlying models of the 'library' which need to be addressed, including:

1 the difficulty of finding a satisfactory definition for 'document' in the electronic environment, where an object may be dynamic and may be made up of many smaller information objects, as when an article refers to images which are held as separate files
2 the boundaries of the 'library', which are very fuzzy, so that it is difficult to know what is a 'library' service. For example, use of a link from the library web pages while using a PC in the physical library would seem to qualify as a 'library service' but it is unclear as to the circumstances in which account should be taken of exactly the same action performed by a library user when at home
3 the number of items delivered may be irrelevant to performance, since users can download many items in the process of browsing through them and discarding most. The traditional information retrieval measures of precision and recall have limited application in such environments. Google has demonstrated this issue conclusively, but there is still controversy over how ranked lists should be assessed
4 readily available statistics are often worse than useless. For example, website 'hits' can be counted in so many different ways and are generated by so

many different applications that interpretation is almost impossible. All that can be said with certainty is that zero hits is a bad thing!

5 the response times experienced by users, frequently viewed as a key user satisfaction issue, are often outside the library's control as delays may be caused by downstream bottlenecks. Extracting true *library* performance data in this area is thus very difficult

6 the convergence of library and computing services, whether or not it happens organizationally, makes the model behind traditional library performance indicators inappropriate.

While all of these difficulties have been recognized, key electronic library performance indicators emerging from the EQUINOX and ISO work include:

- the percentage of the population reached by electronic library services
- the percentage of the library's expenditure directly attributable to electronic services
- documents downloaded
- cost per session and per document downloaded
- virtual visits as a proportion of total visits
- percentage of reference requests submitted electronically
- attendance at user training sessions
- workstation usage rates.

It will be seen that most of these indicators are analogues of the tradi… indicators, with as yet little agreement on how the performance of fund… ally different, and particularly more integrated, services should be asse… Brophy (2001a) remarked:

> The further development of performance indicators will require a reco… of the role and function of the academic library in networked enviro… example, the old paradigm of direct service is being replaced, at lea… disintermediation where the library acts as a broker to set up, … value to services which users access directly at their desk-tops.

Public library performance in the UK

Turning to the UK public library sector, the DCMS introdu… dards in April 2001 and modified the initial set in the ligh…

publication of *Framework for the Future* (DCMS, 2003). Further modifications followed and in 2006 public libraries were expected to meet standards defined in relation to ten criteria:

- the proportion of households living within specified distance of a static library
- aggregate scheduled opening hours per 1,000 population for all libraries
- the percentage of static libraries providing access to electronic information resources connected to the internet
- the total number of electronic workstations with access to the internet and the libraries catalogue (available for public use through both static and mobile libraries, and other service outlets) available to users per 10,000 population
- requests
  — percentage of requests for books met within 7 days
  — percentage of requests for books met within 15 days
  — percentage of requests for books met within 30 days
- number of library visits per 1,000 population
- the percentage of library users 16 and over who view their library service as:
  — very good
  — good
  — adequate
  — poor
  — very poor
- the percentage of library users under 16 who view their library service as:
  — good
  — adequate
  — bad
- annual items added through purchase per 1,000 population
- the time taken to replenish the lending stock on open access or available on loan.

(Department for Culture, Media and Sport, 2006)

Again it is notable that the indicators focus very much on traditional conceptions of the library. They are concerned with the accessibility of physical branch libraries, visits to those libraries, the number of workstations in the library (rather than external ways of accessing services) and indicators of collection strength and currency.

Demand for library services

A key issue for libraries, whether traditional, hybrid or digital, is how to generate and sustain appropriate levels of demand for services. Many libraries, along with numerous other public sector services, are in the situation that their immediate customers do not pay directly for their services. There is thus a question as to which stakeholders require which performance indicators. Brophy and Coulling (1996) put it this way:

> In most settings, the customers pay for goods they receive; in academic institutions and public libraries . . . this is not the case, and care must be taken not to make assumptions that providing the funders with the service they demand will satisfy the actual users and the other stakeholders.

Equally, of course, providing the end-users with the services they want may not satisfy the funders!

Buckland (1988) has written extensively on these issues, particularly on the 'double feedback loop', which separates the responses of library managers and those of users to unsatisfied demand. If demand for a particular library service – perhaps for a particular book – is higher than the service can immediately satisfy, then the librarian may take action to increase the service – perhaps by buying extra copies or by reducing the loan period (in academic libraries usually by placing items in a short loan collection) so that existing copies circulate more rapidly. Quite independently, the user, when faced with the book's unavailability may reduce demand on the library's service by a variety of strategies, such as going to another library, buying a copy, borrowing one from a friend or tutor, or simply giving up. (Incidentally, real-life examples of each of these strategies were discovered by Goodall and Brophy (1997) in their study of franchised course students.) The librarian's actions may stimulate additional, or at least reveal pent-up, demand; the users' actions may reduce demand on the library. However, as Buckland (1988) points out:

> [S]ince library services are normally free, the library's income does not depend directly on the level of demand. Reduced demand, therefore, does not weaken the library as it would a business, where a drop in demand would reduce sales and, therefore, income. Quite the reverse, a reduced demand for a free service reduces the pressure, leaving the existing resources more adequate to cope with the remaining demand. (Similarly, serving increased demand may not be as rewarding as it would be for a commercial business.)

Thus decreased usage can, in some circumstances, lead to increased satisfaction – but is this the aim?

It is interesting to apply this logic to electronic services and this will be considered at greater length later. However, it may be noted here that while a single electronic copy should, bandwidth and other technical factors permitting, be able to serve virtually unlimited demand, other factors start to come into play which tend to uphold the double feedback loop mechanism. For example, the decisive factor may become which of several possible services the user finds it easiest or most pleasant to access – an issue examined in detail later in this chapter when quality attributes are examined.

Quality management

Introduction

A considerable amount of work has been carried out in examining the application of quality management to libraries (see, for example, Milner, Kinnell and Usherwood, 1994; Brophy and Coulling, 1996; Brockman et al., 1997; Brophy et al., 1997). At the heart of this work is the recognition that, as services, the primary motivation for libraries should be to meet the needs of their users as well as is possible. Quality management is based on precisely such a premise, its foundations being laid on definitions of quality which stress that the 'goodness' of a product or service can be measured only in terms of the extent to which it meets the customer's or user's requirements – in formal terms quality is defined as 'fitness for purpose' or 'conformance to requirements'.

Total Quality Management (TQM) stresses a customer focus and continuous improvement as core values. Brophy and Coulling (1996) list ten intertwined facets of TQM which need to be developed simultaneously:

1. Developing a clear purpose for the organization
2. Providing vision, commitment and leadership
3. Encouraging teamwork and involvement by all staff
4. Ensuring that the design of all products and services is customer-oriented
5. Having clear, systematic, unambiguous and universally applied processes
6. Investing in continuous training and development of all staff
7. Monitoring performance continuously and acting on the results
8. Benchmarking achievements against the best in the sector
9. Developing co-operative rather than confrontational relationships with suppliers

10 Careful control of resources and awareness of costs.

In recent years, there has been a noticeable movement towards redefining TQM in terms of 'business excellence' and the 'learning organization'. The latter concept is based on the idea that an organization needs to go beyond the training of individuals, to become a 'learning entity'. The organization itself should be capable of learning, of adapting and changing in response to internal and external stimuli, through facilitating the learning of individuals, teams, sections, departments and ultimately the whole enterprise. Of course organizations themselves cannot think or feel, so what is being suggested is the organization of individual learning in a systematic way that enables the total contribution to be brought to bear on all activities in a planned, yet dynamic fashion. The link to knowledge management, described in Chapter 2, is clear.

Library quality

A considerable number of studies have sought to relate specifically to libraries the understandings of service organizations that have arisen from a quality management perspective. The importance of this approach lies firstly in its very clear focus on customer perspectives – quality is defined in terms of customer purposes and expectations – and secondly in its emphasis on continuous improvement. It is thus concerned with change, but change which is motivated by a closeness to user needs and wants.

Quality management generally builds on systems models and thus, in library terms, fits closely with the systems approach described above. However, its further relevance for present purposes – i.e. for helping to improve understanding of what libraries are for and what role they might play in the future – lies in the definitions of quality itself. While the broader quality management approach has been described by Brophy and Coulling (1996), this tighter focus draws on work initially undertaken by Garvin (1988) in the USA. In essence, it identifies a series of quality attributes: Garvin's initial eight have been modified and expanded to ten attributes in their application to libraries (see Marchand, 1990; Brophy, 1998; Griffiths and Brophy, 2002; Griffiths, 2003; Brophy, 2004b). The aim is to increase understanding of what makes a library service attractive to users and potential users alike and thus to identify critical aspects of service. In the following account, illustrated in Tables 6.1 to 6.10, the initial description of each attribute is followed by two sets of examples. In the left-hand column of each table these are taken from the automobile industry, an area with long experience of quality management approaches and with a need to cope with intense competition and rapid change. The right-hand column is related to library services.

Performance

These are the primary operating attributes of the product or service – what every customer would expect the product to have without having to ask. Their presence has little effect on customer satisfaction, but their absence leads immediately to complaints and dissatisfaction.

Table 6.1 Performance

Automobile	Libraries
• Seats • Gear change • Heater • Interior light	• Catalogue of stock • Logically organized stock • Study space • Knowledgeable staff

The exact definition of these core performance attributes depends, of course, on the individual library and the mission it is trying to accomplish.

Features

These are the secondary operating attributes, which add to a product or service in the customer's eyes and make the whole service more attractive but which are not essential to it.

Table 6.2 Features

Automobile	Libraries
• CD player • Air conditioning • Side airbags • Automatic windscreen wipers	• Link to document delivery from the online catalogue, so that clicking on the item results in it being delivered to the user's home or place of work • Personal notification of new acquisitions • Coffee shop

It is not always easy to distinguish 'performance' characteristics from 'features', especially as what is essential to one customer may be an optional extra to another. Furthermore, over time 'features' tend to become 'performance' attributes – direct delivery of full text is already taking this path, becoming an essential adjunct to library services. Nevertheless there is a valid distinction to be made. One way to check this distinction is to ask, 'Can this aspect of service produce "customer delight"?' Generally, performance attributes are taken for granted – it is only when they are not there that customers notice, and then complain. Features, on the other hand, are usually not noticed when they are absent since the customer did not expect them. When they are provided, customers are surprised at this 'extra' benefit and express delight with the service.

Conformance

The question here is whether the product or service meets the agreed standard. These are both national or international standards (for example, technical standards) and locally determined service standards. The standards themselves, however they are devised, must of course relate to customer requirements.

Table 6.3 Conformance

Automobile	Libraries

• National 'type' standards
• Performance in crash tests
	• Anglo-American Cataloguing Rules, edition 2
	• Z39.50 compliant catalogue
	• Service standards
	  – Average acquisition time
	  – Average ILL delivery time

It is of course important not just to have stated service targets but to determine whether they are being met consistently.

Reliability

Customers place high value on being able to rely on a product or service. For products this usually means that they perform as expected (or better). For services the idea of reliability translates best into 'correct service'.

Table 6.4 Reliability

Automobile	Libraries
• No breakdowns	• Are correct answers given to queries? • Are links on the library's website working correctly?

Reliability also includes service availability – even short periods of unavailability can cause user frustration with a service, especially because expectations of an immediate response are now so high.

Durability

Garvin (1998) defines 'durability' as 'the amount of use the product will provide before it deteriorates to the point where replacement or discard is preferable to repair'. For library services, especially those which are IT based, the question may revolve around longevity of the solution adopted. To some extent this is dependent on technological progress, which may be difficult to predict, but views can be formed on whether a service is within the mainstream of development effort or adopting a more risky approach.

Table 6.5 Durability

Automobile	Libraries
• How prone to rust • Mechanical durability	• Hardback likely to outlast paperback • Long-term support for users' preferred solutions (e.g. for a widely used reference manager system) • Technology has clear development path

Currency

For most users of libraries, the currency of information, i.e. how up-to-date the information provided is when the user retrieves it, is a more pressing issue than durability.

Table 6.6 Currency

Automobile	Libraries
• Is it the latest model? • Does it have the most up-to-date features?	• Latest editions of books • Latest issues of journals • Today's newspapers available when the library opens

Serviceability

When things go wrong, how easy will it be to put them right? How quickly can they be repaired? How much inconvenience will be caused to the customer and at what cost? This last will include not just the direct cost, but the inconvenience and consequential losses the customer faces.

Table 6.7 Serviceability

Automobile	Libraries
• Ease of obtaining spares • Network of garages • Complaints procedures • Comprehensive warranty	• Correction of errors in description or document supply • Courtesy of staff • Receptivity to complaints and suggestions

In general libraries and information services have not had to give a great deal of attention to these issues in the past, but they are becoming of major importance especially where an online information service is being provided on a commercial basis. A particular issue for libraries will be the ability to deliver the 'right' information object in response to poorly formulated queries.

Aesthetics

While this is a highly subjective area, it can be of prime importance to a customer, even if subconsciously. This is why so many commercial services place heavy emphasis on physical design.

Table 6.8 Aesthetics

Automobile	Libraries
• Design (exterior and interior) • Finishes • 'Lifestyle' statements	• Building design, including finishes • Web home page design

A modern, light, airy building, which is well designed and well laid out, can give an impression of quality that can over-ride the actual experience of using the service. Relatively poor service in an aesthetically pleasing environment may be preferred to an average service in a building which is drab and uninviting. First impressions are often the basis for user selection of services, and may have little to do with actual functionality.

Perceived quality

This is one of the most interesting of attributes, because it recognizes that all customers make their judgements on incomplete information. They do not carry out detailed surveys of 'hit rates', or examine rival information retrieval systems' performance or check the percentage of interlibrary loan requests completed within two weeks. They do not read the service's mission statement or service standards and they do their best to by-pass the instructions pages on the website. However, they will quickly come to a judgement about the service based on their preconceptions as users and on the reputation of the service among their colleagues and acquaintances.

Table 6.9 Perceived quality

Automobile	Libraries
• Japanese cars are reliable • German cars are well built • American cars are 'gas guzzlers'	• 'The library is great – the staff are really helpful and nothing's too much trouble' • 'The library is a waste of time – they never have the books you want and the staff always give the impression that you're interrupting them when you ask for help'

Accessibility

The question posed here is, 'Can *this* user make use of *this* service?' Most services and products are designed for the 'standard' customer – tall people may hit their heads on the hanging signs while small users may be unable to lift books off a top shelf. More seriously, a considerable proportion of library users have a disability of some kind and need special consideration if they are to access library services in the electronic era: for example, 2% of the UK population – over a million individuals – have some form of visual impairment.

Table 6.10 Accessibility

Automobile	Libraries
• Seat adjustment • Conversion for disabled users available	• Some of the OPACs have the mouse situated where left-handed users can use it • Large-screen PCs • Audio-based browsers for web access • Braille option instead of print • Text telephone for hearing impaired users

The ten attributes outlined above provide some insights into what is meant by 'quality' in a library context. They reinforce the strong user-orientation of much work in this field but provide additional analysis which helps to demonstrate the issues which are likely to be of particular importance to libraries in the future.

LibQUAL+™

A related approach, arising from the work of Zeithaml, Parasuraman and Berry (1990), has been pursued in the USA and has led to a widely used tool in the academic library sector, LibQUAL+™. The three American researchers, working with customer focus groups in each of four sectors (retail banking, credit cards, securities brokerage and product repair and maintenance) used market research based methodologies to establish the criteria used by customers in assessing the quality of services. Their work is interesting precisely because it deliberately focused on how customers perceive quality in *services* rather than in *products*, and thus has considerable relevance to libraries. It is worth noting, incidentally, that this team of researchers observed that customers find it more difficult to assess the quality of services than the quality of products. By analysing the data from their focus groups, Zeithaml, Parasuraman and Berry were able to identify ten 'dimensions' of service quality, common across all of the services examined, and closely related to Garvin's analysis and the later adaptations described above. These dimensions (adapted from Brophy and Coulling, 1996) were:

1. *Tangibles*: Is the service an attractive place to visit? Are the staff appropriately dressed? Do they use modern, up-to-date equipment?
2. *Reliability*: Is my telephone call returned when the receptionist said it would be? Is my bank statement free of errors? Does the washing machine work when it has been repaired?
3. *Responsiveness*: When a problem occurs, is it quickly put right? Is the company willing to arrange to repair the washing machine at a time to suit me?
4. *Competence*: Do front-line staff give the impression of knowing what they are doing? Similarly, does a repairer appear to know how to diagnose a fault and carry out a repair with confidence?
5. *Courtesy*: Are staff pleasant, even when asked difficult (or what may appear to be ridiculous) questions? Does the repairer wipe his or her shoes rather than trample mud all over my hallway carpet? Do staff manage not to *appear* busy even when they are – so that I gain their attention when I need it?
6. *Credibility*: Does the service enjoy a good reputation – do other people speak well of it? Do I get a credible and worthwhile guarantee with a repair, such that I can have confidence that any problems will be put right quickly and without further expense?
7. *Security*: Is it safe to use the service? For example, is my credit card safe from unauthorized use? Do I have confidence that the repair was properly carried out to an acceptable standard?
8. *Access*: If I have a problem, can I get access to a senior member of staff to

help me resolve the cause? Does the company answer the telephone when I ring? Is it easy to find the repair company's premises?

9 *Communication*: Is the service explained clearly and the options outlined comprehensively? Do the staff avoid using unnecessary jargon? Do they listen to me? If something unexpected occurs and the repair company cannot keep the appointment it has made, does it contact me in good time to rearrange it?

10 *Understanding the customer*: If I am a regular customer, does someone on the staff recognize me? Do they try to understand my individual needs? Do they try to arrange the repair visit to meet my convenience rather than their own?

Zeithaml, Parasuraman and Berry went on to refine their analysis and published a set of five key issues, which have become known as the 'Rater' set from the initial letters of each of the headings:

1 Reliability
2 Assurance
3 Tangibles
4 Empathy
5 Responsiveness.

Perhaps the most critical insight of these researchers was that methodologically quality may be measured by assessing the differences or 'gaps' between customer expectations and customer experience. They developed this observation into a widely adopted methodology called SERVQUAL (Parasuraman, Berry and Zeithaml, 1988).

In recent years the USA's Association of Research Libraries (ARL) has adapted this approach for use in libraries. LibQUAL+™ is described by ARL as 'a suite of services that libraries use to solicit, track, understand, and act upon users' opinions of service quality' (see www.libqual.org). Firmly based on the SERVQUAL methodology described above, LibQUAL+™ has been adopted by a considerable number of academic libraries in the USA and further afield, including in the UK and France.

A key aspect of LibQUAL+™ is the grouping of user satisfaction indicators into three themes:

- *affect of service*: including empathy of staff, responsiveness, assurance and reliability
- *information control*: including the scope of the content made available by the library, convenience, ease of navigation, timeliness, the equipment made available and self reliance
- *the library as place*: including utilitarian space, the building as a symbol and the library as a 'refuge'.

As implementations of LibQUAL+™ have progressed worldwide, the tools have proved flexible enough to accommodate a significant range of local variations. For example, in 2003 the SCONUL participants added five additional questions of their own, concerning:

- access to photocopying and printing facilities
- availability of main texts and readings
- provision for information skills training
- helpfulness of staff in dealing with users' IT problems
- the availability of subject specialist assistance.

In a further development in 2004, SCONUL institutions selected their own five local questions from a range of over a hundred possibilities, thus tuning the survey to each library's particular requirements.

Following on from the successful roll-out of the LibQUAL+™ methodology and system, ARL has embarked on the development of a parallel quality assessment system for digital libraries, to be called DigiQUAL™ (www.digiqual. org/digiqual/index.cfm). At the time of writing this was still under development.

Impact

Academic libraries have long been interested in assessing their impact, and over the years various studies have been undertaken. A new focus for this activity was created as a result of a joint SCONUL/LIRG Workshop held in Scarborough in December 2002. This event resulted in the launching of an 'Impact Implementation Initiative', which was in essence an action research programme undertaken by practitioners with advice from evaluation experts. The latter had many years' experience of conducting library evaluation, and had published two influential volumes entitled *The Effective College Library* (Streatfield and Markless, 1997) and

The Really Effective College Library (Markless and Streatfield, 2000). Deriving from that work, they further developed an 'impact process model' which in effect helped practitioners examine their own interventions in the learning and teaching process – 'a process to help people to decide together what they mean by impact and how impact can be evaluated for their innovation' (Markless and Streatfield, 2006). This approach thus emphasized the importance of investigating the local effects of service interventions.

In the public library sector the widely perceived need to find ways to demonstrate the impact and value of UK public libraries across the whole range of their activities was followed up in a piece of work funded by the Laser Foundation. Undertaken by PricewaterhouseCoopers LLP, the study published its final report in July 2005 (PricewaterhouseCoopers LLP, 2005). It emphasized that in each area identified for investigation both quantitative and qualitative evidence should be collected. For example, when measuring the impact of the public library on older people in the home the following indicators could be used:

- the numbers of older people accessing services for homebound users (in terms of numbers of visits to homebound users, frequency of visits and issues) – a quantitative measure; and
- results of interviews with these users of the service, asking questions such as: 'Does the service from the library improve your life in any way?' and 'Do you feel that this service better enables you to live independently?' – in other words, qualitative evidence.

It is often useful to be able to compare levels of impact across different user groups and for different library services. A methodology to achieve this was developed during an evaluation of the People's Network (Brophy, 2003; 2004a) and further refined after work on the performance of UK academic information services and with public libraries across Europe (Brophy, 2005a). The model places emphasis on assessing how users' behaviour changes as a result of exposure to library services.

It is also noticeable that in recent years there has been a resurgence of interest in the effect of the quality of the library building on impact. Harper (2006) reports one commentator as saying of new public library buildings in the UK:

> A quality product that respects and inspires people really does work. It makes people feel welcome and respected and allows them to use libraries in the way they want . . . Stratford (Newham) and Lowestoft (Suffolk) were conscious attempts to

> change the image of libraries locally, to encourage more and new use in competition with all the other attractions for people's time, and to make them the focus of their communities that they should be.

This again emphasizes that impact needs to be assessed in relation to the local population being served. It is perfectly possible for identical services to have very different impacts in different locations.

One further aspect of library effectiveness is worth mentioning, namely the social and economic impacts that the service has on its community. A variety of studies has been undertaken in recent years (see Chapter 5 of Brophy, 2006) demonstrating that libraries have quite significant social and economic benefits. For example, public libraries can be agents for improving social inclusion as well as significant contributors to economic well-being. Examples of such studies can be found in Usherwood (2002) and J.-M. Griffiths (2006).

Conclusion

Attempts to answer the question 'What is a good library?', whether from systems or quality management viewpoints, demonstrate a twin concern with quantitative measures of (mainly) outputs and with user perceptions. More recently there have been attempts to answer Orr's second question, 'How much good does this library do?' Although user satisfaction, quality attributes and other analyses have started to address this issue, it remains the great unknown of library services. While it is reasonable to infer that users would not continue to use services from which they gained no benefit, the complexity of interactions – particularly in the learning processes which so many libraries claim as their core area of concern – makes the isolation of library contributions difficult. Nevertheless, we are starting to see evidence being produced which demonstrates that libraries have significant effects on their local populations, in both social and economic terms, as well as on individuals.

The evaluation of library services reinforces the conclusions of earlier chapters that the essence of the library is to be found at the nexus of information and use, of information provider and information user and that the successful library is the one which manages services to maximize the benefits to stakeholders, of which the end-user, both as individual and as community, is the most important. Performance measurement retains an emphasis on the quality of collections and delivery from the physical building which is not always found in theoretical studies of libraries' futures, especially in the networked environment. This perspective suggests that the library, as a physical collection and a set of physically located services, still needs to be taken seriously in thinking about how a library service is to be delivered in the 21st century. However, it also demonstrates that concern to achieve impact on user processes, such as learning, is becoming more prominent.

Part 2

Future libraries

7

Linking users to resources

> Library directors . . . face an increasingly complex institutional and informational environment. The population they serve is far from homogeneous in its level of sophistication, information needs and infrastructure requirements. Faculty and graduate students, in particular, seem to be omnivorous in their appetite for information, creative in their strategies for seeking and acquiring information in all forms, and very independent.
>
> (Friedlander, 2002)

Introduction

The examples, models and approaches described in earlier chapters reveal a wide range of perspectives on the concept of the 'library'. Some of these views are driven by technology, some by the library's environment (for instance, the demands of its parent body) while some take a broad managerial, systems or societal perspective. Yet despite the differences within and between sectors, technological approaches and organizational environments, a clear commonality of purpose is revealed. It can be expressed succinctly as a common mission:

> *To enable users to gain access to and use the information that they need.*

The mission is focused first on users and is driven by their needs. It involves ensuring that users are able to access all the information of possible relevance to them, akin to the traditional information retrieval idea of recall – being able to retrieve as much as possible that is relevant despite the heterogeneity of sources and descriptions. The library also enhances that access by limiting and controlling it in ways beneficial to the user – rather like the information retrieval concept of precision, producing a selected but highly relevant set of results, removing the dross and avoiding overloading the user. But it is also important to stress that *use* is behind the access and retrieval processes – it moves the issues into the realm of outcomes and impacts, which earlier chapters suggested were valid and indeed vital issues for librarians to involve themselves in. The basic mission is expanded in the following commentary:

> '[E]nable' may involve delivery to the user, or training in information skills or simply organisation of sources in a way that users find helpful. 'Users' may sometimes be seen as passive, sometimes active and all kinds of terminology may be used to reflect sometimes quite subtle differences of approach – customer, client, patron, and so on. 'Gain access' may again be an active or passive process, may rely on 'pull' ('Come and get it') or 'push' ('Here's what you want') approaches, or more likely on a mix of the two, and certainly includes ensuring that the necessary skills and infrastructure are in place to enable use to take place. 'Information' may include works of the imagination, ideas, concepts, even persuasive literature. 'Need' will be expressed in many ways, and will be interpreted and modified as it is turned into requests for information objects. . . . In all of the processes involved in achieving this mission, the issues of quality, encapsulating factors such as timeliness, relevance, aesthetics, reliability and so on, are important.
>
> (Brophy, 2000a)

Furthermore, there is a growing realization that *use* also involves the *creation* of information objects of various kinds. Indeed, one of the noteworthy aspects of the last few years of service development has been the concern of librarians to support creativity, whether in the scholarly communication process in academia or in the management of knowledge resources in a commercial enterprise or in the reading group in the local neighbourhood. What appear at first to be linear processes in fact resolve into a virtuous circle, where information is used to support the creation of new works which are then added to the wealth of resources shared and made available to the user community in a continuous process.

This common mission is represented in all types of libraries in all the different sectors, whether they are traditional, digital or hybrid services. The aim of this chapter is to develop a generic model of the library as intermediary which will help inform further discussion of what the process of achieving such a mission will entail in the future.

The library as expert intermediary

Virtually all of the descriptions of libraries which are available stress in one way or another that the library 'intermediates' between the user and the information resources which are potentially available, in order to help the user make sense of, and gain access to, information sources. The term 'intermediates' is not used here to suggest that the library forces itself between the user and the information so that barriers are set up. It is rather that the library puts useful processes and procedures in place without which the user would be unable – or able only with great difficulty – to access and use the information. In other words, the library adds value to the process of finding and using information, by making otherwise unknown or inaccessible sources available, by saving the user's time, and so on. This intermediation may, however, be invisible to the user, an issue which will be explored later. So, at its simplest, this function is as shown in Figure 7.1.

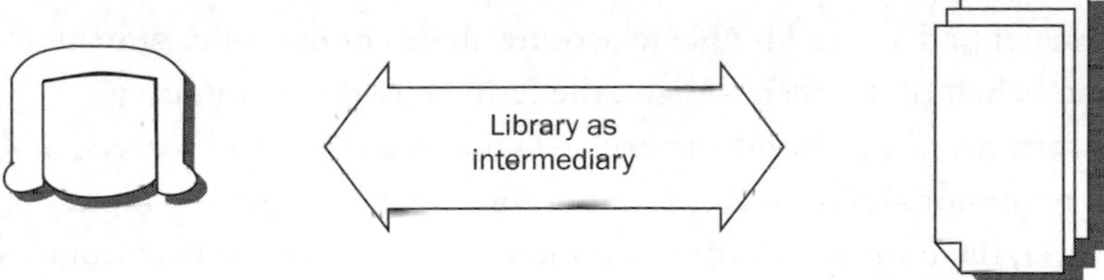

Figure 7.1 The library as intermediary

The terminology used to describe the 'intermediary' role is rather confused. Among the alternative terms in use, each of which has something to offer, are:

1 *Agent*, stressing that the library acts on behalf of the user, going out and finding relevant information, repackaging it and presenting it. In the UK an analogy might be with an 'estate agent' ('realtor' in American terminology) who has detailed knowledge of the market and attempts to fit the would-be purchaser's requirements to the available housing. More broadly, an 'agent' in computing is a piece of software which undertakes actions for a particular user based on knowledge of that user's preferences. This leads to ideas of 'intelligent agents' which can adapt to different environments and learn more about the user's likes and dislikes, ways of working and behaviours. (It is perhaps worth noting that the use of intelligent agents within library services is becoming a topic for considerable debate as part of discussion of Web 2.0 and Library 2.0 – see, for example, Dent, 2007.)
2 *Guide*, with emphasis on helping the user to find useful ways through the information maze, and on information access and use as a learning process.

This term also echoes a mantra that has become common in education, the move of the teacher from being a 'sage on the stage' to a 'guide on the side'. The idea is that users are perfectly capable of pursuing information (and learning) provided they are given appropriate help and guidance at appropriate times. However, it seems to neglect the role of organizing both information and systems.

3 *Mediator*, which carries with it the idea that libraries protect users from the vastness of unstructured resources by interpreting their needs and selectively limiting the materials provided. Again, however, it does not carry with it the role of organizing the content and systems.
4 *Broker*, which places stress on the use of expertise to work on behalf of a user in order to acquire a product. The analogy is with a stock broker who offers investment advice and is able to acquire shares or other investment products on behalf of the client. Again, the term is used in computing circles for software which forms the bridge between a client and servers, or between a requestor and databases or repositories. For some in the library field, however, the term has a rather commercial edge; it also suffers from much the same narrowness as 'guide'.
5 *Gateway* or *portal*, which suggests that the library acts as an entrance to information resources. The problem with this terminology is firstly that libraries do a lot more than simply provide a door which users can pass through and secondly that the term is now used widely for a vast array of different kinds of services.

For the purposes of this chapter the term 'intermediary' is retained, although its limitations are recognized.

Disintermediation

One of the paradoxes of the identification of the intermediary role as core to libraries is that it occurs against a backdrop of 'disintermediation' – which sounds like its exact opposite. This term is used for the process whereby users are encouraged to interact directly with services. So, for example, buying a book from Amazon does not consist of telephoning a human salesperson and negotiating to find the correct title, followed by reading out credit card data, waiting while address details are noted down and so on. Instead the customer interacts directly with the system. Similarly, in libraries the introduction of self-service issue – to take one example – is a process of disintermediation since it removes the need for staff to intermediate between the issue system and the user. The economic advantages of this process are obvious, but it can also bring benefits to the customers, for example, by reducing the need for queuing or by enabling them to be presented with choices and additional services which would be difficult to offer individually in person. Equally, many customers prefer the personal control which direct interaction with a system gives them. Were the phrase not so clumsy, it would be tempting to describe libraries as 'disintermediated intermediaries'!

It is possible to view disintermediation in a different light if the boundaries between 'users' and 'staff' are allowed to become fuzzy. Brophy and Coulling (1996) put it like this:

> Customers are participants in the service, because they can alter the product being delivered and the way in which it is delivered in response to the situation as it develops. . . . Information technology . . . enables services to move from customer–employee relationships to customer-service direct interaction. It is helpful when analysing these customer-service interactions to think of the customer as being (in part) an (unpaid) employee. People deliver services to themselves. This has enormous implications for improving quality provided that the sense of participation and ability to influence design and delivery that would be taken for granted by other employees is nurtured.

The removal of direct interaction between library staff and users is an ongoing trend, although there are some issues associated with it that deserve deeper analysis. For example, there is evidence that users do in fact value a measure of direct human intermediation and that librarians' changing roles need to acknowledge this dimension of service – 'patrons entering the "physical" library often need more help than before' (Melchionda, 2007). Gorman (2003) is emphatic on this point, speaking of 'the vital person-to-person component that has typified reference service across our history. This is an age in which human values are under strain and human contact and sympathy become more prized as they become more rare.'

Taking this factor into account it seems appropriate to continue to use the term 'intermediary' to describe the role of the library of the future but with awareness of its limitations. In particular, although *some* services are directly intermediated, others are organized on behalf of the customer with the library staying in the background, ensuring service availability and that everything runs smoothly – indeed it can be argued that in these cases the intermediary is most successful when the user hardly knows of its existence.

There is ample evidence that many services have seen a parallel shift. In networked environments service users have become used to a paradigm of service delivery which is based on delivery into existing or chosen workflows – and their equivalents for non-work activities, which we could perhaps term 'leisureflows'. A more generic term might be 'lifeflows' – the ways in which people choose to organize their activities for themselves. Where in the past a library or other service could deliver through its own interface, real or virtual, services now have to emerge within other frameworks. For example, in education there is, as we have seen, increasing emphasis on virtual learning environments (VLEs). Students log in at the start of their session and undertake all of their learning online, including watching videoed lectures, asking questions, engaging in discussions and writing essays. The library – which is not prominent within the VLE – may simply be ignored. We will look at the implications of this later in this chapter.

Library users

This brings into focus another issue of terminology, concerned with what have so far been called the 'users'. Again there are many alternatives, this time including:

1 *Customers*, which stresses that users interact with libraries in order to 'purchase' (albeit indirectly) a service and that they have choices – more and more they have opportunities to take their custom elsewhere. However, the notion is controversial in many environments, especially for libraries in education where debates rage as to whether students should be regarded as customers (see Eagle and Brennan, 2007). Nevertheless, the term is also a reminder of the *service* context of libraries with its obvious links to quality management's emphasis on customers, to 'customer care' and so on.
2 *Clients*, emphasizing that the relationship is one between a user and a professional adviser, and that the latter owes some kind of duty to the user. Just as a lawyer must act in the interests of his client, the library user-as-client concept puts emphasis on the librarian working for the user regardless of the employer's interests. So, for example, librarians owe a duty of confidentiality to their users which over-rides their employment duties.
3 *Patrons*, a term which arrived in the UK with American library management systems but which has little common currency among the users themselves. In British English one meaning it carries is that of a 'sponsor' or 'supporter' of a service, rather than a user – as in the Queen is the patron of various charities!
4 *Readers*, which suggests that the primary purpose of the library is to provide

both materials to be read and a place in which to read them. Some would welcome a re-emphasis on this role of the library! Indeed, the British Library still issues *reader* passes to those wanting to use its *Reading* Rooms (see www.bl.uk/services/reading/admissions.html).

5 *Members*, which carries a sense of ownership but is perhaps less appropriate in some sectors than others, especially where the service has a more commercial edge.

There is no agreement on the most appropriate term, for there is value in each of the alternatives, yet each offers only a partial view of a complex, changing relationship between each individual and the library. As Pinfield and Hampson (1999) remarked:

> Libraries carry out a large number of different activities, each of which implies a slightly different relationship with users. It might be said that there are a range of possible relationships. At one end of the range 'transaction-based' activities, such as lending and enquiries, might be described as a 'customer service' relationship with users. At the other end, activities such as providing information skills teaching alongside academics or the selection of major new electronic packages might be described as a 'partnership' relationship.

This book retains the use of the term 'user' but does so in full recognition of its limitations and ambiguities.

User populations

Each library serves a defined group of users. For the public library these may be the members of the local population (defined either by place of residence or by place of work or both). For the academic library the group may be the students and staff of the institution. For a commercial organization it may be the employees. One of the library's first tasks is to establish clearly the criteria by which membership eligibility will be judged. In effect, the library selects, or acknowledges the existence of, a sub-group from the 'universe' of possible or potential users. For example, a university may define its user group as those registered as staff or students of the institution, but may equally determine that members of the public resident in the locality will be eligible for limited services. The universe of possible users is then the total of the members of the institution and the population of the locality. The user population is the sub-group registered with the library. In a few cases, for example, where the user population is defined as all those in the user universe – as for instance in a commercial firm where all members of staff are automatically 'members' of the library but no one else is permitted to use it – then the user universe and user population are coterminous. Usually, however, it is useful to differentiate between the two because the library needs to gather specific information about those registered to use its services, not least if those services include the use of third-party systems with limited access rights, but needs to market services to the wider group.

The user population, once defined, may of course be sub-divided by reference to other criteria – as when undergraduates and academic staff are treated as distinct groups for an academic library's membership purposes or a public library differentiates between adults and children.

Collections

Just as there is a universe of potential users there is also an 'information universe'. This may be thought of as the sum total of recorded information which exists in the world (or maybe beyond if satellite data and data streamed from Mars probes and the like are counted!) and which is potentially available. It includes the books held by the world's libraries, all current and past journal issues, newspapers, databases of various types, the resources of the world wide web, report literature, ephemera such as handbills, patents, recorded visual images whether still or video, audio, realia such as artistic and museum objects, representations in virtual reality, multimedia presentations and so on. For many years librarians have drawn attention to the rapid explosion of published information and to the difficulties this poses for libraries and information services attempting to provide ordered access to the world's information for their users. The advent of digital information, together with the development of worldwide information and communications networks, has brought a new order of magnitude to this problem. While in the past the library's role may have been defined in terms of the collection which it brought together, and which would largely satisfy its clientele, the modern library, as we have seen, is more likely to act as an access interface to the global wealth of information, the 'information universe'.

It should be noted that the information universe also includes proprietary sources which may be restricted to a particular set of users, an example being the laboratory records of a pharmaceutical company which while 'recorded information' and thus part of the information universe are not 'published' in any real sense.

While libraries can act as the interface to this wealth of information, one of their most important tasks is to create order out of potential chaos. They do this by selecting and describing information sources which they will offer to their users. Today libraries select both physical materials to hold in their own stock and virtual materials which they do not own but to which they can provide access and about which they can offer some guarantee (or at least opinion) on quality and availability. The term 'collection' is a convenient way to describe the sources selected by a particular library from the universe of possible sources, bearing in mind the CRADDL definition (Chapter 5). It is worth noting that the libraries have always had the capability to go beyond their initial collection, by buying additional items, or requesting interlibrary loans. However, the speed with which electronic resources can be provided from remote services means that a library's collection must increasingly be treated as dynamic. Chodorow and Lyman (1998) have suggested that 'collection development will increasingly shift toward what might be called continuous live action'. Indeed, a considerable focus of development effort in the digital library community has been on systems which can support dynamic collections – where what the library is able to deliver is constantly changing in accordance with a defined 'collection' policy. The management of this dynamic resource is considered further in Chapter 10.

Within this understanding of the 'collection', the process of making sense of the information universe on behalf of users, partly by mapping and codifying it (including borrowing from the codification of others) and partly by selecting from it those parts which are likely to be of interest and are known, or likely, to be accessible, is critical. It is easy to forget that in the library's traditional role, book selection was often regarded as one of *the* professional tasks (see, for example, Fonfa, 1998).

It cannot be emphasized too strongly that this process of selection is in essence concerned with the provision of quality assurance. The library admits to its collection, whether a static resource or through dynamic access definitions, only those objects which it is satisfied meet a series of quality criteria, remembering that quality is essentially concerned with the 'fit' between a product and its users' requirements. In the traditional library it is possible for libraries to use important cues, such as publisher reputation, and to outsource some of the intellectual work – for example by relying on purchase recommendations, reading lists and the like. In the digital environment cues are far less obvious and reliable, although outsourcing may be achievable by co-operative activities like national subject gateways, the difficulty then being that they are more remote from the individual library's users, and thus less well informed about user needs in that context.

Because information sources may be available conditionally (e.g. only to certain groups of users, or only on payment of a fee, or only if copyright conditions are met) the library may choose to sub-divide the accessible collection depending on the user (increasingly generating this dynamically so that who you are controls what you see), or may attach conditions to what can be viewed. The version of the collection that the individual user sees might be termed a 'conditional collection', which changes and evolves continuously. The actual collection displayed to an individual is then equivalent to the 'information landscape' defined by the Models Information Architecture, as described in Chapter 5.

See Figure 7.2 for the simple intermediary model.

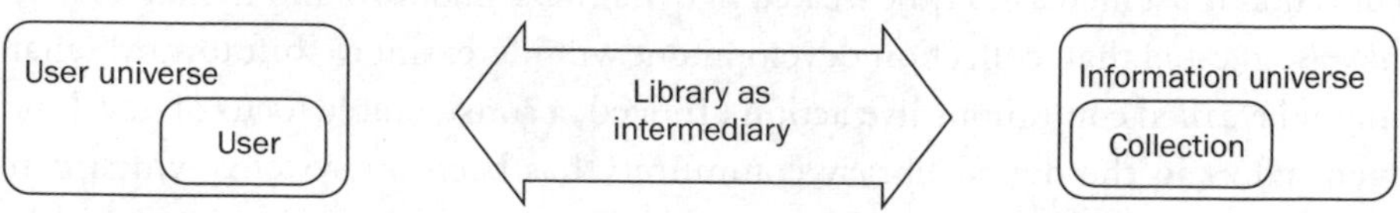

Figure 7.2 User and information populations

What this model neglects, of course, is the direct interactions taking place between the users and the information sources – the disintermediation discussed earlier. Any realistic model has to incorporate this activity – hence Figure. 7.3, emphasizing that the library can only play a part in any individual's use of information.

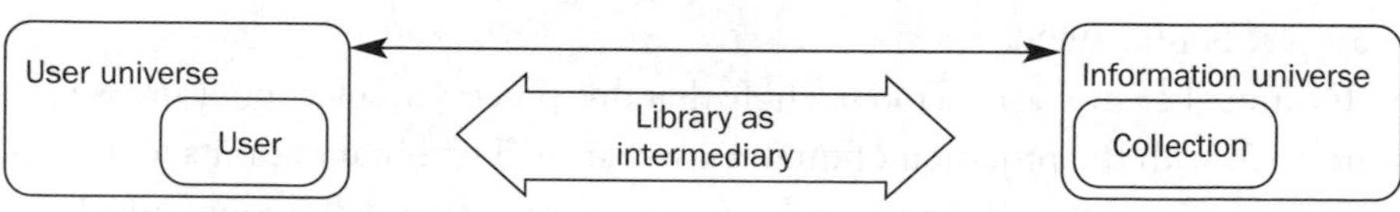

Figure 7.3 Direct as well as library intermediated interaction

Intelligence

The basis of the services the library provides lies in its 'intelligence' about both the user population and the collection. Traditionally, the former requirement has been met by collecting registration data, while the latter has been represented by the library catalogue and associated status data. Registration data would typically include the user's name, address and telephone number while the catalogue would be augmented by location information, such as shelf-mark and status data, which shows whether or not the item is on loan, being rebound or available on the shelves.

In an electronic or hybrid environment, this is insufficient. Ideally, the library needs to have a detailed 'profile' of each member of the user population. This profile might include:

- individual identification data: name, address, telephone and fax numbers, e-mail addresses and so on
- preferences data: level (especially in education), subjects of interest, languages, form (including accessibility requirements such as Braille output), geographical locations for hard copy delivery (for example, home and office, but with selection criteria identified)
- past history of information access, and feedback from use, which may be analysed to predict future interests
- sub-group memberships (linked to a general profile for each sub-group to define borrowing rights, for example)
- credit data, including limits and credit addresses
- public key for cryptographic requirements
- status data related to permitted activities.

When held in a digital directory such intelligence provides the basis for automatic authentication and authorization of users allowing seamless access to a wide variety of potential sources and for proactive delivery of services into life-flow systems.

Intelligence about the collection also needs to be enhanced beyond what was contained in traditional catalogue records. For example, part of this intelligence relates to terms and conditions. One source may charge by items delivered (the classic inter-library loan model) while another may allow unlimited usage but only by a particular sub-group of users. Yet another may impose restrictions on the purpose for which it can be used. The adequate description of the collection is achieved in a number of ways:

- through the way in which the library as a whole and its services are described – perhaps via a web home page or in printed guides and signs, but, following the above argument, also by exposure within user systems
- by describing sub-collections of material to which the user may have access
- through the way objects or descriptions of objects are arranged (whether in

the traditional library, with its books on shelves, or on a web page, or in a list of potentially relevant hits from a database)

- by providing details at a higher level of granularity – at the level of the book or similar object through the catalogue or at the individual paper through, say, an indexing or abstracting service; or possibly, especially with digital objects, at an even higher level of granularity, such as the individual files which make up a multimedia package.

The library must also ensure the reliability of the descriptions it uses. Again, dynamic objects create additional demands on libraries. For example, there may be many, subtly different versions of an object available from different sources, a particular problem with the advent of e-print repositories of various types, so that version control and recording of provenance are of considerable import.

The essence of an intermediary role is to use collected intelligence to create links selectively between the customer and service provider: in a library context, between the user and the information sources. High-quality user and information intelligence will, other things being equal, distinguish the excellent service from the rest. Figure 7.4 illustrates this model.

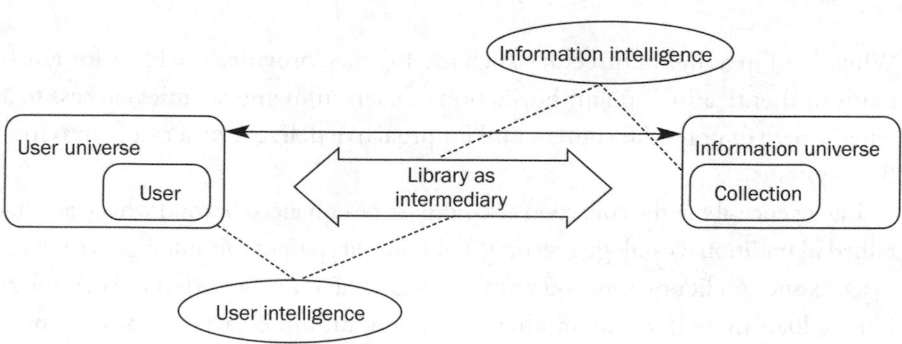

Figure 7.4 The role of user and information 'intelligence'

It is pertinent to add here that user and information intelligence is necessary not just at the micro level, of putting a particular user in touch with a particular piece of information, but also at the macro level where decisions have to be made about the service mix to be offered. For example, managers have to decide whether it would be more efficient to subscribe to an electronic journal, paying per use, or to the paper version, paying once for unlimited use. This is not just a matter of trying to estimate likely numbers of uses, but is also concerned with the nature of likely use – for example, will users be seeking specific papers, or will they wish to browse? Added to this, the life cycle costs of different formats need to be considered, especially where traditional formats impose space and staffing costs. As a result of these decisions, the service mix further down the line – when demands are received from users – will be determined. The decision-making itself is crucially dependent on the quality of intelligence about both users and information sources.

Using information intelligence

At this point it is also helpful to note that many users, whether or not they are the immediate members of the library's user population, will make use of the information intelligence it gathers. Since nearly all of this intelligence is openly available, for example, through an OPAC or library website, there is nothing to stop anyone from using it as an added value service. Indeed many such services are deliberately marketed outside the immediate user population: COPAC, the CURL OPAC, would be a good example. This leads to Figure 7.5.

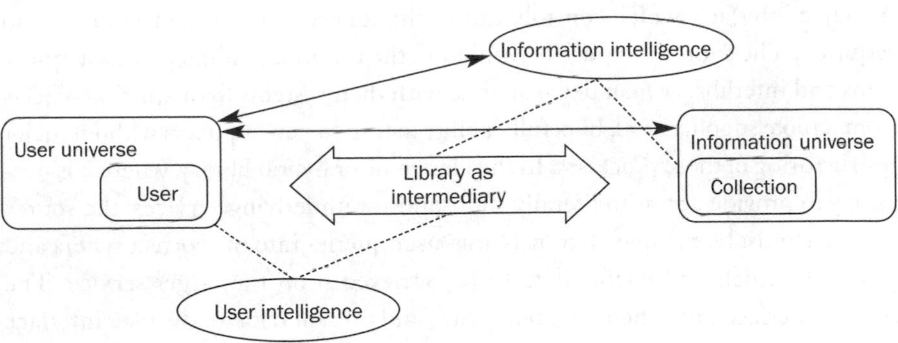

Figure 7.5 Direct use of information intelligence

The user interface

Having determined *who* is to be served and *what* they are to be offered, the library needs to provide the processes which enable users to gain access to their required information and then to make use of it. The users need an interface through which interaction can take place, a real or virtual place where they can interact with the service.

The user interface in a traditional library consists of a welcoming physical building and, within it, places and staff where service demands can be made – ranging from the card catalogue, through shelf guides to enquiry points and an issue desk. Although not always thought of in terms of an 'interface' this is in fact a helpful way to characterize front-of-house library services: they are the places where users interact with the service. As the library moves more towards electronic services so the interfaces start to be delivered electronically. The first may be the library's web home page, initially doing no more than describe services, but increasingly offering a high degree of sophistication. This enables users to formulate complex search strategies, and the library to provide advice and feedback. It may be constructed to reflect the individual user's preferences and interests. Increasingly, as described above, the 'library' interface will be an 'interface within an interface', or at a further level of abstraction, it may be the invisible service behind the user's preferred interface in entirely different systems. In effect, the whole user interface thus becomes a complex but managed array of services, focused on access to information sources but by no means limited to that function.

The source interface

A source interface, which controls and facilitates access to the collection, is also required. The source interface is typified in the traditional library by its acquisitions and interlibrary loan departments, with their systems for acquiring objects from remote suppliers and, hopefully, ability to turn to new suppliers without major restructuring of those processes. In the electronic or hybrid library, where it is necessary to provide access to literally thousands of underlying services, the source interface must be capable of 'translating' user queries into the correct syntax and protocols which will enable data to be retrieved from the target service. The source interface must then negotiate with, and present data to, the user interface just as the traditional library processes books and journals before making them available on the shelves. The model is depicted in Figure 7.6.

The separation of user and source interfaces is an important insight from models of the digital library and itself derives from the client–server approach needed to operate effectively in a networked environment. It is worth repeating here the principle that when these interfaces are properly designed it should be possible to add new resources to the collection without making changes to the user interface – an essential requirement for effective intermediation in a world where there are many millions of remote resources. In effect the ease of adding a book to the stock of a traditional library should be mirrored in the ease with which a new electronic resource can be offered.

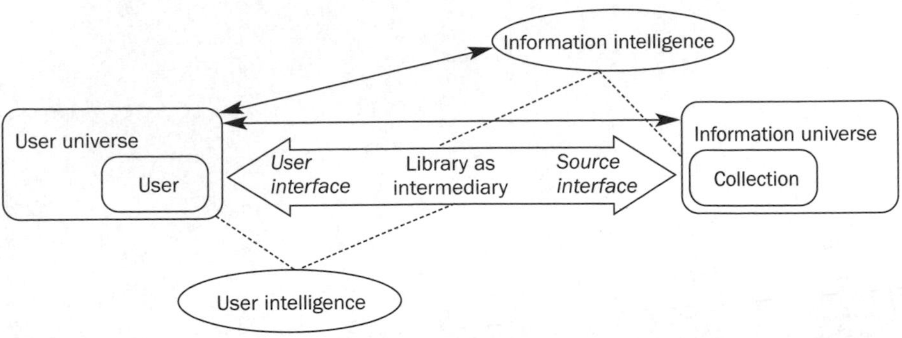

Figure 7.6 Library model with user and source interfaces

With these interfaces in place the library can then enable users to interact with the information resources of their choice.

Conclusion

The intermediary role is well established, but it depends on the ability of the library to organize not just the resources themselves, as in traditional services, but more importantly to gather and organize intelligence about selected information resources *and* about each of the users. In Figure 7.6, however, there is an asymmetry and this provides a clue to the opportunities which are emerging for the library of the future. While users from around the world may access the intelligence the library has gathered and organized about information resources, neither they nor the library's immediate users are able to access intelligence about individuals or about the user population and its sub-groups. A library's competitive advantage lies in its user intelligence – this enables it to tailor services to meet genuine needs, to present them attractively, to innovate effectively and to achieve real impact. The library that neglects its user intelligence is on a slippery slope, since the users, as the model illustrates, are perfectly able to go elsewhere to meet most of their needs.

Conclusion

8
Beyond the intermediary

> Librarians and information managers have a particular role to play. We are concerned with understanding . . . . Our purpose is to serve some community, which means we must relate to the priorities and values of our role in the community.
>
> (Buckland, 2001)

Introduction

In the last chapter a model of the library as the intermediary between users and information resources was developed. There is ample evidence that this remains the most important role which libraries play. However, it is clear from the discussion in earlier chapters that libraries also fulfil a number of other roles. For example, the public library has in recent years emphasized its role in learning and re-emphasized its contribution to the development of basic literacy, especially reading. Academic libraries have made a major commitment to information skills delivery and have developed new buildings which emphasize the facilitation of group work and discussion. Workplace libraries have looked to the encouragement of knowledge transfer through verbal and informal methods which do not require formal publication. It follows that, even if we leave aside the issue of disintermediation (as considered in Chapter 7), a model which depicts the library solely as an intermediary is deficient. So, in this chapter we will look at a different model, designed to capture the richness of library's services, based on a recent study of local libraries and other cultural institutions.

In 2003 the European Commission provided funding for a wide-ranging 'co-ordination action' under the name Cultural Applications: Local Institutions Mediating Electronic Resource Access (CALIMERA). Taking into account the experiences of local libraries, archives and museums in 42 countries in and adjacent to the newly enlarged European Union, one of CALIMERA's tasks was to build a 'research roadmap' demonstrating actions which would be needed to enable this sector to play a full part in the information society. As part of this task, information was gathered on innovative practice in each of those countries, and the results then used to develop a model of library, and other cultural institutions, functions from the point of view of the user. It is this model which is presented here: further details can be found in Brophy (2005b) and on the project website at www.calimera.org.

Figure 8.1 illustrates the user functions which were being supported by this huge range of institutions. It will be noted immediately that only a minority relate directly to the library's role in intermediating between users and published information sources. Note also that the functions are depicted in a circle, to emphasize continuous interactions between them, rather than as a straight line, which might indicate an end-to-end process.

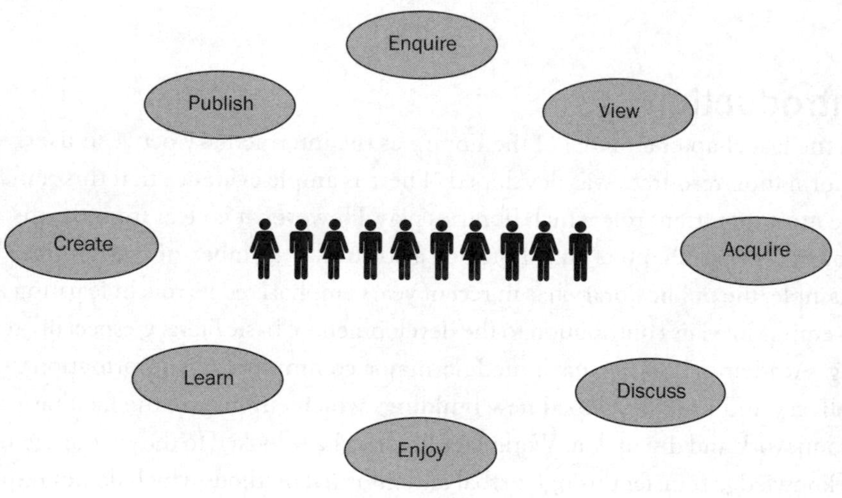

Figure 8.1 User functions from the CALIMERA Co-ordination Action

The functions are as follows:

Enquire

At the most basic level, users of libraries need to be able to explore the services available. This is often the point of initial contact and is akin to an initial consultation with a professional adviser. What kinds of service are available? When is the library open? What facilities does it offer? Are there events that might be of interest? The library frequently also acts as an information or access point for other, non-library services and may be a natural enquiry point for local organizations or for the parent organization as a whole. Users appear to regard library staff as authoritative and neutral, and thus a trusted source for such information.

View and manipulate content

Users need to be able to interact with content and services in a variety of ways. The CALIMERA study confirmed that this remains a much-cited reason for using libraries: the intermediary role. The simplest instance is viewing bibliographic records or full text supplied by the library itself, but multimedia content may involve more complex interactions, perhaps with the user controlling the sequencing of a display, as in the British Library's 'Turning the Pages' application (www.bl.uk/onlinegallery/ttp/ttpbooks.html). At its simplest, manipulation may involve photocopying a book or cutting and pasting from a web page. At the extreme, it becomes fully immersive, requiring the provision of dedicated multimedia workstations.

Acquire content

In many cases the above function of viewing and manipulating content in effect includes acquisition – for example, viewing a PDF document delivers the content of the page to the user's PC, where it may be saved. However, particularly where a financial transaction is involved (for example, with an e-book which provides a taster to enable a user to decide whether or not to buy), acquisition can be seen as separate from viewing. The sequencing of the two processes varies, but again responding to this requirement is part of the intermediary role.

Discuss content

It is here that the traditional library functions start to need extension to meet user demands. There is ample evidence that many users, having acquired content of one kind or another, want to discuss and debate it with others. For virtual services, there is a parallel with Computer-Supported Co-operative Work (CSCW) in the business sector, where discussion, debate and collaboration are critical parts of online user activity. The shift in academic library design towards group study and social areas acknowledges the importance of this approach. Providing facilities like whiteboards and conferencing equipment helps to encourage this kind of interaction. Social spaces in public libraries fulfil the same need.

Enjoy

It is important to remember that many people engage with libraries and similar organizations for pleasure – there does not always have to be serious intent behind engagement, although even then many occasions will afford learning experiences. Reading for pleasure is perhaps the most obvious example, but so too are initiatives like 'Get it Loud in Libraries' designed 'to dispel young people's outdated perceptions of libraries and to bring accessible low-cost live music to the local community' (www.lancashire.gov.uk/libraries/events/LancasterMusic/index.asp).

Learn

Much engagement with libraries is explicitly intended as a learning experience. It may not involve the use of information resources but it can be a direct interaction between teacher and learner, either physically or virtually. A good deal of learning that is mediated by libraries is more informal than that in the most common educational scenarios, such as those offered by schools, colleges and universities. Or the library may be acting in support of other educational providers, for example, by helping students with their work or more formally as an outreach centre. A significant advantage of libraries is that they can offer a non-threatening environment with low thresholds for accessing learning opportunities.

Create

Many library users are interested in expressing and developing their own creativity. Far more than in traditional services, ICTs provide the opportunity for individuals and groups to become active contributors to the networked cultural and information environment. Tools are needed to enable and encourage users to express their creativity by telling stories, generating images, recording verbal reminiscences and building complex presentations using multiple media. A significant proportion of the case studies examined in the CALIMERA work demonstrated this kind of active engagement.

Publish

Expressions of individual creativity need to be shared, debated and discussed – in essence they need to be published. They can thus be made widely available and generate more interest and debate. However, publication cannot be an unmediated process if it is to be legitimate in cultural terms and acceptable according to social, and where appropriate scholarly, norms. Evidence suggests that users equate publication in a mediated service, where there is an element of selection, as much more prestigious than self-publication in an open system, such as YouTube or MySpace. Publication thus becomes an accolade of achievement to the individual and an important means of encouraging involvement and building communities.

Library functions

The user functions described in the above section need to be supported by the range of services that the library can offer. Again, the CALIMERA analysis suggested what these services needed to be, drawing particularly on examples of innovation. Figure 8.2 illustrates them as an outer ring surrounding the user functions. Note, however, that there is no one-to-one mapping implied – a dynamic illustration would show the two rings revolving in opposite directions and sparking interactions at each of the crossover points!

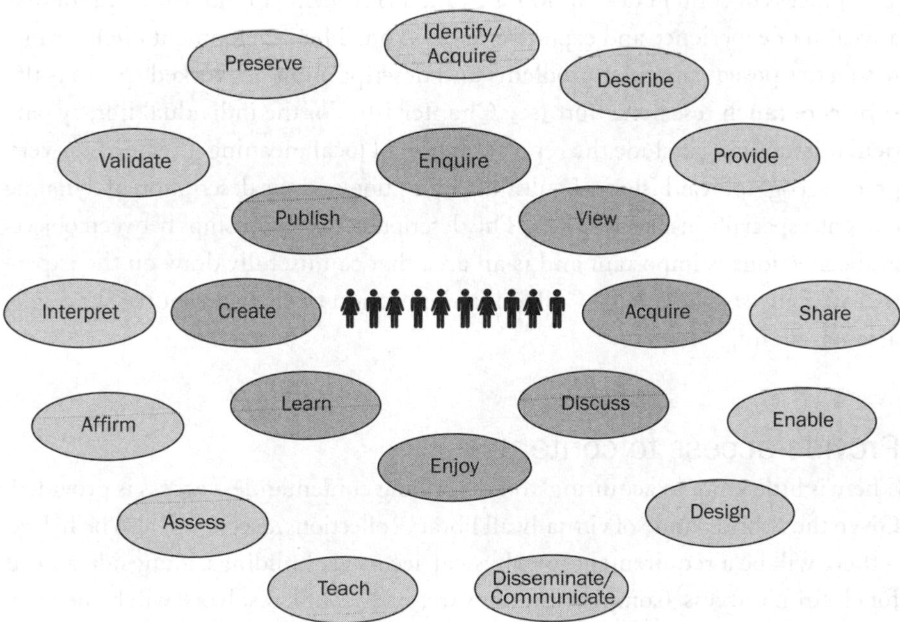

Figure 8.2 User and library functions combined

The library functions required to support the range of user activity are as follows.

Identify and acquire content

A principal role of libraries is to identify and then acquire content within their field of interest. Selection remains a critical, professional task across all sectors, reflecting the difference between a library as an *organized* collection and a mere accumulation of information objects. Classically this content would consist of books, journals, video and audio recordings, etc. on fixed media. Increasingly acquisition of access rights to electronic content is a major feature. This process of building and renewing the collection is thus still seen as central.

The acquisition of content also implies its management. Records need to be created and stored to represent this content, create an audit trail and contribute to content description. Physical and virtual content needs to be curated, which may involve maintaining records of provenance among other tasks.

Describe content

The process of content description is again a classic one for libraries and there is a wealth of experience and expertise to draw on. The development of electronic media has posed particular problems and description in networked spaces is the subject of much research effort (see Chapter 10). For the individual library particular issues may include the representation of local meaning, the need for very precise geographical/historical/cultural description and the description of dynamic content, especially in shared spaces. The description of relationships between objects and collections is important and is an area that can usefully draw on the expertise of archivists and others. Collection description to enable resource sharing is also important.

Provide access to content

There is little point in acquiring and describing content unless access is provided. Given the hybrid nature of virtually all library collections, access will also be hybrid – there will be a requirement for physical access via buildings, alongside a need for electronic access. Complex middleware, such as link resolvers, will be needed. Access itself presupposes the existence of a 'presentation layer' (both physical and virtual) of user-facing services and requires clear understanding of user preferences and capabilities.

Share knowledge between users

Libraries are well placed to enable knowledge-sharing, and indeed most such institutions act as a community resource where people can meet, often to discuss or pursue specific topics or because they have similar interests. This is presumably what the MLA has in mind when it speaks of the public library as being 'at the heart of the community' (Dolan, 2007). There is a significant challenge in complementing these physical meeting points with virtual communities; issues include the role of facilitation versus self-management, the acceptability of different groups in relation to institutional mission and values, and the added services which such groups may require or which may be offered to engage their interest. The difference between a physical and virtual reading group offers a good example.

Enable user activity

Users will often wish to go beyond knowledge-sharing to specific activities, such as the creation of new shared narratives concerning their learning or their local cultures, perhaps in relation to a subject being studied or to a topic like family history. They will need expert assistance and tools to enable this to happen, and to ensure that such products are standards-based, sharable and sustainable in the longer term. The library may wish to capture a proportion of such products as part of emerging collections. A theme running through this and the previous function is that of accessibility, ensuring that all services are usable by all users.

Design presentations

The presentation of individual cultural or learning objects and collections, especially in networked spaces, is an important part of the library's role. Where in the past this might have involved a themed exhibition of physical objects, now it may take place through a website or application, requiring professional design and presentation skills. These presentations may form a 'shop window' for the institution and may determine, or at least influence, its external image. The quality of presentation will also greatly affect the 'stickiness' of a site, i.e. the extent to which visitors/users will return time and again. This is why attention to website design is so important. A vital aspect of design is that it must be user-centred – for example, the presentation design in a school library will be very different from that in a university.

Disseminate and communicate information

A related function is the active dissemination and communication of information about the resources and services of the local institution. Here the challenge is to find ways of engaging with users so as to draw them into lively use of the range of services of relevance to them. A current example would be work to engage scholars in the active support of institutional repositories.

Teach

If libraries see part of their primary role as facilitating learning then they cannot avoid becoming involved in teaching. It is not often stated, but teaching is the unavoidable 'flip side' of the user function of 'learn' and is equally complex. Libraries need to consider their pedagogical stance (in essence the beliefs about learning which are embedded in the teaching they offer) in relation to their users and potential users. Learning objectives need to be thought through and stated. Programmes need to be designed or acquired, delivered in a timely and attractive manner and then reviewed and evaluated. Some teaching may principally be enabling, as in the field of networked learner support; other approaches may be highly didactic. Issues for libraries to consider include the place of assessment (Should those taught gain a qualification?), quality assurance (Who accredits libraries' teaching?) and progression (How do users progress from one level of learning to another in a systematic and planned manner?).

Assess

If it is decided that users' learning should be assessed (and lack of assessment opportunities would severely limit the library's role), mechanisms are needed to achieve this. The library could, at one level, enable self-assessment, which can be effective but has obvious limitations. An alternative might be to link into the assessment regimes of its own institution (if an educational library) or to forge collaborative provision with external educational institutions. Since assessment leads to a formal qualification, there are demands for record keeping and quality assurance, and – in virtual environments – some tricky problems such as user authentication (how do you know that the user is who they say they are?).

Affirm end-user activity

If user created content and narratives are to be included in collections, there is a question as to how their quality can be assured. Libraries may wish to apply some kind of 'kite' or quality mark rather than accepting everything that is offered. The inclusion of their content in collections may be seen by users as itself a 'stamp of approval', in itself recognition of the worth of their creations (as discussed above). Institutional repositories may rely on peer review; if not they need to be clear about the criteria for inclusion and have procedures which they can apply. Systems will need to support and record this process.

Interpret

Many libraries play a role in interpreting their collections, building on their compilations of works by the application of specialist knowledge, for example by curating exhibitions. To achieve this they will draw on external resources and internal expertise. Virtual exhibitions will require appropriate tools to enable local and external knowledge to be brought to bear and interpretations created. More broadly, web pages may be created to guide users to appropriate resources by interpreting them in ways of particular relevance to specific groups of users.

Validate content

Validation is concerned with both authenticity (how a user knows that content is what it purports to be) and standards compliance (ensuring that content is created, stored and made available using open standards enabling current and future interoperability). In networked environments, version control and the validation of dynamic content are particular issues.

Preserve

The final institutional function identified here is again one which libraries have traditionally espoused. The long-term preservation of individual objects and collections raises several well documented issues in both real and virtual spaces, all of which impact on the library (see Chapter 10). In times of economic constraint, placing an appropriate priority on long-term preservation is challenging.

Conclusion

The research described above isolated both the user view of the activities which libraries should support and the library response in terms of functions which need to be established. What is noticeable in this model is that there are many library functions which are not of themselves concerned with the delivery of information objects and thus involve a wide range of activity which goes beyond the intermediary role. Although the latter remains, and will remain at the core of libraries' purposes, the CALIMERA work suggests that it is helpful to draw a much wider picture than that model might suggest.

9

The library user

> On autumnal afternoons we played a version of *What's My Line?* in which two students played a reference librarian and a reader, the object being to find out what the reader wanted to know through a gentle form of interrogation.
>
> 'Morning, sir, how can I help you?'
>
> 'Do you have any books on houses?'
>
> 'I'm sure we do. Do you have any particular kind of house in mind?'
>
> 'Semi-detached.'
>
> Thus the exchange proceeded until the reader finally revealed that what he wanted was to have a bat removed from his loft.
>
> (Taylor, 1993)

Introduction

The library user has been mentioned many times in earlier chapters and the description of the functions needing to be supported in the last chapter was explicitly user centred. However, we have not explored in any detail the general characteristics of library users. This is particularly important in relation to learning, since most library sectors now place an educational purpose at or near the centre of their role.

The user intelligence which libraries maintain in the form of user profiles is often initiated as part of granting membership, frequently limiting the data to name, address and, in educational institutions, status (i.e. student, staff, external, etc.). At this stage the individual has also been identified as a legitimate library user. These records are then used to authorize individual transactions, typically when a request to borrow is made, when the 'material' conditions are compared with the 'user' conditions. So, for example, a 'normal' loan book is matched with a 'staff' status to determine the appropriate loan period.

However, it should be clear from the discussion in earlier chapters that the user community which a library serves, or which forms a potential audience and market for its services, requires much greater attention than this if libraries are to continue to be successful. In a hybrid environment of physical and electronic resources with a vast array of heterogeneous services and the competitive stance of many potential suppliers, whether intra- or extra-organizational, a clear understanding of users is essential if library services are to prosper by offering high-quality services. As discussed in Chapter 6, quality management is based on the idea that every service and every product must be focused on 'fitness for purpose' and 'conformance to requirements', the purposes and requirements being those of the customers or users. As Brophy and Coulling (1996) remarked:

> Before we can legitimately give the tag 'quality' to anything we have first to have thought through what it is that the product or service is to be used for . . . quality for one person is not necessarily quality for another. . . . The concept of choice, the freedom we all have in democratic societies to decide what it is that suits our purposes, our predispositions, our concerns, our preferences is another side of the same basic idea about the word 'quality': so it becomes, when used properly, a statement that the essential *product–customer–purpose* linkage has been established. Fundamentally, quality is concerned with meeting the wants and needs of customers.

It follows that detailed knowledge and understanding of the needs, preferences, skills and reactions of users is utterly fundamental to the future library. The closer the library can get to its users as individuals the more likely it is to find a place in the portfolio of services they choose to use. If libraries get this right then they can become the services of choice for their users.

The situation has become more challenging because many users now expect services to be delivered and integrated into their working and living processes – the workflows, leisureflows and lifeflows described in Chapter 7. So it is not enough for libraries to *offer* services and hope that users will come to use them; they have to establish new ways of providing seamless integration. To date, most discussion of the combination of services in this way has centred on electronic services and workflows, but it applies equally to physical services. The large, highly centralized physical library has become the norm in academia and among public libraries in large metropolitan areas. Yet shifts towards integrated library/ teaching (such as the Saltire Centre at Glasgow Caledonian University, www.gcal.ac.uk/thesaltirecentre) and community libraries (such as Topping Fold in Bury, www.bury.gov.uk/ LeisureAndCulture/ Libraries/BranchLibraries/ToppingFoldLibrary.htm) point towards lifeflow integration of non-virtual services as well. This idea raises a number of questions about how users are perceived and services delivered.

The personalization of services

The trend in the service sector as a whole is towards personalization, whereby systems are designed to recognize the individual user's preferences and to respond accordingly. The motor industry provides an interesting example, where over a long period of time provision has shifted from the apocryphal 'any colour as long as it's black' of the Model T Ford, through mass production of an ever increasing series of pre-defined models, to a situation where many manufacturers allow purchasers to specify the exact model, colour, etc. they require *before* the car is built, with the details selected at a dealership and downloaded direct to the factory. An example of direct application in the information service sector is the use of cookies in web environments, enabling service providers to collect user data once and then to re-use it each time the same user (actually a user at the same workstation, which of course is not quite the same thing!) accesses the service.

In the networked environment, user 'intelligence' is particularly important since it offers the key to a range of added value services. For example, sophisticated user intelligence provides the possibility of making the 'view' of information resources which each user sees personal – the library may know what type of material that particular user has accessed in the past and may tune the initial interface screens to highlight similar, new resources. A simple example is Amazon's recommendations which appear on the opening screen when the user accesses the service a second or subsequent time – without having first to log in. Profiles hold the key to a dynamic collection, as each user can be given a set of electronic privileges as part of membership – users of one type (for example, those signed up with an educational provider) may be offered information sources not available to others. User profiles also hold out the prospect of automated e-commerce, for example, a charged service can be offered automatically if the user profile can be queried to provide the necessary credit rating. Finally, educational libraries in schools, colleges and universities may access personal study skills data, for example to identify the level of study and desirable support materials. In all cases, of course, data may be maintained by the library or, increasingly, accessed through a wider institutional service.

However, personalization is not simply a matter of the service provider or broker collecting user data. It is also concerned with the provision of tools to enable users to personalize their own workspaces. Bookmark files in web browsers are an obvious, though rather crude, example. In effect the user is creating metadata concerning objects and collections of interest. In the case of bookmarks these are usually little more than ordered lists, but more powerful facilities are widely available to enable more sophisticated approaches to be used, and of course social bookmarking services, like Backflip (www.backflip.com) and del.icio.us (http://del.icio.us) are now widespread. As Web 2.0 takes hold, 'the user is participant, partner in dialogue, author and consultant' and this can happen 'regardless of whether the product is physical or virtual' (Karlsen, 2006).

A further type of personalization occurs with 'push' services which are sent directly to the user's web space without being individually requested. The most obvious example of this approach is RSS (Really Simple Syndication) where the user subscribes to 'news' feeds. Feeds from a variety of locations can be combined to provide a highly personalized service. A number of applications are available to present the results to the user – from simple readers like Google's (www.google.com/reader) through personal hosted web pages like Netvibes (www.netvibes.com) and Pageflakes (www.pageflakes.com) to mashups like Yahoo!'s Pipes (http://pipes.yahoo.com/pipes). Such services are of course only the tip of Web 2.0 applications. Again, personalization is critical – this is what lies behind the popularity of social networking sites like MySpace (www.myspace.com) and YouTube (www.youtube.com), and the 3D virtual world, Second Life (http://secondlife.com).

Because most of these services are hosted (i.e. they are on a remote server and are accessed using a standard internet connection, albeit increasingly the need is for a broadband connection) they are portable. This means that users, having created their own personal workspaces, can take them with them wherever they go – all they need is a device, which could be a personal digital assistant (PDA), mobile phone or laptop, and a connection and they can re-immerse themselves in their personal, virtual worlds. So, the familiar workspace created in the office or home environment becomes transferable to a cybercafe, to a public library workstation or onto a laptop. No longer are users limited to the applications which the library, or other provider, has loaded on their workstation.

Mention has already been made of social networking services, but other shared applications are of increasing importance. Where websites were once controlled by a single 'webmaster' to whom content had to be submitted for uploading, collaborative tools like wikis are becoming widespread. A wiki is in essence a website to which anyone with authorization can add, edit and remove content. The best known example is Wikipedia (http://en.wikipedia.org) which has grown hugely to rival long-established encyclopedias like *Britannica* – and studies have suggested that it may be as reliable (see Pickering, 2006; Sanders, 2006).

To date libraries have rarely mirrored this kind of option in their core services, such as the OPAC. However, examples are starting to emerge. For instance:

- the British Library has started a podcasting service, often linked to exhibitions and events (www.bl.uk/onlinegallery/whatson/downloads/index.html)
- Leeds University Library uses a blog hosted on the local Elgg service (an open source networking platform) to keep users informed about developments (http://elgg.leeds.ac.uk/libsocsci/weblog)
- MySpace is used by a number of libraries to promote their services. For example, the innovative LARGE (Leeds Always Reading Group for Everyone) service is featured at http://vids.myspace.com/index.cfm?fuseaction=vids.individual&videoID=2018643873
- many libraries are using instant messaging and Short Message Service (SMS) texting to communicate with users (see www.talis.com/applications/products/message.shtml for a Talis product which handles this)
- the People's Network provides a chat-based Enquire service (www.peoplesnetwork.gov.uk/enquire/index.html) which is staffed on a collaborative basis by public libraries around the UK.

Clearly libraries have a long way to go before they are fully embedded in the technologies which so many users are utilizing every day. In particular, most library applications do not yet support conversational use and data sharing, including the support of individual and group creativity.

Authentication and authorization

Authentication and authorization are the processes of checking the users' identities and rights so that they are able to use a service or particular parts of it. In essence authentication processes ensure that users are who they claim to be, while authorization checks that the authenticated users have the necessary rights (or, possibly, have made the necessary payments) to use the service requested. These processes are essential where libraries wish to allow access to services which are restricted in some way, often through a licence agreement with a publisher.

A particular issue is that with many hundreds of services available, there is a danger that users will have to be issued with a password for each causing password proliferation. To avoid this, national and sectoral authentication schemes have been introduced, of which the ATHENS system (www.athens.ac.uk) in the UK education and health sectors offers a good example. ATHENS provides a centralized server to which authentication requests are passed when a user makes a request which requires this, but is administered locally so that institutions can control the issue of passwords, the privileges given to different groups and the inclusion of resources to which they subscribe.

The advantages of a common, widely implemented and well designed authentication/authorization system are numerous:

- for users there is only one password to remember
- within any one session the user needs to be challenged only once – the user's system should then be able to handle challenges from each underlying source system
- because the user has only one password to remember it is less likely to be lost or forgotten, or accidentally revealed to others (or as happens all too frequently, written on a piece of paper and stuck to the PC!), so improving security and reducing the management overhead
- a well designed system should be scalable across a very wide range of services so that the addition of a new service does not impose any kind or additional requirement on the user.

In order to keep the administrative burden to a minimum it is desirable that the authentication system should enable users to be treated as members of groups. In higher education, for example, it should be possible to set up and vary privileges for, say, all undergraduates – having to change settings for each individual would clearly be an administrative nightmare. It is also desirable that the system should be personal to the user rather than individual to the machine. Thankfully, there has been a marked shift away from authentication based on IP addressing. This was popular because each PC (strictly speaking each internet connection) has an Internet Protocol (IP) address. A university could thus simply declare the range of addresses it uses and a supplier could be sure that the service is being used only at that site. However, IP addressing has serious drawbacks: the major problem for users is that they are unable to use the service off-site. Since, increasingly, people want services accessible at home or via mobile connections IP addressing proved unsatisfactory.

ATHENS is to be replaced by a more flexible system, which allows single sign-on at the local level, in the near future. This will be based on Shibboleth technology (arising from the US Internet2 initiative) which places the onus for authentication back at the local level but provides a standards-based approach to ensure that services can interoperate with it. Institutions are also 'federated', which in effect means that they sign up to common policies and then declare this through their Shibboleth systems. The push for this further development comes from the need to find ways to reflect the increasing complexity of institutional arrangements to serve an extremely diverse body of users and the difficulty of simply adding more complexity to a centralized system. As Joint (2007) put it:

> [D]efinitions of institutional membership that have been available via nationally negotiated licences have been fairly restrictive, centring on the old-fashioned concept of a single, geographically circumscribed place of study and research isolated from commercial activity. These membership definitions have been difficult to apply to the modern educational environment where activities span more than one institution and where commercial spin out companies are seen as an essential function of applied academic research. Institutions wishing to expand into new forms of continuing professional development courses . . . or into foreign campus development . . . need electronic library service arrangements that can support these expansive goals.

Common authentication systems which address the needs of a wide community have a number of additional benefits for various stakeholders. The implementation of the ATHENS system brought significant benefits to service providers, including opportunities for marketing their products and a reduction in their overhead costs as they no longer need to support their own proprietary access control mechanisms. Institutions which use the system also have opportunities for monitoring patterns of use of different services and thus for managing subscriptions.

Data protection and privacy

Data protection legislation has been in force in the UK since 1984 and in some other countries, notably in Scandinavia, for some time before that. The concern behind this legislation is that individuals' personal information should be used only in appropriate circumstances and for legitimate purposes, and that each individual has a right to expect organizations to take all reasonable care to ensure that this happens. Initially restricted to data held in computer systems, the provisions have been extended to all media. The key requirements of the relevant legislation (the Data Protection Act 1998) are that all personal data which is held by organizations or individuals should:

- be fairly and lawfully processed
- be processed for limited purposes
- be adequate, relevant and not excessive
- be accurate and up to date
- not be kept for longer than is necessary
- be processed in line with your rights
- be secure
- be transferred to other countries only with adequate protection.

(www.ico.gov.uk/what_we_cover/data_protection/the_basics.aspx)

In networked environments the opportunities for compromising individuals' privacy are manifold and it is essential that organizations wishing to offer services are able to assure and preferably demonstrate to potential customers that data submitted will not be misused. Libraries may have additional strength as 'trusted intermediaries' provided they maintain the highest standards of care in this regard and ensure that personal data is not passed on, even inadvertently, to other parties. This issue has implications for authentication and authorization services, and provides an added incentive for using devolved systems at the local level.

Issues of privacy, beyond those covered by legislation, are also important. While many of these will be institutional concerns, librarians need to be aware of their own responsibilities. As Shuler (2004) has written, 'within their own buildings, academic librarians need to start thinking about the privacy arrangements with vendors and their community. In particular, as more public services go online and interactive, what is going to happen to all those electronic conversations, if anything, and how might they be used to evaluate the quality of electronic services, if they should be used'. The stand-off between the US Government and Google in 2006 over the former's demand for search engine tracking data provides a singular warning of the potential dangers to personal privacy of seemingly innocent tracking of online activity.

Information behaviour

The role of libraries in facilitating access to information remains central. In order to be effective, however, there is a need for understanding of the ways in which users seek, acquire and utilize information. This question has attracted a huge amount of research and there are many competing as well as complementary theories. This section can do no more than introduce the topic – for extended treatments readers are referred to Case (2002) and Fisher, Erdelez and McKechnie (2005).

First, it is useful to stress that studies of information behaviour cover a huge area of human activity. Case (2002), for example, presents five information seeking scenarios:

- buying products
- finding information in a library
- betting on race horses
- finding the law
- 'I want to know more about cancer'.

It is interesting that Case's examples include two scenarios (the first and third) which would not normally have been associated with libraries, yet which may well involve the use of internet resources – now very much within the province of libraries.

Among the most cited models of information behaviour is that developed by Wilson in the early 1980s (Wilson, 1981). This uses a threefold approach, examining the context of the information user (or would-be user), the system being used and the information resources themselves. Context includes not only the environment in which the individual is operating, but the personal and social situations and perspectives which are brought together in defining an information need. Wilson stressed, however, that it is more helpful to talk of 'information behaviour' than of 'information need' since the former is observable while the latter is not.

In later work, Wilson and his colleagues, mainly at the University of Sheffield, laid stress on information behaviour as a part of problem-solving (Wilson et al., 2002), but also explored the influence of factors such as cognitive styles (Ford et al., 2002).

While this strand of research focused on the behavioural characteristics of users, a range of different variables has been examined in other studies. Kuhlthau (1991) validated a model which showed that users involved in complex information seeking will typically progress through six stages:

- initiation: becoming aware of the need

- selection: identifying the general area of enquiry or problem
- exploration: a variety of inconsistent information is examined
- formulation: the perspective becomes more focused
- collection: systematic gathering of pertinent information
- presentation: the process is completed with new understanding being gained.

Kuhlthau stressed that in these stages there is an interplay of thoughts, feelings and actions and that information seeking must be seen as an holistic activity.

Saracevic, Kantor, Chamis and Trivison (1988) studied learning styles as a basic variable while Steinwachs (1999) examined cultural background. Marchionini (1989) investigated information-searching behaviour in a full-text online system, using different kinds of task based on the idea of 'known item' and 'subject' searching.

In the web environment a number of studies have identified key variables including cognitive style, user experience and task, showing that 'online search experience seems to play a critically important role in improving search performance and developing effective search/navigational tactics' (Kim, 2001). Online searching using Google has been widely studied – Griffiths and Brophy (2005) showed that students have low levels of persistence in this environment – they 'may trade quality of results for effort and time spent searching', a process of satisficing, accepting early results as 'good enough', which may lead to the neglect of key resources.

Library use

The actual processes involved in searching for and retrieving library materials is related to behaviour in more general information environments. Figure 9.1, taken from Brophy (2000b), is a simplified illustration of the processes which may need to be undertaken to enable users to complete an information access and use transaction in this context.

The processes, which apply within both traditional and electronic environments, are described in greater detail below.

1 *Formulate query*: users, possibly with the assistance of library staff, formulate queries to represent the information (or whatever) that they require. This representation of their requirements could be in the form of terms that describe a subject, an author, a 'book like the one I had last

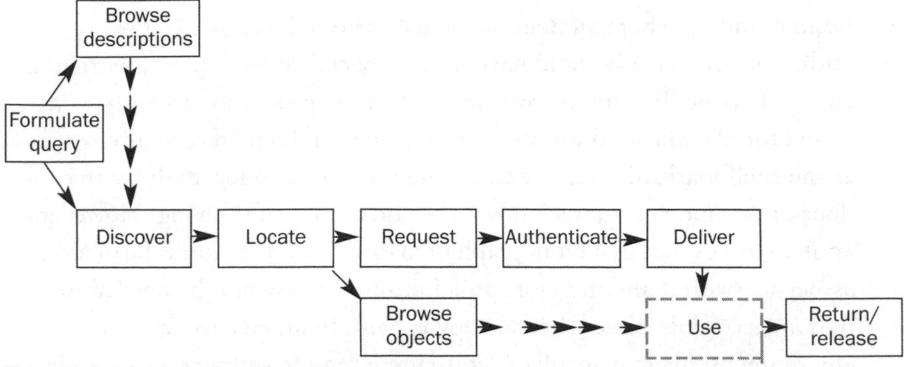

Figure 9.1 Information access and use processes

week', etc. The library has a role in helping users express their requirements in ways that can be used within the subsequent retrieval system, whether it is human, electronic or both. It is important to note here that users will almost certainly need considerable help to express their requirements in 'standard' terminology which can be mapped onto the descriptions used by the underlying services. One of the most common causes of user failure is the query being formulated in a way which the target service cannot interpret or interprets incorrectly – that is not, of course, to blame the user!

2 *Browse descriptions*: at this stage the system responds to the query by offering descriptions of information objects which may meet the requirement, and the user examines them. Classically this would be done by browsing through a section of the card or other printed catalogue, but the OPAC, together with a wide variety of online indexes and other tools, provides much more sophisticated ways of using these sources. Typically browsing of descriptions is by author, subject and/or level to identify a range of items that may be of interest. Much access to the world wide web involves browsing among lists of records of possibly relevant items, before narrowing down the search. The user may not need to go beyond this stage if, for example, descriptions include abstracts or if the query was to establish that a particular author had written a particular book.

3 *Discover*: this is the process of identifying a particular item as being of potential interest and then finding sufficient data about it to enable it to be identified uniquely. Closely linked to browsing, it may also occur through an alerting service bringing items to the attention of the user. With 'known-item' searches, where a user is following up a specific bibliographic reference, it may replace browsing of descriptions.

4 *Locate*: finding where an item, previously selected, is held. In the traditional library this could have been a special collection or a particular bay of shelving. It could be revealed within the process of discovery – as where the classification number given in the catalogue record also serves as the shelf mark, although the user may still have to locate the correct floor of the library and track down the correct bay of shelving. However, an item discovered in a bibliography may not have location information associated with it and therefore an additional step would be needed to find an accessible place where a copy is held. In an electronic environment this may involve identifying a remote supplier. Frequently the library will take on the responsibility of finding the location, as with traditional interlibrary loan services where the user would not be expected to determine the location of a supplying library.

5 *Browse objects*: in a traditional library, once a location had been identified it would be possible to browse through shelves of books or through the issues of a journal, not necessarily to find one in particular, but perhaps to look for ideas. There is some equivalence in browsing through items selected by a web search engine, although in general electronic services are not particularly supportive of this function. Line (2000) remarks: 'Browsing electronic sources has its own merits, but it is a different process from browsing print; it may prove impossible to offer a good electronic surrogate for book browsing.' Where users are able to browse objects, they can of course immediately use them.

6 *Request*: where objects that have been discovered are not immediately available to the user a request for them has to be initiated. For instance, in a traditional library with closed access collections a form may have to be completed to request staff to retrieve the item from the stacks. With electronic services, where delivery of a resource depends increasingly on software systems 'negotiating' to enable users to be given access, it is a core process. As noted above, with some types of resource, such as web pages, the request process may effectively deliver the item to the user.

7 *Authenticate*: the library needs to know that users are who they say they are and that they are authorized to access the material requested. It then needs to ensure that the appropriate 'business process' is put in place to deal with the transaction. Are they members with a right to interlibrary loan requests, for example? In the electronic environment, this might include asking whether the user has the means to pay (credit) to use the system, and then setting up a transaction with appropriate non-

repudiation features. The stage at which authentication and authorization are carried out is dependent on a number of factors. Ideally, in the electronic environment, it occurs when the user logs into the system so that the permissions can be carried through until the end of the session. However, there is also a parallel with traditional services where it is desirable to offer free and open access to many resources without requiring users to identify themselves – this can be fundamental to retaining the open, non-threatening environment on which public libraries in particular pride themselves. In these cases the authentication and authorization may be delayed until the user first generates a request for a restricted item – 'restricted' in this sense meaning that it is not open to all users without question.

8 *Deliver*: the actual process of delivering the requested item to the user. With a book this might involve the completion of a lending transaction; equally it could involve delivering an electronic document as an e-mail attachment in a form in which it can be displayed at the user's workstation. A complication in the electronic environment – which incidentally also applies to exploring descriptions – is that if multiple sources are queried on behalf of the user, there may be all kinds of incompatibilities and duplication between the objects returned. Delivery must therefore interpose some processing in such environments if users are not to be presented with a mass of unstructured data.

9 *Use*: if the above processes form the core of the library's functions as it attempts to create the connection between each user and their ideal information objects, use of those objects provides the whole justification for the existence of libraries and indeed of information objects themselves. Use will be considered in more detail later, but it is worth noting that, for the user, 'use' leads on through processes of extracting and analysing information to personal storage and indexing of personal files and links – the creation of personal hybrid libraries with all the processes that they imply.

10 *Return or release*: in the traditional library the transaction is not complete until the user returns the book, and the staff reshelve it. In many cases there is no real equivalent in the electronic library as each user is provided with their own copy of the information object. However, in some instances a licence restriction (e.g. on numbers of concurrent users) means that the end of the process occurs only when individual users release their connections, thus enabling them to be assigned to others.

In discussing library use it is also worth drawing attention to the phenomenon of 'library anxiety', identified by Mellon (1986). In an academic library context, students reported to Mellon that they felt overwhelmed, lacked confidence, were unable to find their way around the library and were afraid to approach library staff. Onwuegbuzie, Jiao and Bostick (2004) have analysed library anxiety and a number of tools used to measure it in some detail. Their research has informed many information skills programmes. The parallel concept of computer anxiety affects use of electronic services.

Libraries and learning

Most library sectors, as we saw in Chapter 2, place very heavy emphasis on their role in facilitating and supporting learning. This may be informal activity, perhaps within a public library's outreach programme to an under-represented group, or part of the formal educational system, as in a school or university. Research is, of course, a form of learning and the academic library will need to support the whole range of academic activity. To do so effectively librarians need an understanding of pedagogy: the art and science of teaching and learning.

It is clear that, in the emerging knowledge society, traditional conceptions of learning are, if not collapsing, at least in need of revisiting. Obviously there is limited value in acquiring information during the process of formal learning if the information thus gathered will be rapidly superseded and is, in any case, easily accessible from the web. It is of little use learning that 'this is how things are' if tomorrow things will be different. It is not surprising, therefore, that the information-transmission view of learning is breaking down. There are, however, more fundamental issues to consider.

A useful distinction is commonly drawn between objectivist and constructivist pedagogies. Objectivism 'views the world as an ordered structure of entities which exists and has meaning quite apart from the observer or participant. Much of science and technology has traditionally been taught on this basis: what needs to be achieved by learning is a closer and closer approach to complete (and thus "correct") understanding' (Brophy, 2001b).

Constructivist pedagogies focus on interpretation and building understanding. To quote Bednar and her colleagues:

> Learning is a constructive process in which the learner is building an internal representation of knowledge, a personal interpretation of experience. This representation is constantly open to change, its structure and linkages forming the

> foundation to which other knowledge structures are appended. Learning is an active process in which meaning is developed on the basis of experience. This view of knowledge does not necessarily deny the existence of the real world . . . but contends that all we know of the world are human interpretations of our experience of the world. . . . learning must be situated in a rich context, reflective of real world contexts for this constructive process to occur.
>
> (Bednar et al., 1993)

So, on this understanding, learning is an active process in which learners place their interpretations of their learning into the context of their previous understandings and world views and are enabled both to modify their knowledge and views and to transfer their understanding to new contexts – what Streibel (1991) calls 'situated cognition'. This is one of the reasons that information skills development works best when it is embedded – the learner is able to respond to the challenge of making the learning fit their world view, thus making it relevant.

Coupled with this shift towards constructivism is renewed interest in learning or cognitive styles and learning models, the classic work being that of Pask (1976, 1988) and of Kolb (1984). Pask argued that individuals take one of two basic approaches to learning. 'Holists' tend to look at the relationships between topics so as to build up a conceptual overview into which details can be fitted later. 'Serialists' take things in sequence, analysing one thing at a time so as to build up an overall picture in small steps. Ford (2000) linked these ideas with ideas about 'deep' and 'surface' learning and field dependent/independent cognitive styles (Witkin et al., 1977) to examine information system use in virtual environments, including hypertext navigation and database searching.

But focusing on individual learners addresses only part of the issue. What both the objectivist and simple constructivist approaches underplay is the fact that human activity is almost always a social process. Johnson and his colleagues reminded us nearly 20 years ago that 'learning is a social process that occurs through interpersonal interaction within a cooperative context. Individuals, working together, construct shared understandings and knowledge' (Johnson, Johnson and Smith, 1991). And this brings us back full circle to Wittgenstein and his emphasis on shared language and shared experience (see Chapter 3). We do not learn in isolation but within a process of interplay between individuals collaborating or competing. Learning takes place by participation in communities and the undertaking of developed social practices. At the core of these practices lies shared language and shared discourse. This suggests that learning needs to be designed in the context of the learner's social engagement. Ideas such as 'communities of practice' support this viewpoint.

Networked learning

The term 'networked learning' can be used to describe all those methods of delivering learning which rely on information and communications technologies. The term is in widespread use although there is some ambiguity in its application, since a traditional, on-campus student who makes use of an electronic information resource in the university library could be regarded as a 'networked learner'. Usually, however, the term implies some measure of online interaction with a tutor and other learners as part of the learning event.

Although enormous claims are made for networked learning the evidence for its efficacy is as yet mixed. In their evocatively titled paper, 'Students' Distress with a Web-based Distance Education Course', Hara and Klung (2000) suggest that 'we need more student-centred studies of distance education that are designed to teach us how the appropriate use of technology and pedagogy could make distance education more beneficial for more students'. There is nothing to suggest that the need has lessened since those words were written.

A distinction needs to be made between synchronous and asynchronous learning, the former requiring all students to be available at the same time (as, for example, with a video conference or online chat) and the latter allowing students to contribute at their own time (as, for example, with e-mail or text). This distinction is quite crucial in evaluating some of the claims made for networked learning – for example, students cannot learn at the place, pace and time of their choosing if synchronous techniques are in use.

Educational researchers suggest that networked learning has both strengths and limitations. Work by the Centre for Studies in Advanced Learning Technology (CSALT) team at Lancaster University (CSALT, 2000), Sproull and Kiesler (1991), Levy (1998) and others suggests that some of the strengths and limitations of networked learning may be as follows:

- Strengths
  - —promotes interactivity while providing flexibility in terms of time and place
  - —promotes active engagement by all learners
  - —encourages openness and reduces the inhibition of talking and/or

presenting face-to-face which can be a major disincentive to some learners
—promotes reflective learning by requiring learners to consider what others in the group are saying
—can automatically create a permanent record of discussions to which tutors, and possibly students, can refer
—provides new opportunities for group learning, especially for part-time students and those with other responsibilities, such as students with families who live off-campus
—promotes social interaction as a side-benefit, for example through the use of e-mail to establish social as well as learning relationships
—gives easy access to the global resources of the web and other digital information
—provides better access for some under-represented groups
—changes relationships in learning: the tutor changes from being the 'sage on the stage' to the 'guide on the side' or, more appropriately, to a carefully selected mix of both roles.

- Limitations

—lack of what is known as 'expressive richness' in contributions: typed text lacks the nuances of the face-to-face spoken word
—lack of immediacy, especially for asynchronous communications, so that a contributor can be left wondering how others are reacting
—excessive immediacy, especially for synchronous communications, where impulsive messaging may adversely affect the discourse and some may be more impulsive than others
—reduced barriers to confrontational behaviour – it is easier for individuals to be domineering without immediate challenge
—synchronous 'conversation' may proceed too quickly for some students – an issue noted by Hara and Klung (2000) – and too slowly for others
—groups may take a long time to achieve consensus on a decision since temporal cues, such as the end of a scheduled meeting, may be missing
—it requires access to equipment and network connections and some competence in their use, neither of which can be assumed
—its style of communication – predominantly through short text messages – does not suit everyone even after long practice (there is a learning styles issue here which is currently under-researched)
—there may be differing and possibly conflicting styles of communication within a discourse, which some participants may find difficult

—the lack of visual and other cues may make communication impersonal and may make it difficult to understand underlying 'messages' which are not explicit (in extreme cases this can result in students 'disconnecting' from the class)
—the lack of timetabling (unlike in traditional learning) may make it more difficult to gain the commitment needed from all participants where activity is predominantly asynchronous
—management of networked learning can be extremely onerous – how, for example, should a tutor deal with e-mail arriving from literally hundreds or even thousands of online students at all hours of the day and night?
—feedback to students may be inadequate, especially where negative comments need to be given within the ambit of pastoral concern.

The CSALT team suggests that it is 'rather dangerous to make any strong claims about the strengths and limitations of networked learning . . . these are "claims in principle" rather than guarantees'. However, with so many issues to consider, the design of appropriate library services for networked learning will quite clearly need considerable further research and development effort.

Lifelong learning

One of the reasons that it is important to concentrate attention on learning itself is that the role of libraries in supporting learning throughout life continues to be emphasized. The public library sector's 'Inspiring Learning for All' initiative was discussed in Chapter 2 and speaks of 'placing learning at the heart of the museum, archive or library' and of demonstrating 'that the museum, archive or library is a learning organization' (MLA, 2004b). Brophy, Craven and Fisher (1998) defined the concept of lifelong learning as 'a deliberate progression throughout the life of an individual, where the initial acquisition of knowledge and skills is reviewed and upgraded continuously, to meet challenges set by an ever changing society'.

There is also a growing consensus around the idea that not only should steps be taken to encourage learning that is lifelong, but that lifelong learning should be an aspiration for all citizens. Over ten years ago Jean-Claude Paye, then Secretary-General of the OECD, wrote (1995):

> Continuing to expand education and training systems that rely upon learning opportunities limited to early life . . . will not suffice as a strategy for meeting

> today's challenges . . . Much has been said over the years about lifelong learning but, in truth, it is still a reality for only a tiny segment of the populations of OECD countries. The huge task now facing OECD Governments is to make it a reality for a progressively expanding part of the population, so that it eventually becomes a reality for all.

There seems to be general acceptance that libraries have considerable potential to assist in the achievement of these visions. Furthermore, this would appear to be an area where the mix of technological systems and human expertise that characterizes libraries very much comes into its own. As Brophy and MacDougall (2000) commented:

> The issue for libraries will be to provide a range of services which support lifelong learners who choose to learn in any one of many modes, and probably in a personal mix of all those available. The term 'hybrid', coming into common use to describe the types of media (traditional and electronic) with which libraries will deal, may equally be applied to the learning processes which they support.

Information literacy

Users cannot operate within networked environments without some basic skills. Literacy is the first of these, for without the ability to read – an issue noted in Chapter 2 in relation to the public library's role – no one can participate meaningfully in the Information Society. But literacy must extend beyond the simple ability to read. As Balsamo (1998) put it, 'the construction of meaning is a complex behavior that is dependent on the embodied knowledge of individuals – in short, embodied literacy . . . Literacy is the ability to make significant connections, to form interpretations, to evaluate situations, and to provide context.'

So literacy must go well beyond basic reading, writing and numeracy skills. 'Functional literacy' refers to the ability to function in an advanced society – the OECD has used a threefold definition (Organisation for Economic Co-operation and Development, 1995) which was adopted for the major International Adult Literacy Survey (IALS):

1 *Prose literacy* – the knowledge and skills needed to understand and use information from texts including editorials, news stories, poems and fiction
2 *Document literacy* – the knowledge and skills required to locate and use

information contained in various formats, including job applications, payroll forms, transportation schedules, maps, tables and graphics

3 *Quantitative literacy* – the knowledge and skills required to apply arithmetic operations, either alone or sequentially, to numbers embedded in printed materials, such as balancing a chequebook, figuring out a tip, completing an order form or determining the amount of interest on a loan from an advertisement.

Information literacy is clearly related to the first two of these areas, although the relationship is not straightforward. SCONUL defines it in the following terms: '[I]nformation literacy encompasses library user education, information skills training and education, and those areas of personal, transferable or key skills relating to the use and manipulation of information in the context of learning, teaching and research issues in higher education' (2006b). CILIP has an alternative definition: 'Information literacy is knowing when and why you need information, where to find it, and how to evaluate, use and communicate it in an ethical manner' (2004c). World-wide, information literacy has become a key issue in many countries, notably in Australia and the USA, and was the subject of an expert meeting under the aegis of UNESCO, IFLA and the US National Forum on Information Literacy, resulting in the 'Alexandria Declaration' (UNESCO, 2006) as part of the World Summit on the Information Society initiative (see Chapter 10). The Declaration stated, *inter alia*, that 'vigorous investment in information literacy and lifelong learning strategies creates public value and is essential to the development of the Information Society'.

There is plenty of evidence, albeit much of it anecdotal, that students coming through our school and university systems lack the necessary information skills to learn effectively. For example, in the USA, a recent large scale study reported that 'college students and high-school students preparing to enter college are sorely lacking in the skills needed to retrieve, analyze, and communicate information that is available online . . . only 13 percent of the test-takers were information literate' (Foster, 2006).

A SCONUL briefing paper identified seven 'Pillars of Information Literacy', as follows:

1 The ability to recognise a need for information.
2 The ability to distinguish ways in which the information 'gap' may be addressed.
    - Knowledge of appropriate kinds of resources, both print and non-print.

- Selection of resources with 'best fit' for task at hand.
- The ability to understand the issues affecting accessibility of sources.

3 The ability to construct strategies for locating information.
- To articulate information need to match against resources.
- To develop a systematic method appropriate for the need.
- To understand the principles of construction and generation of databases.

4 The ability to locate and access information.
- To develop appropriate searching techniques (e.g. use of Boolean searching).
- To use communication and information technologies, including international academic networks.
- To use abstracting and indexing services, citation indexes and databases.
- To use current awareness methods to keep up to date.

5 The ability to compare and evaluate information obtained from different sources.
- Awareness of bias and authority issues.
- Awareness of the peer review process of scholarly publishing.
- Appropriate extraction of information matching the information need.

6 The ability to organise, apply and communicate information to others in ways appropriate to the situation.
- To cite bibliographic references in project reports and theses.
- To construct a personal bibliographic system.
- To apply information to the problem at hand.
- To communicate effectively using the appropriate medium.
- To understand issues of copyright and plagiarism.

7 The ability to synthesise and build upon existing information, contributing to the creation of new knowledge.

(Society of College, National and University Libraries, 1999)

A difficulty for libraries is that the concept of information literacy, as distinct from other literacies, is not widely accepted beyond the profession. Others use terms like 'media literacy', defined by Ofcom (2007) as 'the ability to access, understand and create communications in a variety of contexts', although clearly there are significant differences as well as overlaps between the concepts. Candy (2006) has proposed that we draw the concepts of information literacy and ICT (information and communications technology) literacy together under the banner of 'digital literacy', but others would argue that this loses the emphasis on handling traditional materials which balances approaches to information literacy. What is clear, however, is that libraries need to be key players in ensuring that their users have the competencies and skills needed to make full use of information resources in all their complexity. Whether they can go beyond the skills needed to access and use information and help create an 'information literate society' is perhaps a more open question. Nevertheless, across all sectors libraries have scored considerable successes in promoting information skills in recent years. Projects like Big Blue (www.library.mmu.ac.uk/bigblue), an information skills development initiative, have had considerable impact and demonstrated the direct role of the librarian in delivering learning.

The evidence suggests that there are two related and essential requirements for success in library delivery of information literacy programmes. The first is embedding; the second situatedness. Embedding implies that information skills tuition must be an integral part of the taught curriculum. Situatedness implies that they are relevant to the subject and task in hand. Thus Smith and Presser (2005) have noted, in the context of teaching information skills to law students, 'the importance of embedding information skills teaching in the curriculum, reinforced by core law assessment tasks, so that students immediately see the relevance and applicability of the skills they are developing'.

Wakefield (2007), also speaking of law students, notes that successful information skills training impacts on other library services: 'the number of law enquiries at helpdesks has dropped as students learn basic research skills via the tutorials. Demand for more in-depth, one-to-one help sessions has increased, as students experiment with a wider range of resources and use more complex functions of a database or e-resource.'

Of course librarians cannot achieve information literacy on their own. Leaving aside definitional issues, there is a growing realization that the key lies in embedding the librarian, not just the library's contribution. Staff at Edge Hill University in the UK, for example, speak of a 'vision of a multi-professional team of academics, learning technologists and information specialists creating a learning environment and learning experiences with the learner at the centre' (Davey, 2006).

Conclusion

Consideration of the user universe leads rapidly from a consideration of the range of online services with which users interact, and the authentication and other services put in place to facilitate seamless access, to broader consideration of the main purpose of libraries, which leads to a requirement for understanding of learning and how it takes place. In hybrid environments, understanding of both traditional, face-to-face, and networked learning is crucial and this leads naturally to a need to engage with users in relation to their skills and competencies. There is a considerable challenge for librarians, across most sectors, to develop their direct involvement in the delivery of learning. In all sectors, understanding of pedagogical principles will help librarians to be more effective in designing and delivering their services and demonstrating the relevance and importance of information literacy.

10
The information universe

> Information gently but relentlessly drizzles down on us in an invisible, impalpable electric rain.
>
> (von Baeyer, 2004)

> A library is thought in cold storage.
>
> (Attributed to Herbert Samuel)

Introduction

The idea of an 'information universe' was introduced in Chapter 7, as a way of referring to the sum totality of all the information sources available throughout the world, in whatever format. Overlaying this universe of information there is a wide variety of structures, including:

- the structuring of data into information objects
- the aggregation of information objects into collections (traditionally, most information objects – or at least their surrogates – were represented in more than one collection)
- descriptive information, itself part of the information universe, which imposes meaning on the object and collection spaces
- data and structures related to rights, including commercial information such as pricing data and intellectual property rights such as copyright
- services of many different types based on underlying objects, collections and aggregates of collections, and including search, retrieve and delivery services
- governmental, legal and commercial structures, which relate to the acquisition, possession and retransmission of classes of information objects defined in various ways, for example, by commercial interests and national security.

Libraries are heavily involved in this structuring process. In the past their involvement was centred on the selection of a sub-set of the objects available, providing description and structure to the ensuing collection, and taking steps to make it available to a defined user population. However, once libraries shift their focus away from collection building (in the sense of building collections of physical artefacts) towards the role of intermediaries that provide their users with access to remote sources, then their interests must also shift. Libraries cannot remain neutral while others design the systems and services on which they will rely. As a result, libraries must now take a very real and close interest in their regional, national and international information environments. It is the role of libraries in building these broader information environments which is the subject of this chapter. It begins, however, by considering the broad policy context as evidenced by the development of national information policies.

Information policies

In the emerging and rapidly evolving Information Society it is becoming apparent that failure to plan strategically at international and national level could be disastrous. The interests of societies and their governments intermesh with a strong information sector, and even if market economics play a major role, governments cannot simply stand by and hope that appropriate structures emerge.

To make matters more complex the inter-relationships between sectors and information providers mean that there is an enormous number of stakeholders to consider. Users frequently cross neat boundaries, shifting from being a citizen looking for, say, government information, to being a consumer of entertainment, to being a student within an online learning environment, to being a researcher seeking current survey data. Furthermore, users may become producers – by putting up web pages, or perhaps by creating an artistic object. And as producers their interests may conflict with those they have as consumers, for example in the handling of intellectual property rights (IPR). Into this confusing mix of roles has to be added the interests of major corporate producers – publishers, film producers, newspaper proprietors and others, many of them operating across national boundaries. Yet another group of stakeholders consists of the 'information transport' agencies: broadcasters, Internet Service Providers (ISPs), cable companies and telecommunications companies.

The legislative frameworks which nations put in place are themselves a source of additional complexity. There are few guiding principles. Freedom of access to information is a fine banner, until it trips over confidentiality, privacy or the trading of information as a valuable commodity – and if the last is denied, the whole basis of the new information society is removed.

These complexities have been recognized by governments and international agencies. Thus it was that, in 1995, eight principles were agreed as the basis for work to develop a Global Information Infrastructure (GII) (G-7 Information Society Conference, 1995):

- promoting dynamic competition
- encouraging private investment
- defining appropriate regulatory frameworks
- providing open access to networks.

while

- ensuring universal provision of and access to services
- promoting equality of opportunity to the citizen
- promoting diversity of content including cultural and linguistic diversity
- recognizing the necessity of worldwide cooperation with particular attention to less-developed nations.

Following a number of other initiatives the UN organized the World Summit on the Information Society (WSIS), held from 2003 to 2005, mainly through meetings in Geneva and Tunis. The initial meetings were particularly concerned with internet governance. A formal 'Declaration of Commitment' issued from the Tunis meeting included the following statement:

> We reaffirm our desire and commitment to build a people-centred, inclusive and development-oriented Information Society, premised on the purposes and principles of the Charter of the United Nations, international law and multilateralism, and respecting fully and upholding the Universal Declaration of Human Rights, so that people everywhere can create, access, utilize and share information and knowledge, to achieve their full potential and to attain the internationally agreed development goals and objectives, including the Millennium Development Goals.
>
> (www.itu.int/wsis/docs2/tunis/off/7.pdf)

Eleven action lines emerged from these meetings:

- the role of governments and all stakeholders in the promotion of ICTs for development
- the information and communication infrastructure
- access to information and knowledge
- capacity building
- building confidence and security in the use of ICTs
- enabling environments
- ICT applications (e-government, e-business, e-learning, e-health, e-employment, e-environment, e-agriculture, e-science)
- cultural diversity and identity, linguistic diversity and local content
- media
- ethical dimensions of the Information Society
- international and regional co-operation.

Clearly, virtually all of these themes impact on libraries and contain issues which greatly affect both the nature of the library and its development. It would be beyond the scope of this book to examine them all, but the emphasis in the Tunis Commitment on a 'people-centred, inclusive' information society makes this area an obvious one for librarianship, with its longstanding commitment to the principle of inclusion, to pursue.

Exclusion from full participation in society can take many forms, some direct and some indirect. The UK's Department for Culture, Media and Sport (DCMS) noted in one of its early statements that while social exclusion is frequently experienced as an individual problem – a 'personal misfortune' – the evidence suggests that it is best tackled as a community issue as 'successful policies for social inclusion must encourage people to take joint action on issues affecting their neighbourhood' (DCMS, 1999). Furthermore it noted that:

> a key feature of a sustainable community is its connections. People living in affluent communities tend to have good road systems, trouble-free service from public utilities, access to quality education and health services, access to legal and financial services, access to leisure opportunities, access to political processes, and access to information and communication channels. By contrast, a feature of life in the least integrated communities is that such connections are not well-established.

Although these comments were made in the context of a policy paper on public libraries, their import is considerably broader.

National information policies do not consist of a single master plan. Rather they are the summation of a series of components which together contribute to a more or less coherent whole. Rowlands (1997) suggests that it is useful to consider:

1 *Infrastructural policies* which apply across the whole of society. These would include taxation policy, employment law, etc.
2 *Horizontal information policies*, which apply across the information sector. An example would be the provision of public libraries.
3 *Vertical information policies*, which are specific to a sector such as, perhaps, the health sector.

It is probably also useful to add to this taxonomy *international* and *sub-national policies*, the latter including those developed at regional or state (as opposed to federal) level since all of these also impact on one another. Information policy then needs to be seen as the sum total of these various strands and the interplay between them.

For all the above reasons, but also because individual information services are often planned nationally – the People's Network (www.peoplesnetwork.gov.uk) and the National Library for Health (NLH, www.library.nhs.uk) being good examples in the UK – a series of issues has to be addressed by librarians that simply do not occur in traditional, localized libraries. There is a need to provide a 'managed environment' within which resources, both traditional and electronic, are provided by and to libraries and others in a co-ordinated fashion. The role of national libraries, which in the past have taken the main responsibility for developing collections of last resort, is still emerging but could be highly significant.

In the UK the picture is complicated by the fact that while in theory the MLA, which is responsible to the Department for Culture, Media and Sport (DCMS), is the voice of libraries in government in fact it really represents only the public library sector, and to some extent the British Library. Academic libraries, with their huge resources and key role in supporting research and teaching, report through their institutions to the Department for Innovation, Universities and Skills, health libraries report ultimately to the Department of Health and so on. This diversity is both a weakness and a strength, since it makes it possible to lobby legitimately to different arms of government but makes it difficult to speak with one voice.

Information infrastructures

The infrastructures which make it possible for libraries to provide access to the information universe are of course varied and complex. The internet itself is not a network but an interconnected network of networks which exchange data using internationally agreed standards like the Internet Protocol (IP). It uses packet-switching technologies so that data can be routed in many different ways to reach its destination, thus avoiding bottlenecks and system failures. Its design has proved tremendously resilient.

The growth of traffic on the internet inevitably led to problems with limited bandwidth and congestion at peak times, as well as concerns over security and privacy. Governments, universities and private companies have overcome some of these problems by building private networks, such as the Joint Academic Network (JANET, www.ukerna.ac.uk), to which all UK universities are linked, and NHSNet/N3 (www.connectingforhealth.nhs.uk), linking UK hospitals and Internet2 in the USA (www.internet2.edu). The UK's eScience Grid (www.grid-support.ac.uk) has been put in place to provide high-level computational and software resources for researchers' use of data, with an emphasis on huge datasets from such applications as satellite observation and atomic physics. The use of mobile networks has mushroomed with wireless connectivity becoming widespread, leading to the development of more and more location-independent services.

It is difficult to keep pace with the growth and development of information and communications infrastructure. End-user hardware is of course far more powerful than even the largest computers were a quarter of a century ago. Computing power doubles every 18 months or so in accordance with Moore's Law (named after the co-founder of Intel) and the pace shows no real sign of slackening. Storage capacities have increased to the extent that cost is rarely now an issue except for very large applications, so the local storage of information is not usually constrained by available digital space. Graphical user interfaces and applications software have developed to the stage where little additional training is needed to manipulate most kinds of digital information resource, and much of the underlying technology can, in any case, be hidden from the user. Access to computers is widespread, in the office, in the home, through cybercafés, through public libraries, in educational institutions and via laptops, personal digital assistants and increasingly sophisticated mobile phones. Most are capable of acting as internet clients and it has become virtually impossible – and fairly meaningless – to calculate the total number in use. Actual use may be a better indicator. The best estimates for internet connectivity (defined somewhat variably, but most surveys appear to use a definition of 'have used the internet at least once in the last month') put the internet population at 1.1

billion worldwide in 2007, out of a total population of 6.6 billion, i.e. about 16% of the world's population is connected to the internet (www.internetworldstats.com/stats.htm). In North America internet penetration has reached just under 70% of the population, while in Europe the figure is 39%.

Web 2.0

The world wide web has grown spectacularly since its invention less than 20 years ago as a way for scientists at CERN to share their work. As a powerful, worldwide communications tool it is virtually unparalleled, enabling people in every country of the world to publish and share information. It is also gaining increasing use as a platform for virtual commerce. However, it has some noteworthy limitations. Firstly, despite its original design as a means of communication, it is mostly one-way. The majority of use consists of a small number of people publishing and a huge number of people browsing and consuming. Secondly, most websites are monolithic, in the sense that they present their information in the same way to every visitor, unless the human user chooses to select a different view. Thirdly, websites are built with a clear hierarchical structure; they cannot easily serve up content to other applications on request. Fourthly, websites use essentially static data, rather than being able to process it. All this is beginning to change and much of this new approach is promoted under the banner of 'Web 2.0'.

The idea of Web 2.0 is closely intertwined with the related concept of the 'semantic web'. Indeed, the terms are often used interchangeably, although in fact they do not have quite the same meaning. The concept of the semantic web lies in the idea that instead of simply sharing documents with meaning to human beings, the basic stuff of the web should consist of data to which machine-readable meaning has been attached. The inventor of the web, Tim Berners-Lee, and his colleagues published a paper in 2001 in which they argued that 'the Semantic Web will bring structure to the meaningful content of Web pages, creating an environment where software agents roaming from page to page can readily carry out sophisticated tasks for users' (Berners-Lee, Hendler and Lassila, 2001). Thus, the central idea is that by adding meaning to web objects, software agents will be able to act on behalf of users to deliver sophisticated services. However, in order to express meaning we need shared language, as was argued in relation to the delivery of library services in Chapter 3. It is not surprising, therefore, to find that in a follow-up paper published in 2006 (Shadbolt, Hall and Berners-Lee, 2006) Berners-Lee and his colleagues devoted most of their attention to the development of ontologies, conceptualizations of meaning which can be shared between disciplines and across social, geographical and other boundaries:

> For example, life sciences research demands the integration of diverse and heterogeneous data sets that originate from distinct communities of scientists in separate subfields. Scientists, researchers, and regulatory authorities in genomics, proteomics, clinical drug trials, and epidemiology all need a way to integrate these components. This is being achieved in large part through the adoption of common conceptualizations referred to as ontologies. In the past five years, the argument in favor of using ontologies has been won – numerous initiatives are developing ontologies for biology (for example, see http://obo.sourceforge.net), medicine, genomics, and related fields. These communities are developing language standards that can be deployed on the Web.
>
> (Shadbolt, Hall and Berners-Lee, 2006)

Although the debate on Web 2.0 has included this central feature, it has tended to place much more emphasis on the social dimension of the web. The term was coined in 2003 by Tim O'Reilly, who went on to argue that 'the central principle behind the success of the giants born in the Web 1.0 era who have survived to lead the Web 2.0 era appears to be this, that they have embraced the power of the web to harness collective intelligence' (O'Reilly, 2005). Again, this term is open to multiple interpretations, but commentators frequently point to social networking sites, such as YouTube and Facebook, as offering examples of the kinds of services which Web 2.0 encompasses. Anderson (2006) identifies six 'big ideas' behind Web 2.0:

- individual production and user generated content
- harnessing the power of the crowd (O'Reilly's 'collective intelligence'), including the 'wisdom of crowds' ('what fans of the TV show *Who Wants to be a Millionaire* would call "ask the audience"')
- data on an epic scale
- the architecture of participation
- network effects, power laws and the 'Long Tail'. (This includes the notion that as more people join in using a service on the network so each gets more value. The Long Tail encapsulates the idea that on the internet there is a huge number of people with a very small amount of unique or otherwise valuable data, and that the networks enable this value to be

realized by making connections with the small number of people who may be interested.)
- openness.

There is not room here to go into the detailed discussion on each of these characteristics of Web 2.0, but it can be seen that they include ideas which have a real bearing on *library* services. Take the idea of the Long Tail (the term comes from the title of an article by Anderson, 2004). Many libraries possess a small number of rare items. In terms of the number of times each is requested this is a tiny part of their business. Before the web enabled catalogues to be opened up worldwide these items received very limited exposure. But now their whereabouts is known to anyone interested. So not only can we aggregate these rare item requests into a significant volume of business in their own right, but the tail grows by enabling a greater number of interested readers to find them. What we have is a combination of much wider exposure and much easier access, provided, of course, that we can manage our libraries cost-effectively to deliver within this environment. With physical artefacts this means a more efficient interlibrary loan system or careful selection of items for digitization. As Dempsey (2006b) puts it: 'libraries collectively manage a long tail of research, learning and cultural materials . . . we need to do more work to make sure that this long tail is directly available to improve the work and lives of our users'.

Ideas like this have led, perhaps inevitably, to discussion of 'Library 2.0', a term coined by Casey in 2005 when he referred in his blog to the work of 'Librarians without Borders', a Canadian group helping to build a library in Angola with the stated aim of improving 'access to information resources regardless of language, religion, or geography, by forming partnerships with community organizations in developing regions' (Casey, 2005). Miller (2006) sees Library 2.0 in the following terms:

> Blogs, wikis and RSS are often held up as exemplary manifestations of Web 2.0. A reader of a blog or a wiki is provided with tools to add a comment or even, in the case of the wiki, to edit the content . . . Library 2.0 means harnessing this type of participation so that libraries can benefit from increasingly rich collaborative cataloguing efforts, such as including contributions from partner libraries as well as adding rich enhancements, such as book jackets or movie files, to records from publishers and others.

However, there is some ambiguity among commentators over whether Library

2.0 is 'Web 2.0 for libraries' in this sense or should be seen as a more philosophical approach which borrows Web 2.0 concepts such as user-centredness. So Casey and Savastinuk (2006) comment that: 'the heart of Library 2.0 is user-centred change. It is a model for library service that encourages constant and purposeful change, inviting user participation in the creation of both the physical and the virtual services they want, supported by consistently evaluating services. It also attempts to reach new users and better serve current ones through improved customer-driven offerings.'

Of course much of this is a matter of emphasis. What is apparent is that leading libraries and library service suppliers are starting to develop Web 2.0 like components. A simple example would be OCLC WorldCat's support for user reviews, modelled on Amazon's similar feature.

Organization of content

Taking the UK academic sector as an example, digital content acquisition (including in that term the acquisition of access rights, that is ignoring the question as to whether the data is hosted locally or remotely) has gone through considerable evolution. It began with access to remote, usually bibliographic, data services such as MEDLINE – some libraries acquired tapes of records and ran them on a local machine as an alternative to accessing the remote server. During the 1980s the common pattern was for mediated online searching, the over-riding issue being one of constraining costs – charged on some kind of usage basis – and the end result being very little use. Aston University Library pioneered the wide-scale use of full text with the ADONIS biomedical periodical service, installed in 1992–3 using a CD-ROM jukebox. CD-ROM datasets rapidly achieved wide penetration, initially in standalone mode, later becoming networked. The breakthrough which CD-ROMs delivered was not so much the technology as the shift in economic model – for almost the first time access to digital resources was not constrained by per use charges. It was this concept of 'free at the point of use' which was to prove crucial in the next stage.

The first major higher education data service in the UK was established at Bath University in the early 1990s. Currently there are two national academic datacentres – EDINA in Edinburgh (www.edina.ac.uk) and MIMAS in Manchester (www.mimas.ac.uk). As an example of the types of service available, MIMAS currently (mid-2007) offers:

- discovery tools, such as COPAC, ISI Web of Knowledge and Intute

- journal collections, such as Journal STORage (JSTOR)
- learning materials, including the national Jorum repository and the National Learning Network (NLN) materials from Becta
- primary research data, such as the Economic and Social Data Service (ESDS), International Data Service (IDS) and the UK Census data
- geospatial data, such as the Landmap service for satellite data images
- services for librarians, including the National Electronic Journal Licensing Service (NESLi2).

The economic model underlying these services ensures that the dataset will be free at the point of use even though various charging models are used to bill institutions. This carries on the model referred to above and developed during the early days of electronic library services.

The two data centres do not, of course, have a monopoly on data services. Other national services include the UK Data Archive at the University of Essex (www.data-archive.ac.uk) and the National Centre for Text Mining (NaCTeM, www.nactem.ac.uk), operated jointly by the Universities of Liverpool and Manchester. In addition, institutions continue to exploit the full range of other commercial services.

By and large these services follow the traditional creator–publisher–intermediary–user model and deal with discrete information objects. However, there is now a vast range of digital objects which pose new problems. As long ago as 1998, Lyman and Chodorow remarked that 'the system of scholarly communication governing the flow of information and knowledge within the academic community . . . has become unstable'. The same authors drew attention to the difficulty, in a digital, networked environment, of defining a 'publication': 'the electronic format encourages constant change – addition, subtraction, alteration – and its organization is fundamentally different from the one used in printed materials'.

This neatly summarizes the challenge for libraries used to dealing with formally 'published', discrete objects. What does 'publication' mean in an era when anyone can put anything up on the web? What is the 'object' when it may be here today, and still here tomorrow but in a subtly different form? At what level of granularity should objects be described and delivered?

Information environments

Although the organization of the delivery of major resources into data services, as described above, addresses a number of technical and contractual issues, it is fairly clear that further organization is needed if libraries are to be able to provide access to the growing mass of services on offer, if issues of interoperability are to be tackled systematically and if, nationally, maximum efficiency is to be obtained from investment. For this reason attention has turned in a number of countries to the management and organization of distributed resources. One example would be Denmark's Electronic Research Library (DEFF) which Kvaerndrup (2000) describes as a 'large, coherent, electronic library structure providing integrated information services' – see also Öhström (2006). Another, discussed in greater detail below, is the JISC Information Environment (IE) in the UK.

Just as the design of traditional libraries depends on the application of some reasonably well understood general principles, the development of information environments needs to take account of a number of common issues. The key ones for the purpose of the present discussion are scalability, sustainability, interoperability (described below) and personalization (described in Chapter 9).

Scalability refers to the ability of solutions to be implemented widely across a whole service or across a sector, such as the whole of higher education, or perhaps across all library and information services. Many projects which work well with small numbers of users fail to 'scale', either because the software cannot support larger numbers or because the operational and managerial overheads are too high. For example, a project which relied on users having a particular type of hardware (say a particular sound card) could not be scaled across higher education, though it might just scale across one institution – until the users demanded access from home. More frequently it is the sheer effort required to support a service which prevents it scaling. Experience shows that failure to scale is one of the most frequent reasons for failure to turn electronic library experiments into viable services.

Sustainability is the ability of a service to be supported over the long term. Will it be possible for the project firstly to be maintained as a service and secondly to 'grow' with the needs of the users? The first point emphasizes that, although extra effort may be required to set up the service, it will then need to operate with minimal overheads and minimal support as one of a portfolio of services offered by the library. Services must be able to cope with all possible forms of 'stress' – handling failures gracefully (so that the whole system does not crash each time an error occurs), operating in a wide variety of environments and with a source of ready maintenance advice when problems occur. The second recognizes that the environment and the supporting technologies will develop and change over time, so that the new service needs to be maintained and to grow alongside it.

The concepts of scalability and sustainability are linked. So, for example, a careful analysis of both the existing technological base of higher education and its likely development, if considered early in the design of a project, can go a long way to ensure that it is both scalable and sustainable.

But these are not the only issues. Of even greater importance is the whole question of *interoperability* – the ability of services to work together effectively and efficiently, so that software can be used to interrogate one service and integrate the results with those from another to enable the user to receive a seamless service. In the UK the Interoperability Focus at UKOLN has been established to assist services to address this issue (see www.ukoln.ac.uk/interop-focus/about). It is suggested that interoperability can best be viewed from six separate viewpoints (see Miller, 2000):

1 *Technical interoperability* is concerned with the standards needed to enable systems to interact and information to be stored, transported and communicated between and across them.
2 *Semantic interoperability* is concerned with bringing standardization to the ways in which terms are used to describe objects or concepts. For example, the use of a thesaurus may assist interoperability at this level. A particular issue is that while terminology may be used consistently within a subject domain, it is frequently used differently between domains. This work on shared ontologies is important.
3 *Political/human interoperability* relates to the exercise of control over resources, such as decisions on whether to make them available, and to the ability of staff to handle complex systems which each pose different problems if the end product is to be brought together as an integrated service.
4 *Inter-community interoperability* is concerned with facilitating sharing of information objects and collections across communities, such as libraries, museums, art galleries and other 'memory institutions'.
5 *Legal interoperability* relates particularly to where legislation differs between countries, for example in the areas of data protection and freedom of information.
6 *International interoperability* includes issues such as language and culture.

Accessible interoperability is related to the use of standard 'display' features which are designed to meet the needs of individual users, i.e. ensuring that each object presented to the user is consistent in its accessibility requirements and does not require the user to switch between different applications. For example, a user who is blind and who has installed voice-output software should not have to switch applications to 'read' different objects. The World Wide Web Consortium (W3C) has been active in developing the Web Accessibility Initiative (WAI) and its Web Content Accessibility Guidelines (WCAG). Libraries have been prominent among organizations attempting to take accessibility requirements seriously, as Brophy and Craven (2007) remark:

> Library researchers have been prominent in exploring ways of improving Web accessibility for the last decade. They have brought to the field an overriding concern for a user-centered approach, which has led to a series of user-focused studies showing precisely where common approaches to Web design have been failing those with disabilities . . . A combination of improvements to access technology and adoption of 'design for all' principles, coupled with staff and user training and awareness raising, has been shown to have significant, positive results. Over this period of time, libraries throughout the UK and elsewhere have been encouraged to mainstream accessibility, and, partly as a result of new legislation, to maintain the issue high among their priorities.

As Cervone (2006) has said of federated search (see page 197) 'we must quickly come up with better tools to integrate these services into the user's information-seeking environment, be that the library Web site, a course management system, or some other information portal of the patron. If not, other services such as Google Scholar and Microsoft Academic Live will quickly fill the void and another opportunity for libraries will have been lost.'

Open access

The old paradigm under which scholars effectively give their published work away to publishers who promptly sell it back to their institutional libraries, often at huge prices, is coming under the spotlight. Stevan Harnad, Director of the Cognitive Sciences Centre at the University of Southampton, is the leading UK proponent of a new system of scholarly communication under which authors would simply make their papers available freely on the web, making expensive academic journals a thing of the past (Harnad, 2000):

> In the PostGutenberg era of global digital networks . . . there is at last an alternative, and not only researchers, but research itself, and hence all of society, would be the losers if we failed to take full advantage of it. For now we no longer

> have to rely on the expensive, inefficient and access-limiting technology of print on paper to disseminate research findings. They can be *self-archived* by their authors in public online archives . . . and thereby made accessible to one and all without any financial firewalls. [*Original emphasis*]

In the past decade the open access movement has made rapid progress (see Chapter 2), although there is still a long way to go. A seminal event was the opening of the Berlin Declaration on Open Access to Knowledge in the Sciences and Humanities for signature (http://oa.mpg.de/openaccess-berlin/berlindeclaration.html). The goals stated in the Declaration are:

> Our mission of disseminating knowledge is only half complete if the information is not made widely and readily available to society. New possibilities of knowledge dissemination not only through the classical form but also and increasingly through the open access paradigm via the internet have to be supported. We define open access as a comprehensive source of human knowledge and cultural heritage that has been approved by the scientific community. In order to realize the vision of a global and accessible representation of knowledge, the future Web has to be sustainable, interactive, and transparent. Content and software tools must be openly accessible and compatible.

Carr et al. (2006) argue that open access self-archiving offers at least five benefits:

- early advantage (early self-archiving produces both earlier and more citations)
- usage advantage (more downloads for open access articles, correlated with later citations)
- competitive advantage (relative citation advantage of open access over non-open access articles)
- quality advantage (the open access advantage is higher, the higher the quality of the article)
- quality bias (authors selectively self-archiving their higher quality articles).

These issues have been debated long and hard, and the debate will no doubt continue. Meanwhile, actual use of repositories – in terms of items deposited by authors or on their behalf – has been disappointing. As a result there is now a move, backed by the UK Research Councils, to make deposit mandatory.

E-print repositories are by no means the only kind of repository which libraries may be involved with. Collections of reusable learning objects are developing slowly, most notably through the higher/further education Jorum (www.jorum.ac.uk) and the post-16 level National Learning Network (NLN, www.nln.ac.uk). As with any kind of digital object, the metadata accompanying the learning objects is critical in enabling it to be identified, evaluated for re-use and retrieved. There is also debate about what the difference between an information object and a learning object is. McGreal (2004) suggests the following definition to create boundaries around what may legitimately be termed a learning object:

> Any reusable digital resource that is encapsulated in a lesson or assemblage of lessons grouped in units, modules, courses, and even programmes. A lesson can be defined as a piece of instruction, normally including a learning purpose or purposes.

For librarians, a particular issue is that the metadata standards in use for learning objects differ from those used for information objects, although work on interoperability is ongoing. This does mean, however, that providing access to the full range of objects is challenging and as yet few libraries appear to have integrated access to learning objects into their search and delivery systems.

Repositories as a whole pose a series of problems or issues which need to be tackled:

1 While self-archiving by authors is a laudable aim, evidence to date suggests that they are remarkably reluctant to do this and that so far the effort required appears to outweigh the perceived benefits. Some libraries have undertaken the work of depositing on behalf of authors but this would be an expensive route to take in the long term. The 'stick' of mandatory deposit may be helpful, but academics are not easily herded and more 'carrots' may need to be found.
2 Because repositories may contain pre-prints, direct copies of published papers and post-prints, the last with later comments attached, it is not always clear what version the repository is holding. To add to the problems, it may be very difficult to reproduce the published version from the files which the author actually submits.
3 Since many repositories are institutionally based they will contain items from a wide variety of subject domains. Achieving consistency of description such that federated searching across a wide range of repositories

will retrieve the relevant items will be extremely difficult, if only because of variations in subject description. Yet interoperability between repositories is critical to the success of the open access movement.

4 There is some concern that repository owners could be tempted to take monopolistic actions where they have the only copies of publications in a given field. Although unlikely, this could affect subjects where, say, a learned society runs the repository and finds it needs to generate revenue.
5 There is a tension between open access and long-term preservation. Repositories can fulfil both functions, but their policies and practices need to be clear.

None of these are insuperable problems, of course, but they pose challenges for libraries to address if they are to secure this strand of work as part of their long-term service portfolio.

Supporting creativity

The institutional repository offers an interesting example of the way in which libraries are starting to become much more involved in supporting the creation and publication of information objects. Whereas in the past libraries have been at the end of the information chain, taking published work into their collections, making it available and preserving it, they are now starting to occupy some of the space at the beginning of the process. Indeed, in many ways it is becoming more apt to think in terms of a virtuous circle, with each stage reinforcing the others, rather than a longitudinal chain. This was one reason that the CALIMERA model (Chapter 8) was depicted as a pair of interlocked circles.

It is not just in the academic sector that this change is observable. Among public libraries there has been considerable development of services which support the creativity of users. Evidence for this comes from many quarters. For example, the Northamptonshire Black History Project, winner of the 2005 Libraries Change Lives Award (www.cilip.org.uk/NR/exeres/A45385F0-A6E8-4F4C-80AD-9E426144362E.htm), demonstrated how communities can be encouraged to create resources of their own.

The inference of this, and similar examples, is that users often interact with libraries in a bid to *produce* information objects of their own, as well as to use objects created by others. A more general example of this activity is in the area of genealogy, where many users want to explore their family history in order to create a family tree and, very often, to produce a collection of images and text to describe their antecedents and the worlds they inhabited.

This idea has been taken forward on a somewhat broader scale by a number of projects and service developments which encourage users to see themselves as contributors to the collection. As Butters, Hulme and Brophy (2007) put it:

> The involvement of non-experts in creating recordings of cultural heritage, in whatever medium, so as to capture the experience of 'ordinary citizens' in their own terms, could lead to richer and more illuminating collections as new insights and previously hidden information is revealed. This democratises the creation of cultural heritage, removing it from an elitist monopoly, and provides new perspectives on local, regional, national and international events. Advantages of this approach to building collections include greater relevance to the lives of ordinary people, while individuals gain a sense of achievement from seeing their work published.

Examples of such services include 'Moving Here', concerned with memories of immigration (www.movinghere.org.uk), 'WW2: People's War' (www.bbc.co.uk/ww2peopleswar), the City Stories project in the USA (www.citystories.com) and the Cultural Objects in Networked Environments (COINE) project in Europe (www.uoc.edu/in3/coine/eng/index.html). An evaluation of the last of these concluded that COINE had been successful in proving 'the viability and attractiveness of the concept of offering ordinary citizens the tools and opportunities to tell their own stories in a digital environment' (Butters, Hulme and Brophy, 2007).

For libraries, in their role as intermediaries, the critical issue is of course the content which needs to be delivered either in analogue form or across the internet. It is to this issue that we turn next.

Content

Libraries have traditionally organized content for themselves in their collections. As we have seen the collection has been central to their operations and has served a number of purposes, including preservation, the provision of access, bibliographic identification and prestige. But, as has already been remarked, the availability of electronic documents changes things fundamentally:

> [T]he effect of having electronic documents is to make local storage optional rather than necessary. This means that we can realistically begin to think nationally or, in

> more technical terms, network-wide – as broadly as there is networked access. Since electronic documents do not need to be locally held and since the needs of users in different locations vary, the most plausible approach is that of viewing the totality of electronic documents as being, in effect, one great big distributed collection.
>
> (Buckland, 1992)

The digital content available in the world is organized in many different ways and has to be accessed through a variety of mechanisms. It is simplest for descriptive purposes to divide content into that available freely, such as most websites, and that subject to some kind of restriction, such as many electronic journals and databases. Libraries have tended to put their emphasis on the organization of the latter type of content but this is being challenged by the significance of openly available sources, including some journals, material in e-print repositories and dynamic content, such as blogs and wikis.

Information objects

The concept of an 'information object' was introduced in Chapter 1, where it was used to describe any object, including physical books and journals, electronic documents and multimedia, which might form part of a library collection. The term is a useful one, but it is helpful to try to define it more precisely, especially as these broadly defined information objects will be the raw materials with which libraries will continue to deal. This section is mainly concerned with digital information objects, because that is where the most challenging issues lie, but it is worth stressing that analogue objects, including traditional books, will almost certainly remain a key part of nearly all libraries' collections and services. Indeed, it is useful to recall that an effect of concentrating on individual 'objects' can be to lose sight of – and even destroy – the purpose of the work in question. Most books, for example, are much more than collections of individual chapters. The organization of objects at this micro level is all-important to their coherence and meaning. A book cannot simply be deconstructed into discrete chunks, each handled independently, in the way that individual journal papers can. The level of granularity at which digital objects are treated is discussed later, but similar arguments apply to analogue media.

It is also worth noting that the digitization of analogue objects opens up the possibility of enrichment by providing deep context. For example, historical documents may be indexed by place and date, and tools provided to enable researchers to cluster such objects in novel ways. A digitized resource may thus be much more than the simple equivalent of the original object.

Of course, libraries have had the problem of defining information objects, albeit writ small, in the past when they have created or acquired 'items' where the physical manifestation of an item does not coincide with the smallest unit of useful information. An example would be a bound volume of a journal, or even a single issue, where the useful 'item' from the user's point of view is usually the individual article while the 'item' for the library (as represented in its catalogue and physically manifested on its shelves) is the volume or issue. The same argument could be applied to an edited collection of essays or to a database of bibliographic or other records. A complexity is that the library's 'item' may evolve over time into a different manifestation, as when the individual journal issues are bound into a volume – the library then ceases to regard the issues as items and treats the bound volume as the basic unit, even though the users' interests have not changed.

In the electronic information field the situation has become even more complex. A web page provides a good example. It may consist of a series of frames, each of which may contain text, images, sound files or other embedded 'objects'. What, in these circumstances, should be regarded as the basic 'information object'? This is a particularly difficult question because the same image, or piece of text, could well be regarded as an information object in its own right in one circumstance, but as an embedded (and in effect inseparable) part of an intellectual and indeed physical construct (the whole web page for example) in another. Web pages also display another problematic property for libraries and users, in that they do not persist. Unlike physical books and journals, and some electronic formats like CD-ROM, there is no guarantee that a web page that exists today will still exist, anywhere in the world, tomorrow. Furthermore, even if the page does survive its location may have changed, rendering it inaccessible.

Yet more complexity lies in the existence of varied forms or editions of information objects. Libraries are used to handling new editions of books, but the complexity of the digital world goes far beyond this. For example, a web page is increasingly likely to be created dynamically when it is requested, with no two occurrences – even if delivered to the same user in response to an identical request – being identical. Even where the content is identical, a document may be packaged in different ways – so, for example, documents available for downloading from the web may be offered in PDF or HTML versions. Should the librarian treat these as different information objects? If so, how should the relationship between them be expressed? In order to make some sense of this situation, it is useful to have some working definitions. As yet these cannot allow for every possible eventuality, but consensus is emerging around ways to handle, describe and locate information objects.

Many of the difficulties arise because the systems which have been developed in the print-on-paper world no longer apply in the electronic, and still less in the hybrid information universe. Paskin (1999) has suggested that in place of the printed object we now need to think in terms of three 'spaces' in which 'the same' article appears:

- Information space = the work as intangible entity (ideas)
- Cyberspace = digital manifestation (electronic, made of bits)
- 'Paper space' = physical manifestation (cellulose and ink, made of atoms).

The logical approach is clearly to have a unique identifier for the first of these instances and then some way to reference the digital and paper manifestations of it from that basic definition ('paper' being used here to represent any non-digital formats). A number of approaches are being explored to achieve this, and these will be described briefly below.

First, however, it is important to note that this does not solve the question of the level of granularity at which a 'work' should be recognized – is the basic unit, for example, the book, the chapter, the illustration, the sentence or something else? A practical suggestion is that we define a 'document like object' (DLO) (Caplan, 1995; Carpenter, 2003) which is, in essence, a common sense approach to the basic useful unit – so it might be, say, a journal article, a web page or a video presentation. Paskin (1999) suggested that it may also be useful to define a lower level of object, the 'component of a document' which may become especially useful as multimedia packages become more commonly used, as well as the higher level 'cluster of documents' which is represented by, for example, a database or journal volume. However, more recently the issue of persistent identifiers for data, especially in e-science, has complicated the picture still further. Where, for example, the digital object is a database which is changing continuously and where the principal application may be data mining, achieving persistence requires considerable thought and effort at the design stage and throughout the lifecycle. It is also pertinent to add that much discussion of this area refers not just to 'information objects' but rather to 'digital objects', on the basis that, once digitized, all objects are, at least in principle, capable of being handled in the same way. However, noting that it is difficult to conceive of a digital object which did not have the potential to convey information and that the term 'information object' is inclusive of non-digital resources, that remains the preferred term for this discussion.

Libraries have used 'document identifiers' for many years. For example, the International Standard Book Number (ISBN) and International Standard Serial Number (ISSN) are used to identify a specific edition of a particular book and a specific journal title uniquely. These are examples of what are sometimes called 'intelligent' or 'compound' identifiers, because the numbers themselves contain meaning. Provided the structure is known, and there is access to a table of values, the publisher can be deduced from the number itself without recourse to the actual item. By contrast, a 'simple' identifier is just a number – the accessions number used by many libraries in the past was an example, since it was simply assigned in sequence and nothing could be deduced from it by itself. The use of identifiers to convey meaning is discussed below.

ISBNs and ISSNs are also good examples of identification systems which are of limited usefulness because of the particular stakeholder view they embody. For example, they are usually of little interest to the user, since it is impossible to resolve the request for 'a copy of *The Pilgrim's Progress*' by a single ISBN. The only library users who are likely to find them helpful are scholars who need a particular edition – but even then the varied practice among publishers with regard to reprints and versions makes this usage hazardous. Use of separate ISBNs for hard cover and paperback editions is undoubtedly useful to publishers and booksellers, but much less so to other stakeholders. What is needed is an identifier system which has much broader applicability.

It was noted in Chapter 5 that perhaps the most critical issue is to separate the unique identifier of a digital object from the pointer to its location. Uniform Resource Locations (URLs) do not persist if the object's location changes, for example, when a resource moves from one server to another or when a website is reorganized. Although pointers can be created from the old location to the new, in practice this happens infrequently. In effect, instead of (or rather alongside) URLs we need a system of Uniform Resource Names (URNs) for objects with independent resolvers to supply locations.

Persistent Uniform Resource Locators (PURLs) are designed to resolve this problem so are of particular interest to librarians. In essence the PURL stays with the document forever, while a resolution service maintains the location information. A client request for a document using a PURL or URN in effect queries the resolution service, which then supplies the location. PURLs should be regarded as an interim measure to provide a resolution to current problems, though they are proving quite persistent. For more information see http://purl.org.

The Digital Object Identifier (DOI) system is compatible with the Uniform Resource Name (URN) and Uniform Resource Identifier (URI) specifications, offering the ability to add descriptive data and applicable to any environment (i.e. not designed specifically for the web). It assigns an alphanumeric character string to each object to identify it uniquely and a 'handle', which is a mechanism for resolving the identifier into a location (see www.handle.net). The International DOI Foundation, based in Geneva, is responsible for the standard, for approving naming conventions across different sectors and for appointing resolution (location) agencies.

Finally, it is worth observing that users as well as objects may usefully be assigned persistent identifiers. An example of this within a Shibboleth authentication implementation is described by Moyle (2006).

Document formats

Even if the problem of identifying objects uniquely can be resolved, libraries would still be faced with handling, and enabling their users to handle, a vast array of different document formats. Leaving aside non-digital media (paper, film, magnetic tape and so on) the range of electronic formats remains huge. It also changes rapidly. For example, the text document formats .doc and .rtf appeared to be adopted almost universally until Microsoft launched .docx with Office 2007. Some publishers immediately warned authors that they could not accept submissions in that format! Nor are the problems limited to electronic objects. The current (2007) 'format war' between Blu-ray and HD (High Definition) DVD formats offers a good example.

It is difficult to be sure of the impacts of this proliferation of document standards on libraries. Most mainstream formats are supported by standard client software, such as the mainstream web browsers (if not directly then by means of plug-ins) so that few problems should be experienced. However, there are serious issues for the library's role as a preservation agency and this is discussed further later in this chapter.

XML

XML (eXtensible Markup Language) was developed largely in response to the acknowledged shortcomings of HyperText Markup Language (HTML), which is concerned primarily with the *appearance* or *presentation* of a web page on a screen rather than with what the *content* actually is. HTML was never designed for the kind of complex task which has now become routine on the web, for example, where a company wants to upload orders from customers or interact in real time with a remote site. The data is simply not tagged in a way which is meaningful to another computer – for instance, there are no universally recognized tags for the content of a personal record. Because HTML tags have to be approved by an international committee the process of adding a new one is time-consuming and laborious, and in any case it is highly unlikely that a specialist tag – say for an application specific to libraries dealing with incunabula – would be approved. One deleterious result of this was that because the only way to communicate such information was to embed it within the web page, when just one element changed the whole page had to be re-transmitted. For example, when trying to book a flight or train ticket, if an error was detected in the page sent by the user to the server, the whole page had to be sent back with an indication of an error inserted. This could, of course, go on for considerable time, to everyone's frustration.

XML, which is within the Standard Generalized Markup Language (SGML) family and recommended by the World Wide Web Consortium (W3C), is designed to provide the shell or framework within which anyone can create a specialized markup language of their own, so that any community can create its own tags and thus impart meaning to a document. In effect XML is a meta-language. There are no predefined tags, as there are in HTML. In order to define a new XML 'language' it is necessary to agree three aspects: the tags themselves and their meaning, how they are allowed to be nested within each other and how they are to be processed. The first two of these are contained in the language's Document Type Definition (DTD), as with any SGML application, although DTDs are being replaced with XML schemas. The processing of XML-encoded data, for example for display purposes, can then be carried out by reference to stylesheets, defined in a standard called eXtensible Stylesheet Language (XSL). The concept of namespaces is important as a means of sharing the meaning of tags (e.g. to define what 'name' means across a range of application spaces which may wish to share processable data). The fundamental point, however, is that because XML tags are meaningful in terms of data content, XML documents are ideally suited to machine processing.

There are many reasons for the importance to libraries of this new approach, since it allows information objects to be analysed and manipulated and permits much more sophisticated handling of metadata objects. A simple example of the advantages to users would be the ability of client software to interpret data and output it more appropriately for a blind or visually impaired user. Current HTML causes problems because the display tags, such as '<H1> . . . </H1>', are of little use to non-visual displays. XML can therefore assist in making information and other services much more inclusive than in the past.

Metadata

Metadata – 'data about data' – consists of descriptions of information 'objects' (whether books, web pages, audio tapes or whatever). The term is usually applied to *structured* data since without structure it is impossible to process the information contained in a metadata record.

Metadata serves a number of purposes: it aids resource discovery (i.e. establishing the existence of an information object which may fulfil a user's needs); it assists the user to evaluate the object, without necessarily having to access the object itself; it enables the user to check the object's availability (to that user); it describes the terms under which the object may be used as it enables a location for the object to be determined. In the traditional academic library catalogue the use of metadata might be typified by a search to discover a book title of potential interest. Information on author, language, publisher and date of publication might be used to form a preliminary view of its likely value; a note might indicate that it is in a restricted collection not normally available to undergraduates; while a shelf mark would provide its exact location and a loan category indicator would inform the user of the permitted length of loan.

Apart from the user's interests, metadata also provides the owners of the objects with a means of asserting their rights. It may state ownership, intellectual property rights, terms for use and so on. It may also assist those responsible for managing collections of objects – including librarians – by describing features such as frequency of use or condition, when circulation staff add a note to an item record.

Libraries have thus long created metadata in the form of catalogue entries and have generally bought in further metadata, especially in relation to journal papers, in the form of published indexing and abstracting services. However, many other parties are involved in the production and utilization of metadata: publishers, abstract and indexing service providers, archives, internet search engine companies, document supply services, booksellers, subscription agents, governments and many more. All of these stakeholders have their own approaches to metadata and most have developed their own standards, usually based on their particular view of the information chain. For example, libraries have developed metadata based largely on the description of book titles, publishers and wholesalers have developed metadata suited to electronic trading (including pricing) and governments have encouraged the development of content labelling.

In the networked information environment metadata has become more and more important, since it holds the key not only to providing individuals with descriptions for them to browse but more importantly to the use of software to locate relevant information, to negotiate terms for its supply, to request it and to receive it.

It is important to note that metadata standards need to encompass two distinct issues: the *structural format* of a metadata record (which fields are valid, their syntax, and so on) and the *content*. Both issues have received considerable attention from librarians with the development of thesauri, cataloguing rules, various subject heading lists, etc.; some of the most important examples of these are considered next.

MARC

The MARC (MAchine Readable Cataloguing) standard has been in use for well over a quarter of a century, and nearly all large libraries now make use of it, often buying in records from the national library or other supplier. It is by far the longest established computer-readable metadata standard, but on the negative side it is not particularly well suited to describing electronic documents. MARC was designed for the *exchange* of bibliographic and other related information in machine readable form, although it is often regarded as an internal format also. A further complication is that MARC is really a family of formats based on ISO 2709 (ISO, 1996), although USMARC is now dominant.

It is worth noting that the Z39.50 'search and retrieve' standard (see page 196) was originally developed as a means of searching remote MARC databases, although it can be used more generically. The question for libraries is not so much whether MARC will persist – it is not under serious threat – but how it can be handled alongside other approaches, especially those designed for digital objects, including 'non-library' objects such as learning materials. Its complexity, although well suited to the bibliographic requirements of libraries, is too high for it to be applied widely outside that arena.

Resource Description Framework

A generic approach to description syntax called the Resource Description Framework (RDF), approved by the World Wide Web Consortium (W3C), provides a structure which can be used within any application area in the networked information environment, including for such requirements as e-commerce, digital signatures and content rating systems. Indeed, it is generic enough to describe relationships between virtually anything, including people, and not necessarily only those in networked space. It provides the structure within which meaning can be exposed, and thus forms a foundation for the semantic web. The aim is to ensure that metadata which can be processed by software is created to common standards.

RDF, which uses XML syntax, is based on a model which requires metadata statements to be grouped together as 'triples', consisting of a subject (the object being described, e.g. a particular web page), a property-type (a property of that resource, e.g. an author) and a value (of that property, e.g. John Smith – rather like the object of a sentence). However, triples can also be arranged in complex structures, for example by replacing the value by another triple.

One way of thinking about XML and RDF is to conceive of XML as the means by which *structure* is added to web pages (or other documents) while RDF is used to express *meaning*. The URI system *identifies* each resource (but not necessarily its location). Anyone can define a new tag in XML and declare it in the DTD; anyone can make assertions about an object in RDF so that its relationship to other objects can be understood and processed. Together they provide the necessary language to build Web 2.0.

Dublin Core

Dublin Core (http://purl.org/metadata/dublin_core), so-called because the first meeting of the Working Group which designed it was held in Dublin, Ohio, was developed to improve resource discovery on the world wide web. It is in effect a standard schema within RDF. Unlike MARC it was deliberately designed to be simple and uses only 15 'elements' – title, creator, publisher, subject, description, source, language, relation, coverage, date, type, format, identifier, contributor and rights. It is also intended to be generic, and goes beyond the type of objects found in libraries to include museums, art galleries, etc. – in effect it can be used to provide a description of any information object. For example, rather than 'author' it uses the concept of 'creator': 'the person or organization primarily responsible for the intellectual content of the resource'.

It is also possible to use what is known as 'Qualified Dublin Core', in which an element value is associated with an externally defined scheme, although this clearly requires agreement among the user communities involved to be effective.

Dublin Core raises a number of issues that need to be resolved. The most important is whether this simple, or, some would say, simplistic, approach to description can possibly provide sufficient richness to enable sophisticated retrieval of objects.

Librarians have catalogued resources at a far higher level of detail and with stringent quality control for a reason, so it seems hopeful to suggest that Dublin Core will produce comparable results. The problem is compounded by a lack of consistency in element content as opposed to structure.

The Anglo-American Cataloguing Rules

Probably the best developed set of rules for describing library-type materials, the Anglo-American Cataloguing Rules (second edition, known as AACR2), based on the concepts established in the International Standard Bibliographic Description (ISBD), are used by most libraries. The rules are particularly important in providing a neutral, standard way of describing names, titles and other elements of a bibliographic record. Currently, work is underway to develop Resource Description and Access (RDA) which will be more suited to the digital environment.

The importance of AACR2 is that, while it was never designed for a digital or even hybrid environment, it represents the main, coherent body of work which has established how variants, for example in names, should be handled so as to ensure that all records referring to the same entity use the same form – the obvious example being to bring all works by William Shakespeare together under the same main entry heading so that all can be retrieved when that name, or a variant of it which is referenced to the main heading, is used in a query. AACR2 also defines the order of bibliographic elements and the separators to be used between fields.

Other approaches to cataloguing

The examples above concentrate on what might be described as the standard or classic library approaches to cataloguing. They are focused on the description of the printed book as the primary information object, and adapted more or less satisfactorily to other media, although RDA is breaking out of this straitjacket. However, other traditions have developed their own approaches. For example in the museums sector the Spectrum standard, developed by the MDA, is widely used in the UK although there are also proprietary approaches in use. Similarly, the archives community has exploited the Encoded Archival Description (EAD) standard, which can be mapped to Dublin Core or to MARC.

The importance of these approaches for the library of the future, of course, lies in the nature of digital objects themselves. In networked environments what is retrieved and presented to the user may be a digital representation of a library object such as a book, of an archival object such as a manuscript or of a museum object such as a glass vase. Each could relate to an enquiry on, let us say, Roman Britain. Each could, assuming the use of appropriate object standards, be displayed to the user. Interoperability between them is essential to enable a single search to display a comprehensive result set.

Subject classification

Classification, along with cataloguing, is core territory for the professional librarian. It is important when considering the technologies of the future library to acknowledge the groundwork done by librarians and others in establishing the principles and application of subject classification. The description of the meaning of content, rather than its structure, is crucial to successful retrieval for many purposes, whenever a known item search is impossible because the user does not know which items might satisfy an enquiry. The simplest but crudest way to handle this requirement is to use keyword based retrieval, but the limitations of this approach are well known.

The problems which need to be solved in this area revolve around the systematic description of either the whole of knowledge (as with the Dewey Decimal Classification or the Library of Congress Classification) or a specific domain within it. Achieving interoperability through the use of standard terminology, or through ontologies which support shared understanding of concepts, is a major area of research and development effort. Vocabulary control, or the use of thesauri both to guide subject description (indexing thesauri) and to permit cross-interpretation of enquiries within and between domains (search thesauri), is a crucial issue to be tackled within the networked domain. For both applications there is debate about the use of natural language terms, including the usefulness of folksonomies, which are in essence taxonomies created by users collaboratively, and systems for mapping between natural language and controlled vocabularies. Existing standard schemes, such as the Library of Congress Subject Headings (LCSH), Medical Subject Headings (MeSH) and the Education Resources Information Center (ERIC) thesaurus in education, may provide the basis for this work, although there are syntactic variations which have appeared over time and which cause significant problems. Equally, as librarians know, the necessity to update classification schemes from time to time results in the subject descriptions of older material being incompatible with newer material. As yet, this problem has not been addressed successfully in the digital environment, but it is an area in which librarians can make a crucial contribution.

Rights metadata

Efforts are being made to develop standard ways of associating rights information with digital objects and Digital Rights Management (DRM) has become a huge field, not least because of commercial interests. This is both familiar and new territory for libraries. They have long been concerned with protecting copyright but facilitating fair dealing, for example when providing photocopying services, but by and large they have not had to police individual users' re-use of electronic objects, nor to protect their users' rights as creators of content. As machine readable rights metadata becomes associated with digital objects, however, library systems need to be able to process it and relate it to user profiles, to incoming requests and to associated authorization processes.

Rights can be expressed in either human readable or machine readable form or both. This is illustrated by Creative Commons licences (www.creativecommons.org.uk) which appear on many websites and allow authors to express their permissions, from 'All Rights Reserved' through to 'Attribution' with the latter simply requiring anyone who uses the content for any purpose to acknowledge the source. Creators of content can also use Digital Rights Expression Languages (DRELs) to encode the ways in which objects can be used. DRELs are then interpreted automatically by a DRM system. This approach is commonly encountered in commercial applications, such as Apple's Fairplay and Microsoft's WMA, where rights such as 'may be downloaded up to three times' can be policed automatically.

Rights management is likely to be an issue of increasing concern for libraries, not least as their role in education starts to extend into the re-use of learning objects created elsewhere and as their users start to seek advice on the protection of their intellectual property and other rights. Libraries which succeed in securing responsibility for institutional repositories will inevitably be drawn into this arena.

Managing objects and metadata

Associating objects, identifiers, metadata and locations

It will be clear from the above discussion that one of the major challenges facing libraries – indeed facing the networked information world as a whole – will be associating each object with its identifier, with metadata describing it and with locations where the object may be retrieved. It is worth noting that there are a number of different mechanisms available to achieve this. The RDF model, to take one pertinent example, suggests that metadata can be associated with objects in at least four different ways:

- by embedding it within the object, as in HTML where the metadata tag forms part of the HTML page
- by holding the metadata separately from the object but delivering it with the object when that is requested – as with the HTTP GET or HEAD commands
- by holding the metadata separately from the object and requiring a separate request for it – for example, using an HTTP GET request to a service bureau
- by embedding the object within the metadata, known as 'wrapping'; an example of this is provided for within RDF itself.

A particular complexity is that for any given object, use may be made of more than one of these methods, and each can be used more than once. So, for example, there may be metadata held by more than one service bureau as well as embedded metadata.

Collection description

A particular issue in the electronic environment is to find standard ways in which *collections* can be described. As the number of searchable resources (library catalogues, websites, other datasets and so on) expands, it is no longer feasible to rely on the user selecting particular collections to search manually. Nor is it a scalable approach for librarians to list resources of possible interest on a web page. What is needed are ways of describing collections so that software can handle selection, at least within parameters set by the user. Collection descriptions need to provide for subject, level, scope, geographical location, access policy and a whole range of other attributes and need to cover collections of analogue, digital and hybrid resources. The search of suitable collections can then be adjusted dynamically by software which examines a registry of collection descriptions and chooses which to search.

Work in this area has been funded by the JISC through UKOLN's Collection Description Focus and operationalized, for collections and other services, through the Information Environment Service Registry (IESR). A collection description schema was developed during the Research Support Libraries Programme (RSLP) and this has formed the basis for subsequent work.

Finding and delivering the content

Introduction

The range of services, including in this category the free content which does not need to be subject to negotiated licences, is now so large that it is clear that added value services are needed to enable users to cope with the plethora of provision. As far as open web resources are concerned the Intute service (www.intute.ac.uk) offers an excellent example of collaboration at the national level. Rather than every library having to evaluate each resource, the workload is effectively pooled and paid for collaboratively by 'top-slicing' university grants through the JISC Services budget. Each resource included in Intute has been quality-checked by an experienced professional (librarian or subject expert) and professionally catalogued, thus selecting 'the best of the web'. One of the add-on services is MyIntute, enabling personalization through save facilities and an alerting service.

As far as individual libraries are concerned, the Online Public Access Catalogue (OPAC) remains the interface of choice for most access. Built on the traditional concept of library systems, with modules for acquisitions, cataloguing, circulation and so on, the OPAC is basically a public view on the library collection. However, most OPACs lag well behind the sophistication of the typical web interface with which users are now familiar and rapid development is needed to bring them into the Web 2.0 world. As Breeding (2007) put it, 'one of the most biting indictments of all is that I hear stories about users who find library OPACs so unfriendly that they often go to places like Amazon.com to look for books of interest, and then flip over to the catalog to see if those titles are owned by their libraries'. Or, to quote Tennant of the California Digital Library, 'we need to focus more energy on important, systemic changes rather than cosmetic ones. If your system is more difficult to search and less effective than Amazon.com (and whose isn't?), then you have work to do' (Tennant, 2005).

Why is this so? It is partly to do with interface design but also the fault of limited functionality. For example, if a user mis-types a request in Google's interface, they are presented with alternatives that make an, often very accurate, attempt to present what is needed. Library OPACs too often simply give a nil return. A similar result occurs where the library genuinely does not possess the requested item – yet Amazon or Google would automatically suggest alternatives, Amazon opening up alternative supply possibilities through its Marketplace.

One solution to the lack of functionality of OPACs is to make the library data available within another organization's website. So, for example, Amazon's display could flag whether the book someone is looking for is available in their local library. This is the concept which Chad and Miller (2005) suggest in their paper on Library 2.0:

> Why can't information on books and other resources available to borrow appear in online bookstores as an alternative to buying? Equally, why can't information on books and other resources available to buy appear in library systems as an alternative to waiting for an item that is already on loan or only available via ILL? What role might there be for the library in mediating these choices with or on behalf of the user?

Searching for and retrieving digital objects

The problem of identifying the existence of an appropriate digital object (discovery) remains at the core of information access and thus at the heart of many library services. It is beyond the scope of this book to go into the detail of information retrieval systems, although it must be noted that highly sophisticated approaches to text, image, audio, multimedia and other objects are being developed. For example, shape recognition technologies, drawing in part from work on satellite-based earth observation, are maturing to the extent that they have become practical approaches to the retrieval of images from large databases. Despite this most users are likely to make use of general search engines, such as Google and Yahoo!, or specialized data services, such as ISI Web of Knowledge or Elsevier's Scirus, as well as, to some extent, library OPACs.

For libraries a major problem is to ensure that users gain access to a copy of each resource they request which best meets their needs and is most economic for the service provider, in this case the library itself or its parent institution. This is the *appropriate copy* problem. For example, if a library takes out a subscription to an electronic journal it needs to ensure that its users can find that copy, rather than buying individual articles from a broker or other supplier. Similarly it will wish to avoid users requesting a work by interlibrary loan when it is available in the library's stock. The resolution of this problem lies in the deployment of link resolvers maintained by the local library, making use of OpenURLs to resolve requests to the preferred source. The OpenURL itself consists of the address of the link resolver and the bibliographic data needed to identify the requested resource.

Cross-searching

For libraries, the provision of access to electronic resources which are not in their immediate ownership has in the past required users to navigate to and within a huge range of different interfaces. To some extent this is still true, but the concept of cross-searching widely heterogeneous resources is now well established – a single user interface enabling access to a wide variety of underlying services.

Increasingly library systems need to be able to take a query from a user and use it to search a selection of databases before returning results to the user in an ordered form, for example by removing duplicate entries and flagging relevance, or perhaps indicating geographic location on a map, especially if what is presented is locations for hard copy.

Interoperability between heterogeneous services is a complex issue. At its heart lies the implementation of standards and protocols, including ontologies and terminologies which work across different application domains. Issues such as authentication were described above.

Search and retrieve

The main communications standard used for searching across library systems is Z39.50 (an American NISO standard but with international acceptance) which assumes the use of a client/server (in Z39.50 parlance an origin/target) model. In essence the client (e.g. the user PC or local library system) requests a service from the server (e.g. a remote library catalogue system). The server performs functions on behalf of the client, as specified in the request, and returns a result set – this may then be interpreted by the client software and turned into, for example, a display of catalogue records. The client only needs to 'understand' the Z39.50 syntax in order to query any compliant server. For distributed systems this is of course essential.

Critically, the client does not have to be an end-user oriented system, but can be another piece of middleware. Provided both client and server are Z39.50 compliant it should in theory be possible for any client to query any server and receive back an interpretable set of results, thus enabling complex querying across multiple heterogeneous datasets and subsequent processing. In practice it has proved difficult to achieve this, partly because of different implementations of the standard by software suppliers, and partly because of incompatibilities in the internal structure and content of records returned by the server. The complexity of Z39.50 is one reason that attention has switched towards SRW (Search &

Retrieve Web Service), which uses standard web development tools such as SOAP and WSDL and replaces the baseline of MARC with XML.

A real problem with most federated search systems is slow speed of response, especially if the presentation of results is delayed until the slowest server has responded. Users have become accustomed to the almost instantaneous response provided by Google and other search engines, and are unwilling to wait even a few seconds.

Union catalogues

Union catalogues have been used to indicate the holdings of groups of libraries for at least a century. As well as direct user access, they have been the mainstay of many interlibrary lending systems, used to find locations and thus for routing requests. In recent years there has been a resurgence of interest in the union catalogue approach, with high-profile examples like OCLC's WorldCat and UK Research Libraries' COPAC making a major contribution to service delivery. In essence the union catalogue relies on member libraries contributing records of additions to stock and withdrawals which are then combined to provide a list of items held and their locations. Among the limitations of this approach have been a general tendency to under-report withdrawals and the lack of current availability information. As one of Hartley and Booth's (2006) interviewees remarked: 'When I'm looking for a book I'm looking for whether it's available or on hold, short loan or long loan. I'm interested in whether I can go there and get it or put a hold on it.' However, the ability to interact directly with the individual catalogue online to find status data, a task which the interface should perform automatically for the user, is helping to overcome these problems.

Harvesting

An alternative to searching catalogues in real time and to consortial agreements to contribute data to a shared union catalogue is for metadata to be harvested from catalogues (or other sources), combined into a new database and then used to answer queries. This approach resolves the response time and other issues of Z39.50 and contribution problems with union catalogues. It does not, however, entirely resolve the item status problem – even a new overnight harvest will not pick up on items borrowed or returned during the subsequent day.

In effect this is the approach which the major search engines take. They harvest the web for descriptive data, build their own indexes and use them to respond to queries. However, the critical development for libraries came with the deployment of a new standard, the Open Archives Initiative Protocol for Metadata Harvesting (OAI-PMH). This enables services to be built on aggregated data from a wide range of sources, originally using simple Dublin Core to provide the description standard although now greatly extended. For each library, facilitating such harvesting enables them to expose their metadata much more widely and thus build their demand base. Lagoze and Van de Sompel (2003) quote Clifford Lynch, Executive Director of CNI, as describing OAI-PMH as 'a vital component of the digital information infrastructure'.

The harvesting approach is not without its problems, however. By and large, libraries create metadata records primarily for internal use and such views on their collections are not always suitable for use within a shared collection. Shreeves, Riley and Milewicz (2006) argue that:

> metadata should be simply a view of the resource, and that view may change depending on audience, use, and context. Unfortunately many libraries, museums, and other cultural heritage institutions have treated a metadata record as a monolithic item – a single record with all descriptive, technical, and administrative information about the resource included – and share this single record rather than a version of it most appropriate for the intended use.

This suggests that a more sophisticated approach to the creation and deployment of local catalogue data is needed, something libraries will be challenged to undertake if they aspire to take a role as part of global information space.

An interesting issue which has yet to be resolved is the efficiency of a distributed search of multiple targets as against the building of union catalogues to enable direct searching, albeit of a surrogate, and the regular harvesting of metadata. What is clear is that users judge all these systems against the benchmark of popular search engines. As Hartley and Booth (2006) remark of participants in their study of union catalogues, they:

> use internet search engines more frequently than they do either OPACs or bibliographic databases . . . Comments from participants indicated clearly that their expectations of union catalogues, and indeed other information resources, are influenced by their experiences with internet search engines. One user expressed the view that user-friendliness was determined by similarity of behaviour and functionality to Web search engines and another indicated that if a specific

information resource did not produce useful information rapidly then the respondent would turn to Google.

Preservation

The long-term preservation of information objects has in the past been a responsibility not only of libraries but also of other kinds of 'memory institution' – museums, art galleries, archives and others. While not all libraries and information services have played a significant part in this activity in the past, some seeing their role only in terms of the provision of access to current literature, the need for long-term preservation is widely recognized.

The 1998 European Parliament Green Paper on *The Role of Libraries in the Modern World* (Rynänen, 1998) saw this preservation role as fundamental (although omitting to mention the role of other memory institutions): 'the unique function of libraries is to acquire, organize, offer for use and preserve publicly available material . . . in such a way that, when it is needed, it can be found and put to use. No other institution carries out this long-term, systematic work.'

At that time the need to think seriously about, and act on, requirements for preserving digital objects was only just starting to be recognized. There are a number of problems which need to be addressed:

- physical deterioration of the medium on which the data is stored. For example, there is still considerable uncertainty about the expected shelf life of CD-ROMs
- technological change, which makes reading equipment obsolete and thus may make archives virtually inaccessible; for example, it is highly unlikely that CD-ROM players will still be widely available in 10 or 20 years' time
- dynamic content, since digital content may change rapidly. An example would be a website offering a range of goods for sale, where updating of each page results in the loss of earlier versions. (In fact the pages would be created dynamically from a database, itself dynamic and almost certainly unpreserved.)
- non-persistent identifiers (as discussed above), which mean that if a web page or other object is moved to another site, or re-addressed within a site, it becomes effectively lost
- security, especially loss by fire or water damage, of materials where only one master copy is held

- responsibility, since it is by no means obvious that the archival functions of libraries with traditional media can be carried over into the electronic era; for example, who should assume responsibility for archiving publicly available, but not publicly funded, websites?

It is important to note that in this context 'digital preservation' is a term used to describe the preservation of digital objects. The over-riding aim of this activity is to ensure that information held in digital form remains accessible into the distant future. There are separate issues concerned with the use of digital technologies to preserve traditional objects, for example by creating page images of manuscripts – this is the approach of services like JSTOR. This initiative, originally funded by the Andrew W. Mellon Foundation, has developed a digital archive now approaching 1000 scholarly journals, including some of the earliest scientific journals such as the *Philosophical Transactions of the Royal Society of London*. For each journal the archive begins with the first published issues and covers material up to a 'moving wall' set at between one and five years before the current volume. Because the operation concentrates on older material it avoids competition with publishers, who have generally been willing to negotiate contracts with JSTOR.

The eLib CEDARS (CURL Exemplars in Digital ArchiveS, www.curl.ac.uk/projects/cedars.htm) project was among the first significant attempts to address the problems of digital preservation in the sense of long-term preservation of 'born digital' materials. In 2001 the Digital Preservation Coalition (DPC) was created. It has commented:

> while there is as yet only largely anecdotal evidence, it is certain that many potentially valuable digital materials have already been lost. Some of these may have disappeared without ever having reached a wider audience than the original creators . . . At the very least, this constitutes failure fully to maximise the potential benefits of the investment expended in creating these digital materials.
>
> (Digital Preservation Coalition, 2007)

It is important for libraries to determine how broadly they should interpret their remit. An obvious question arises in the context of e-science data, generated in huge volumes and much, though not all, being of long-term value. The Research Information Network (RIN) has recently published a set of principles which includes the statement, 'digital research data of long term value arising from current and future research should be preserved and remain accessible for current and future generations' (2007), although it is by no means clear as to who will take this responsibility. Among the complexities the report points to is the issue of dynamic datasets: 'As digital research data are increasingly updated, amended and annotated over their lifecycle both by data creators and by subsequent users, provenance protocols and audit trails are needed to indicate clearly who has annotated or amended data, how and when'.

The DPC has developed a decision tree (available at www.dpconline.org/graphics/handbook/dec-tree.html) to help libraries and others manage their digital preservation responsibilities. It suggests that there are four areas which need to be considered in decision-making on the preservation of any digital object: selection, rights and responsibilities, technical issues and associated costs and documentation and metadata.

Selection

Digital preservation is expensive and it will not be possible to preserve everything. Nor, indeed is this desirable – it is sometimes forgotten that the essence of any archive is selective preservation and much of the intellectual effort needed lies in that selection process. However, there is increasing emphasis on making at least tentative decisions on long-term preservation at the acquisition stage – in other words using a life-cycle approach which examines acquisition, management, retention and preservation responsibilities and costs at the start of the process. This approach falls within the meaning of the more general term 'digital curation', defined by the Digital Curation Centre (DCC, www.dcc.ac.uk) as 'maintaining and adding value to a trusted body of digital information for current and future use; specifically . . . the active management and appraisal of data over the life-cycle of scholarly and scientific materials'.

Rights and responsibilities

Even the action of copying a digital object onto a new medium for security can breach intellectual property rights (IPR). Doing so for preservation purposes, unless there is a statutory exemption (and of course the library exemptions which relate to printed works are not applicable in the digital environment), may infringe the rights of the copyright holder of the content, but could also infringe rights relating to the software platform. In addition, libraries acquire a right to use digital information objects under a licence rather than the ownership of a copy purchased with traditional media.

Technical preservation

A number of different methods of digital preservation are available, which can helpfully be considered as: *migration* – where an information object is transferred from its native technological base to another; *emulation* – where software is provided to enable the old format to be interpreted in a new technological framework; and *technology preservation* which involves maintaining the old hardware/software platform as well as the content. Each of these approaches has its problems. Migration may destroy or alter part of the original structure and content, is expensive if there are large numbers of objects and if it has to be repeated, and is less and less feasible as objects become increasingly complex. Emulation is difficult because digital environments are inherently complex and becoming more so (trying to emulate pre-DOS environments in Windows XP is no easy matter, for example) so that the emulation may lose or alter features of the original, or simply not work with all objects. Technology preservation is unscalable as the number of platforms used historically increases, and in any case maintaining hardware – for example, a CD-ROM drive – for tens and hundreds of years is fraught with difficulty.

Metadata

Metadata for preservation purposes differs from that required for access in a number of ways. For example, it needs to encode provenance (who has had ownership or custody of the object – where it came from); authenticity (to ensure that users can be sure that it is what it purports to be); preservation activity (what actions have been taken to preserve it); renderability (specifying the technical environment needed to render the digital object(s)); and current rights (which may differ from the original). The Open Archival Information System (OAIS) Reference Model (ISO 14721:2003), which has been widely adopted in the digital preservation community, includes an Information Model which offers a framework for preservation metadata (see Ball, 2006, for more details).

Summary

Digital preservation is an expensive business and one which usually has few immediate tangible, as opposed to long-term, benefits. Recognizing this, the JISC recently funded work to develop a model for demonstrating what the benefits are. As Currall and McKinney (2006) remark: '[D]ecision-makers need to have very good reasons to divert resources from primary activities to digital preservation practices, and being able to answer "why" is more than a matter of saying: "because it is important" '. The *espida* model (www.gla.ac.uk/espida/index.shtml), based on Kaplan and Norton's Balanced Scorecard (Kaplan and Norton, 1992), is a tool to demonstrate that benefits take many forms other than the directly financial.

There is one further preservation issue which is worth exploring, namely that while information objects need to be preserved and there needs to be some form of certification of their integrity, associated metadata is also subject to change (or, rather, the world which the metadata describes changes independently of the object and its description). There is a rather nice example of this in the archives of the Scottish Cultural Resources Access Network (SCRAN) in Edinburgh, where some old film footage of the world's last sea-going paddle-steamer, *Waverley*, shows the ship progressing down the Clyde. After a while the image cuts to a young singer playing guitar. The original metadata identifies the item by the location and name of the ship. Only later, when the singer had made his reputation as the comedian Billy Connolly, would the description be enhanced to identify him as a subject. The object itself has not changed, but its significance has. How can metadata be updated to reflect such changes in the significance of the vast range of electronic resources which will be preserved?

Conclusion

The information universe is far more than a random agglomeration of data; it requires a massive effort to enable its effective exploitation. National, and indeed international, policy frameworks are needed to enable society to ensure that access is both inclusive and efficient, and that legitimate e-commerce can flourish. Long-term strategies are required to develop the organizational infrastructure needed to create a new kind of national and global resource. Libraries have a role to play in this endeavour, not only as intermediaries in the information access process but as architects and builders of the structured information universe itself. A huge range of issues has to be addressed, in collaboration with many other communities of interested parties.

11
Envoi

> One must never lose time in vainly regretting the past nor in complaining about the changes which cause us discomfort, for change is the very essence of life.
>
> (Attributed to Anatole France)

Introduction

In the first edition of this book, I suggested that 'the core of library and information services is to be found . . . in the intermediary role between users and the information universe'. Seven years later that verdict stands but seems inadequate to describe the panorama of service possibilities which beckons those responsible for libraries. Therein, of course, lies a very real danger. Too often libraries have tried to be everything to everyone, and succeeded only in overstretching themselves and thus inviting well aimed criticism of their shortcomings.

Libraries are, fundamentally, services. What they do is intended, whether in the short or long term, to benefit people of all ages and backgrounds. They are quite clearly in the business of helping their users to develop knowledge and understanding. Both of these, services and knowledge, are firmly at the centre of community development, whether globally or locally. Su and Lin (2006) write, 'the offering of knowledge based service and the continuous enhancement of its quality have provided businesses with an avenue for differentiation from their competitors'. But libraries are not just businesses in a narrow sense. They are different from online booksellers, from bookshops, from museums, from community centres and from classrooms. Libraries are unique.

Yet libraries are also at risk. Chapter 1 outlined ten threats to libraries. They do not need to be reiterated here. From e-science to primary school history, from YouTube to Second Life, users are exploiting new ways to create, manage and use information in ways which very often have no obvious library dimension.

This final chapter does not attempt to address each individual issue, but instead makes some suggestions as to the ways in which libraries in the 21st century need to progress, based on the myriad issues portrayed, albeit briefly, in preceding chapters.

Move from being user-centric to being lifeflow-centred

The proposition that libraries should be user centred has been accepted so completely that it is hardly likely to be challenged. However, it seems from much observation of users and how they act, especially in networked environments, that it is time to move on with our concept of engagement with users. Information and communications technologies are now part of everyday life. Services are delivered through favourite applications like Google and MySpace to location-independent devices like mobile phones and PDAs. Personal and community e-spaces are combining social networking with personal filespace and applications. VLEs are changing students' and staff's experience of interaction with information resources, leaving little incentive to navigate across to user-unfriendly library OPACs. As Shedlock and Walton (2004) reported, 'faculty do not want to work too hard to find information . . . "Please do not make me look for more helpful information about what I need – just give it to me right up front" '.

A better analogy for library services may therefore draw on the idea that the only meaningful model is one which rejects the idea of 'standing outside, looking in' in favour of that of immersion. The immersive library, a term used in Chapter 3, seeks to have a presence within the normal living environment of its users. The idea is best developed in terms of workflow integration and can be seen in many emerging Virtual Research Environments (VREs), defined by the JISC as:

> a set of online tools and other network resources and technologies interoperating with each other to support or enhance the processes of a wide range of research practitioners within and across disciplinary and institutional boundaries. A key characteristic of a VRE is that it facilitates collaboration amongst researchers and research teams providing them with more effective means of collaboratively collecting, manipulating and managing data, as well as collaborative knowledge creation.
>
> (2007b)

To be effective in lifeflow integration it is essential that everything possible is done to fit each service encounter into the user's personal interests. It is argued in Chapter 7 that a library's intelligence about its users, what it knows of them, is virtually all they have which is unique. Exploiting this information to deliver services into the natural environment in which users spend their lives provides one of the key challenges for library development.

Learn the language

The concept of language games was introduced early in this book (Chapter 3) quite deliberately, because it emphasizes that librarians will be credible only where they can demonstrate a deep understanding of their users' discourse. This is true whether we are speaking of the knowledge officer in a commercial information service, the subject librarian in an academic library or the community librarian in a public library. In some circumstances a formal qualification in a specialized domain may be essential to fulfil this task, but the best librarians have shown in the past that they possess the skills to learn the users' language, to enter the discourse of a discipline, and so become valued members of the users' teams. Again the library, through its staff, is immersive.

Support creativity

For decades libraries put enormous effort into building catalogues so that their users could search for and find the books and other resources in their stock. The model being pursued was that of information delivery (what is sometimes termed the 'demand to delivery', or d2d, paradigm), enabling a user to come with a request for an item or for information on a subject and to leave with a relevant book or photocopy. That model persists but is utterly inadequate in a world where, within ten years, Google will be providing sophisticated searches of the whole of the world's literature, connecting users seamlessly to most full-text resources, with the local library providing the middleware (and thus invisible to the user) subscription, authentication and authorization services. Of course there will still be demand for physical books, and the proportion of an individual library's service mix devoted to that will depend on local circumstances, requiring careful management.

However, as the examples cited in this book have demonstrated, there is a considerable opportunity for libraries to play a much larger role in supporting their users' creativity, what we might term a 'creation to content', or c2c, paradigm. The most obvious example is the academic sector's institutional repositories and it is heartening that, by and large, it has been the library which has been given the responsibility for managing this service. But examples like COINE and Moving Here (see Chapter 10), and the way in which family history has mushroomed as an activity in public libraries, demonstrate that users, and potential but currently unengaged users, see the library as a trustworthy and expert player in helping their self-expression. Grasping this opportunity will enable libraries to close the circle, so that they support the whole creation–publication–use–creation cycle. The added value services which could be contributed to this model of service are almost limitless.

Join the broader literacy movement

Libraries have made great strides in developing the concept of information literacy and some have persuaded their immediate stakeholders to give formal recognition to this work. Public libraries have been closely involved with basic literacy work, especially in relation to reading, for many years. However, particularly in the former area, libraries have for too long ploughed their own furrow, failing to recognize that tackling literacy needs a co-ordinated effort from a range of disciplines, not least from pedagogical experts. Information literacy needs to be seen as one component, or one way of looking at, the whole question of users' ability to function in a complex, technology- and information-intensive world. Ind since the glory of libraries for well over a hundred years has been their pr tion of reading, it is odd that we have not taken that as the starting point fo literacy agenda, and telling that many involved in promoting reading, in the National Literacy Trust, do not themselves use the term 'information In addition, if libraries are to support creativity then the literacies ne express that creativity need to be made much more prominent. So the is to become much more collaborative and integrative in approach.

Understand learning

Formal education has turned away from overly didactic approac constructivist, participatory and active learning. Librarians ne deep understanding of why this change has occurred and its i delivery of all of their services.

One of the remarkable linking themes which emerged fr Chapter 2 on libraries across the sectors was that almost al contribution to society in educational terms. Panizzi wa regarding the national library in Britain. It formed the academic libraries' Follett Report, where on the very first page there is the statement, 'it is impossible to imagine any university or college functioning effectively without a good library service'. School libraries have emerged from the, often warm, shelter of the English Department to become 'a tangible expression of the school's ethos and values, its approaches to equality of opportunity, the moral and spiritual development of children and young people and its educational purposes' (Tilke, 1998). Workplace libraries are placing increasing emphasis on their role in enabling employees to *learn* – this is, after all, the whole point of knowledge management and the underlying assumption of evidence-based practice. If, as has been suggested, lifelong learning is set to become *the* policy agenda for all nations in the 21st century, libraries should be well positioned to develop a firm place within society, within corporations and within educational and other institutions – in fact across the whole organizational, societal and personal landscape. That place will be secured not solely by their role as information intermediaries, but by becoming 'learning centres' and perhaps 'centres of learning'.

But learning is not passive. It has impacts on individuals and on societies, and part of learning is learning how to share, to go beyond the educational consumer into membership of what might be called a 'learning network'. Such networks – characterized by interactions between people, regardless of the technology used – complete the information chain and turn it into a virtuous circle where publishing reinforces learning, and learning becomes a shared experience. Individuals become publishers – maybe only within their own small network, maybe growing in confidence to publish within their own local or domain communities, maybe contributing across a wider stage. The community information intermediary would seem ideally placed to provide not just infrastructure – for anyone can publish on the web – but authority (which may be localized), descriptive metadata, security, privacy and preservation.

The library as place

While technology steals the headlines, people still live in real places and use real objects. Consider this comment on the role of the library as a meeting place:

> The public library as an open forum in society, where anyone can go without having to do anything in particular, is an aspect seldom discussed. Libraries are often spoken about as an intermediary of knowledge and information or as a place where children are encouraged to read. In a paper Göran Greider makes the observation that there is a noticeable difference whether a society has a public

> space in the form of a library, even to those that never venture there. He goes on to say that it 'marks the presence of the public in the social wilderness'.
>
> (Corneliuson, 2005)

Thus the Norfolk and Norwich Millennium Library was designed as part of The Forum, providing space for learning organizations, a café and restaurant, tourist information and a heritage centre as well as simply being a place to meet. Or take Handsworth public library in Birmingham, a refurbishment of a listed building: 'the library treats each zone as a separate entity to create environments that reflect the needs of the users. Some parts are traditional in feel, others are funky and bright to reflect the desire of the teenage users and the children's library is like "the best children's bedroom you ever saw" ' (www.designinglibraries.org.uk/view/index.php?id=45550ca663aa8).

It is easy, in the excitement of cyberspace, to lose sight of the fact that physical places remain important and are where people actually live out their lives. In academic institutions, the library – centrally situated on the campus – often becomes the meeting place for staff and students. This lies behind the design of new libraries, often aligned with related user-oriented functions, like the Saltire Centre referred to in Chapter 4 which offers '1,800 seats . . . designed to provide users with a variety of different spaces, from noisy social interaction areas for group work, to places for silent study' (www.gcal.ac.uk/thesaltirecentre/building/index.html).

This value of the library as place, and as a symbol of something much greater than the role of information intermediary might suggest, can be found everywhere. The Ruskin Library at Lancaster University, built at the top of a hill as the entrance road reveals the university, makes a statement of the enduring value which the library represents:

> The linear arrangement is deliberately church-like with entrance, treasury and reading room standing for narthex, choir and sanctuary. The public have access from a double height entrance to the first floor gallery which is arranged as two spaces connected through the treasury by a glass bridge . . . Lighting will be kept to a minimum to preserve the archive . . . the only sunlight allowed into the building will be at sunset which will illuminate the metal soffit running through the centre of the building.
>
> (MacCormac Jamieson Prichard, 1995)

Libraries say something important about the communities which build them.

Until human beings disappear entirely into cyberspace, it seems likely that this role will remain.

Put technology in its place

A large part of this book has been concerned with information and communications technologies and I make no apologies for that. It reflects both the transformation of information creation, storage and supply in the last quarter century and the sometimes bewildering rate of change of technology. However, while there is undoubtedly a place for some virtual libraries, the evidence surely points to the future of most libraries as hybrid (in that rather inelegant and already somewhat dated term). The danger is that so much attention is paid to virtual services that the need to serve people *in person* becomes neglected. Enquirers are fobbed off with a search on the internet instead of receiving personal service. Learners are pointed to an e-resource instead of being encouraged to discuss their understanding in a rich experience of real interaction with others. The image of the library on its website becomes more important than the customer service delivered at the issue counter. Hits on the website are used as evidence equivalent to the number of books borrowed. The space devoted to physical information objects is taken over by PCs.

It is not that a focus on being technologically up to date is wrong, but that the balance needs to be preserved. For most libraries, the core constituency is still physically on the doorstep, even if many of them are only occasional visitors. Technology needs to enhance the service those people receive.

There is a well known adage in the commercial sector: never be the first to take up an innovation, let someone else do that, learn from their mistakes and then enter the market quickly enough to benefit from a relative lack of competition. It is not a bad strategy. Its relevance for libraries lies in the fact that they do not themselves spend significant amounts on research and development but borrow from other disciplines as needed to deliver their services. To cope with the unknown, the innovation that will displace the mobile phone or social networking, they need simply to be aware of what is developing and ready to move quickly when a technology, or a social movement, is sufficiently established. This may take a very short time or it may take years. As an example, background research into the use of radio frequency identification device (RFID) technology in libraries was undertaken in 1996 but took ten years to reach viable operational deployment. Link resolvers, on the other hand, were deployed quite quickly after the need for them was identified. The role of expert organizations, like UKOLN, in environmental scanning and alerting the community to developments, their significance and their deployment is thus vital to the health of libraries.

Form alliances

But local is not everything. Libraries have actually been remarkably successful at forming collaborations locally, regionally, nationally and internationally. On the national scale both the research, development and service activity of the JISC in the academic sector and the roll-out of the People's Network among public libraries testify to the benefits of collaborative activity. The prominence of UK representatives among international standards and other fora demonstrates the influence that librarians can wield. At the local level links to educational providers and between libraries, as for example with joint use libraries such as that at Easterhouse in Glasgow, demonstrate the potential of collaboration. There the Scottish Library and Information Council is testing the 'implications for lifelong learning in public library services where users have ready access to information about learning opportunities and sources of professional learning support' (Green and Kearney, 2007). Libraries cannot go it alone and their future strength will depend on the alliances they forge.

Conclusion

Libraries are hugely complex organizations which need to operate across many boundaries but have few, if any, unique services. Yet they have survived for millennia, changing to meet new circumstances and adapting to their users' needs. They are there for the long term, not only in their duty to preserve humankind's recorded memory but as centres of expertise in accessing, using and, increasingly, creating information and knowledge. Doomsday scenarios have come and gone, yet excellent libraries keep renewing themselves. The challenge for all librarians is to find that judicious blend of traditional service and courageous innovation which will secure their libraries' future.

Bibliography

Abram, S. (1998) Post Information Age Positioning for Special Librarians: Is knowledge management the answer? In *Knowledge Management: a new competitive asset*, Economist Intelligence Unit, 179–90.

American Library Association (1996) *Library Bill of Rights*, www.ala.org/work/freedom/lbr.html.

American Library Association (2007a) *Interpretations of the 'Library Bill of Rights'*, www.ala.org/ala/oif/statementspols/statementsif/interpretations/Default675.htm.

American Library Association (2007b) *Diversity in Collection Development: an interpretation of the 'Library Bill of Rights'*, www.ala.org/Template.cfm?Section=interpretations&Template=/ContentManagement/ContentDisplay.cfm&ContentID=103209.

American Library Association (2007c) *Evaluating Library Collections: an interpretation of the 'Library Bill of Rights'*, www.ala.org/Template.cfm?Section=interpretations&Template=/ContentManagement/ContentDisplay.cfm&ContentID=103211.

Anderson, C. (2004) The Long Tail, *Wired*, http://web.archive.org/web/20041127085645/www.wired.com/wired/archive/12.10/tail.html.

Anderson, P. (2006) *What is Web 2.0? Ideas, technologies and implications for education*, London, Joint Information Systems Committee, www.jisc.ac.uk/media/documents/techwatch/tsw0701.pdf.

Arms, C. R. (1996) Historical Collections for the National Digital Library: lessons and challenges at the Library of Congress, *D-Lib Magazine*, (April), www.dlib.org/dlib/april96/loc/04c-arms.html and www.dlib.org/dlib/may96/loc/05c-arms.html.

Arms, W. Y. (1995) Key Concepts in the Architecture of the Digital Library, *D-Lib Magazine*, (July), www.dlib.org/dlib/July95/07arms.html.

Arms, W. Y. (2000) *Digital Libraries*, Cambridge MA, MIT Press.

Arms, W. Y. (2005) *Digital Libraries*, Cambridge MA, MIT Press (updated online edn: www.cs.cornell.edu/wya/DigLib/index.html).

Arms, W. Y., Blanchi, C. and Overly, E. A. (1997) An Architecture for Information in Digital Libraries, *D-Lib Magazine*, (February), www.dlib.org/dlib/february97/cnri/02arms1.html.

Audit Commission (1997) *Due for Renewal: a report on the library service*, Audit Commission.

Ball, A. (2006) *Briefing Paper: the OAIS Reference Model*, Bath, UKOLN, www.ukoln.ac.uk/projects/grand-challenge/papers/oaisBriefing.pdf.

Balsamo, A. (1998) Myths of Information: the cultural impact of new information technologies. In: Porter, A. L. and Read, W. H. (eds), *The Information Revolution: current and future consequences*, Ablex.

Barratt, L. (2004) New Guidelines, New Challenges in Schools, *Library & Information Update*, **3** (9), 30–1, www.cilip.org.uk/publications/updatemagazine/archive/archive2004/september/article2.htm.

Bednar, A., Cunningham, D., Duffy, T. and Perry, J. D. (1993) Theory into Practice: How do we link? In Duffy, T. and Jonassen, D. (eds), *Constructivism and the Technology of Instruction*, Lawrence Erlbaum Associates, 19.

Bell, D. (1973) *The Coming of the Post-Industrial Society*, Basic Books.

Bellinger, G. (2004) *Knowledge Management: emerging perspectives*, www.systems-thinking.org/kmgmt/kmgmt.htm.

Berndtson, M. (2003) The Role of the Public Library as a Space for the Future, *Scandinavian Library Quarterly*, **36** (3), www.splq.info/issues/vol36_3/03.htm.

Berners-Lee, T. (1999) *Weaving the Web*, Orion Business Books.

Berners-Lee, T. et al. (2005) *Journal Publishing and Author Self-Archiving: peaceful co-existence and fruitful collaboration*, Southampton, University of Southampton, School of Electronics and Computer Science, http://eprints.ecs.soton.ac.uk/11160/04/ejop-alpsp.html.

Berners-Lee, T., Hendler, J. and Lassila, O. (2001) The Semantic Web: a new form of Web content that is meaningful to computers will unleash a revolution of new possibilities, *Scientific American*, May 27 2001, www.sciam.com/article.cfm?articleID=00048144-10D2-1C70-84A9809EC588EF21&catID=2.

Bertot, J., McClure, C. R. and Ryan, J. (2000) *Developing Statistics and*

Performance Measures for the Networked Environment: final report, Washington DC, Institute of Museum and Library Services.

Booth, A. (2003) Bridging the Research-Practice Gap? The role of evidence based librarianship, *The New Review of Information and Library Research*, **9**, 3–23.

Breeding, M. (2007) Thinking About Your Next OPAC, *Computers in Libraries*, **27** (4), 28–30.

British Medical Journal (1996) Evidence-Based Medicine, *British Medical Journal*, **312**, 71–2.

Brockman, J. et al. (1997) *Quality Management and Benchmarking in the Information Sector: results of recent research*, London, Bowker-Saur.

Brogan, M. (2006) *Contexts and Contributions: building the distributed library*, Washington, Digital Library Federation, www.diglib.org/pubs/dlf106/dlf106.pdf.

Brophy, P. (1991) The Mission of the Academic Library, *British Journal of Academic Librarianship*, **6** (3), 135–47.

Brophy, P. (1998) It May be Electronic but is it any Good? Measuring the performance of electronic services, *Robots to Knowbots: the wider automation agenda. Proceedings of the Victorian Association for Library Automation 9th Biennial Conference, January 28–30 1998*, Melbourne, Australia, VALA, 217–30.

Brophy, P. (2000a) Towards a Generic Model of Information and Library Services in the Information Age, *Journal of Documentation*, **56** (2), 161–84.

Brophy, P. (2000b) *The Library in the Twenty-First Century: new services for the information age*, London, Library Association Publishing.

Brophy, P. (2001a) Assessing the Performance of Electronic Library Services: the EQUINOX project, *The New Review of Academic Librarianship*, **7**, 3–18.

Brophy, P. (2001b) Networked Learning, *Journal of Documentation*, **57** (1), 130–56.

Brophy, P. (2003) *The People's Network: a turning point for public libraries: first findings*. Resource: The Council for Museums, Archives and Libraries, www.mla.gov.uk/resources/assets//P/pnreport_pdf_4288.pdf.

Brophy, P. (2004a) *The People's Network: moving forward*, Resource: The Council for Museums, Archives and Libraries, www.mla.gov.uk/resources/assets//I/id1414rep_pdf_4287.pdf.

Brophy, P. (2004b) The Quality of Libraries, *Die effective Bibliothek*, Munich, K. G. Saur, 30–46.

Brophy, P. (2005a) The Development of a Model for Assessing the Level of Impact of Information and Library Services, *Library and Information Research*, **29** (93), 43–9.

Brophy, P. (2005b) *Research Roadmap: deliverable D7 of the Calimera project*, Calimera Consortium, www.calimera.org/Lists/Resources Library/Technologies and research for local cultural services/Calimera Research Roadmap v5 Final.zip.

Brophy, P. (2006) *Measuring Library Performance: principles and techniques*, London, Facet Publishing.

Brophy, P. (2007) Narrative-Based Practice, *Evidence Based Library and Information Practice*, **2** (1), 149–58, http://ejournals.library.ualberta.ca/index.php/EBLIP/article/view/137/248.

Brophy, P. and Coulling, K. (1996) *Quality Management for Information and Library Managers*, Aldershot, Gower.

Brophy, P. and Craven, J. (2007) Web Accessibility, *Library Trends*, **55** (4), 950–72.

Brophy, P., Craven, J. and Fisher, S. (1998) *The Development of UK Academic Library Services in the Context of Lifelong Learning: final report*, Library Information Technology Centre, South Bank University on behalf of JISC.

Brophy, P. and Fisher, S. (1998) The Hybrid Library, *The New Review of Information and Library Research*, **4**, 3–15.

Brophy, P. and MacDougall, A. (2000) Lifelong Learning and Libraries, *The New Review of Libraries and Lifelong Learning*, **1**, 3–18.

Brophy, P. and Wynne, P. M. (1997) *Management Information Systems and Performance Measurement for the Electronic Library*, Library Information Technology Centre on behalf of the Higher Education Funding Councils' Joint Information Systems Committee.

Brophy, P. et al. (1997) *EQLIPSE: evaluation and quality in library performance: system for Europe: final report and final functional specification*, CERLIM, Manchester Metropolitan University.

Brown, J. S. (2005) Commencement Speech: University of Michigan 2005, www.johnseelybrown.com/UM05.pdf.

Buckland, M.K. (1992) *Redesigning Library Services: a manifesto*, Chicago IL, American Library Association, http://sunsite.berkeley.edu/Literature/Library/Redesiging/html.html.

Buckland, M. K. (1988) *Library Services in Theory and Context*, 2nd edn, Pergamon Press.

Buckland, M. K. (2001) *The Heritage of Public Librarianship*, www.ischool.berkeley.edu/~buckland/Nordic01.pdf.

Burnhill, P. and Law, D. (2005) SUNCAT Rising: UK serials union catalogue to assist document access, *Interlending & Document Supply*, **33** (4), 203–7.

Butters, G., Hulme, A. and Brophy, P. (2007) Supporting Creativity in Networked Environments: the COINE project, *Ariadne*, **51**, www.ariadne.ac.uk/issue51/brophy-et-al.

Cambridge University Press (2006) *Annual Report and Accounts for the Sixteen Months Ended 30 April 2006*, Cambridge, Cambridge University Press.

Candela, L. et al. (2007) Setting the Foundations of Digital Libraries: the DELOS Manifesto. *D-Lib Magazine*, **13** (3/4), www.dlib.org/dlib/march07/castelli/03castelli.html.

Candy, P. C. (2006) Running Amok with a Chainsaw: a personal perspective on information literacy (in three acts). Paper presented at the LILAC 2006 Conference, University of Leeds, 27–29 March 2006, www.cilip.org.uk/NR/rdonlyres/E59CDDA1-C0CB-42D6-86A4-79DF82CA90E4/0/Candy.ppt.

Caplan, P. (1995) You Call it Corn, We Call it Syntax: independent metadata for document-like objects, *The Public-Access Computer Systems Review*, **6** (4), 19–23, http://info.lib.uh.edu/pacsrev.html.

Carpenter, L. (2003) OAI for Beginners – the Open Archives Forum online tutorial, www.oaforum.org/tutorial/english/intro.htm.

Carr, T. et al. (2006) *Repositories for Institutional Open Access: mandated deposit policies*, http://eprints.ecs.soton.ac.uk/13099/02/abs77.pdf.

Case, D. O. (2002) *Looking for Information: a survey of research on information seeking, needs, and behavior*, London, Academic Press.

Casey, M. (2005) *Librarians Without Borders*, www.librarycrunch.com/2005/09.

Casey, M. and Savastinuk, L. C. (2006) Library 2.0: service for the next generation library, *Library Journal*, www.libraryjournal.com/article/CA6365200.html.

Castels, M. (1998) *The Information Age: economy, society and culture*, Blackwell.

Centre for Studies in Advanced Learning Technology (CSALT) (2000) *Effective Networked Learning in Higher Education: notes and guidelines*, Lancaster University, http://csalt.lancs.ac.uk/jisc.

Cervone, F. (2006) Exploring the Federated Search at Northwestern University Library, *Serials Review*, **32** (4), 247–54.

Chad, K. and Miller, P. (2005) *Do Libraries Matter? The rise of Library 2.0*, Birmingham, Talis, www.talis.com/applications/downloads/white_papers/DoLibrariesMatter.pdf.

Chartered Institute of Library and Information Professionals (2002) *Start with the Child*, London, CILIP, www.cilip.org.uk/NR/rdonlyres/D94ED35A-81DB-4421-9815-74F2B454A7AB/0/startwiththechild.pdf.

Chartered Institute of Library and Information Professionals (2004a) *CILIP Royal Charter*, London, CILIP, www.cilip.org.uk/aboutcilip/charterMissionGoals/charter.htm.

Chartered Institute of Library and Information Professionals (2004b) *Mission Statement: what we stand for*, London, CILIP, www.cilip.org.uk/aboutcilip/charterMissionGoals.

Chartered Institute of Library and Information Professionals (2004c) *A Short Introduction to Information Literacy*, London, CILIP, www.cilip.org.uk/professionalguidance/informationliteracy/definition/introduction.htm.

Chartered Institute of Library and Information Professionals (2007) *Professional Guidance, Policy and Research*, London, CILIP, www.cilip.org.uk/professionalguidance.

Childers, T. and Van House, N. A. (1989) Dimensions of Public Library Effectiveness, *Library and Information Science Research*, **11**(3), 273–301.

Chodorow, S. and Lyman, P. (1998) The Responsibilities of Universities. In Hawkins, B. L. and Battin, P., *The Mirage of Continuity: reconfiguring academic information resources for the 21st century*, Council on Library and Information Resources and Association of American Universities, 61–78.

Chowdhury, G. G. and Chowdhury, S. (2002) *Introduction to Digital Libraries*, London, Facet Publishing.

Clapp, V. W. (1964) *The Future of the Research Libraries*, Urbana IL, University of Illinois Press.

Coates, T. (2004) *Who's in Charge? Responsibility for the public library service*, London, Argonaut Press.

Cochrane, P. (1999) What is the Future of Man, Woman and Machine? *RSA Journal*, 2 (4), 64–9.

Comedia (1993) *Borrowed Time: the future of public libraries in the UK*, Bourne Green, Comedia.

Committee on Higher Education (1963) *Higher Education: report of the committee appointed by the Prime Minister under the chairmanship of Lord Robbins 1961–1963*, (The Robbins Report) (Cmnd 2154), HMSO.

Corneliuson, C. (2005) Reality Chat: the library as a meeting place, *Scandinavian Public Library Quarterly*, **38** (4), www.splq.info/issues/vol38_4/05.htm.

Council of Chief State School Officers (1961) *Responsibilities of State Departments of Education for School Library Services: a policy statement*, Council of Chief State School Officers, cited in Gaver, M. V. (1972) United States. In Lowrie, J. E. (ed.) *School Libraries: international developments*, Scarecrow Press, 228–42.

Currall, J. and McKinney, P. (2006) Investing in Value: a perspective on digital preservation, *D-Lib Magazine*, **12** (4), www.dlib.org/dlib/april06/mckinney/04mckinney.html.

Dahl, M., Banerjee, K. and Spalti, M. (2006) *Digital Libraries: integrating content and systems*, London, Chandos.

Davey, J. (2006) Teams and Technologies: developing eLearning in the current climate. Paper presented at the MMIT Group Conference, Liverpool John Moores University, 11 December 2006, http://data.bolton.ac.uk/learning/mmitnw/seminars/vle1206jd2.pps.

Davies, A. (2003) Oxford Libraries Conference: Library Space, the final frontier? *SCONUL Newsletter*, **28**, 89–90.

De Kerckhove, D. (1997) *Connected Intelligence: the arrival of the web society*, Somerville House.

Deegan, M. and Tanner, S. (2002) *Digital Futures: strategies for the information age*, London, Library Association Publishing.

Dempsey, L. (2006a) The (Digital) Library Environment: ten years after, *Ariadne*, **46**, www.ariadne.ac.uk/issue46/dempsey.

Dempsey, L. (2006b) Libraries and the Long Tail: some thoughts about libraries in a network age, *D-Lib Magazine*, **12** (4), www.dlib.org/dlib/april06/dempsey/04dempsey.html.

Dempsey, L., Russell, R. and Murray, R. (1999) Utopian Place of Criticism? Brokering Access to Network Information, *Journal of Documentation*, **55** (1), 33–70.

Dent, V. A. (2007) Intelligent Agent Concepts in the Modern Library, *Library Hi-Tech*, **25** (1), 108–25.

Department for Culture, Media and Sport (1999) *Libraries for All: social inclusion in public libraries*, Department for Culture, Media and Sport.

Department for Culture, Media and Sport (2003) *Framework for the Future: libraries, learning and information in the next decade*, London, Department for Culture, Media and Sport.

Department for Culture, Media and Sport (2006) Public Library Service Standards, London, Department for Culture, Media and Sport, www.culture.gov.uk/NR/rdonlyres/07070797-AE22-4064-8BAF-FEEE2ABA99F9/0/libstandards_06.pdf.

Department of Culture, Arts and Leisure (2002) *Tomorrow's Libraries*, Belfast, Department of Culture, Arts and Leisure.

Department of National Heritage (1997) *Reading the Future: public libraries review*, HMSO.

Digital Preservation Coalition (2007) *The Handbook*, London, DPC, www.dpconline.org/graphics/handbook.

Dolan, J. (2007) *A Blueprint for Excellence: public libraries 2008–2011: connecting people to knowledge and inspiration*, London, MLA, www.mla.gov.uk/resources/assets/B/blueprint_v2_11233.pdf.

Duff, A. S. (1998) Daniel Bell's Theory of the Information Society, *Journal of Information Science*, **24** (6), 373–93.

Dyson, E. (1997) *Release 2.0: a design for living in the digital age*, Broadway.

Eagle, L. and Brennan, R. (2007) Are Students Customers? TQM and marketing perspectives, *Quality Assurance in Education*, **15** (1), 44–60.

Eldredge, J. D. (2002) Evidence-Based Librarianship: What might we expect in the years ahead? *Health Information Libraries Journal*, **19** (2), 71–7.

Ellis, D. (1989) A Behavioural Approach to Information Retrieval System Design, *Journal of Documentation*, **45** (3), 171–212.

ESYS Consulting (2000) *Summative Evaluation of Phase 3 of the eLib Initiative: final report*, London, ESYS Consulting, www.ukoln.ac.uk/services/elib/papers/other/summative-phase-3/elib-eval-main.pdf.

European Commission (2007) *Communication from the Commission to the European Parliament, the Council and the European Economic and Social Committee on Scientific Information in the Digital Age: access, dissemination and preservation* (Document SEC(2007)181), Brussels, European Commission, http://ec.europa.eu/research/science-society/document_library/pdf_06/communication-022007_en.pdf.

Eve, J. and Brophy, P. (2001) *The Value and Impact of End-User IT Services in Public Libraries*, London, Resource, www.cerlim.ac.uk/projects/vital/report.pdf.

Ezard, J. (2006) Libraries Turn a New Leaf to Avoid Extinction, *The Guardian*, 4 July, http://books.guardian.co.uk/news/articles/0,,1811980,00.html.

Fisher, K. E., Erdelez, S. and McKechnie, L. (E. F.) (eds) (2005) *Theories of Information Behavior*, Medford NJ, Information Today.

Fonfa, R. (1998) From Faculty to Librarian Materials Selection: an element in the professionalization of librarianship. In Mech, T. F. and McCabe, G. B. (eds), *Leadership and Academic Libraries*, Greenwood Press.

Ford, N. (2000) Cognitive Styles and Virtual Environments, *Journal of the American Society for Information Science*, **51** (6), 543–57.

Ford, N. et al. (2002) Information Seeking and Mediated Searching. Part 4. Cognitive styles in information seeking, *Journal of the American Society for Information Science and Technology*, **53** (9), 728–35.

Foster, A. (2006) Students Lack 'Information Literacy', Testing Service's Study Finds, *Chronicle of Higher Education*, **53** (10), A36, www.chronicle.com/daily/2006/10/2006101701t.htm.

Friedlander, A. (2002) *Dimensions and Use of the Scholarly Information Environment: introduction to a data set assembled by the Digital Library Federation and Outsell, Inc*, Washington DC, Digital Library Federation and Council on Library and Information Resources.

G-7 Information Society Conference (1995) *Chair's Conclusions*, www.ispo.cec.be/g7/keydocs/G7en.html.

Garvin, D. A. (1988) *Managing Quality*, Free Press.

Gaver, M. V. (1972) United States. In Lowrie, J. E. (ed.) *School Libraries: international developments*, Scarecrow Press, 228–42.

Ginsparg, P. (1997) First Steps in Electronic Research Communication. In Dowler, L. *Gateways to Knowledge: the role of academic libraries in teaching, learning, and research*, MIT Press, 43–58.

Goldenburg-Hart, D. (2004) *Libraries and Changing Research Practices: a report of the ARL/CNI Forum on e-research and cyberinfrastructure*. http://dlist.sir.arizona.edu/770/01/ARL237_3.htm.

Goodall, D. and Brophy, P. (1997) *A Comparable Experience? Library support for franchised courses in higher education* (British Library Research and Innovation Report 33), Centre for Research in Library and Information Management, University of Central Lancashire.

Gorman, M. (2003) *The Enduring Library: technology, tradition, and the quest for balance*, Chicago IL, American Library Association.

Goulding, A. (2006) Public Libraries in England: a valuable public service or a service in distress? *Journal of Librarianship and Information Science*, **38** (1), 3–5.

Green, C. and Kearney, C. (2007) Service Provision: getting the measure of the bridge, *Information Scotland*, **5** (1), www.slainte.org.uk/publications/serials/infoscot/vol5(1)/vol5(1)article9.htm.

Green, H. and Hannon, C. (2007) *Their Space: education for a digital generation*, London, Demos.

Greenberg, D. (1998) Camel Drivers and Gatecrashers. In Hawkins, B. L. and Battin, P., *The Mirage of Continuity: reconfiguring academic information resources for the 21st century*, Council on Library and Information Resources and Association of American Universities, 105–116.

Griffiths, J. R. (2003) Evaluation of the JISC Information Environment: student perceptions of services, *Information Research*, **8** (4) http://informationr.net/ir/8-4/paper160.html.

Griffiths, J. R. and Brophy, P. (2002) Student Searching Behaviour in the JISC Information Environment, *Ariadne*, **33**.

Griffiths, J. R. and Brophy, P. (2005) Student Searching Behaviour and the Web: use of academic resources and Google, *Library Trends*, **53** (4), 539–54.

Griffiths, J.-M. (2006) Outcomes and Impacts, Dollars and Sense: Are libraries measuring up? In Brophy, P., Craven, J. and Markland, M. (eds), *Libraries without Walls 6: evaluating the distributed delivery of library services*, London, Facet Publishing, 110–18.

Grimes, D. J. (1998) *Academic Library Centrality: user success through service, access and tradition*, American Library Association.

Hara, N. and Klung, R. (2000) Students' Distress with a Web-Based Distance Education Course, www.slis.indiana.edu/CSI/wp00-01.html.

Harnad, S. (2000) E-knowledge: freeing the refereed journal corpus online, *Computer Law and Security Report*, **16** (2), 78–87, www.cogsci.soton.ac.uk/~harnad/Papers/Harnad/harnad00.scinejm.htm.

Harper, P. (2006) Library Design has Arrived, *Library & Information Update,* **5** (7/8), 35–9.

Harris, M. H. and Hanna, S. A. (1993) *Into the Future: the foundations of library and information services in the post-industrial era*, Ablex.

Hartley, R. J. and Booth, H. (2006) Users and Union Catalogues, *Journal of Librarianship and Information Science*, **38** (1), 7–20.

Hawgood, J. and Morley, R. (1969) *Project for Evaluating the Benefits from University Libraries*, OSTI Report 5056, University of Durham.

Helms-Park, R., Radia, P. and Stapleton, P. (2007) A Preliminary Assessment of Google Scholar as a Source of EAP Students' Research Materials, *The Internet and Higher Education*, **10** (1), 65–76.

Higham, N. (1980) *The Library in the University: observations on a service*, London, Deutsch.

Higher Education Funding Council for England, Scottish Higher Education Funding Council, Higher Education Funding Council for Wales and the Department of Education for Northern Ireland (1993) *Joint Funding Councils' Libraries Review Group: report* (The Follett Report), HEFCE.

House of Commons (2005) *Culture, Media and Sport: third report*, House of Commons, www.parliament.the-stationery-office.co.uk/pa/cm200405/cmselect/cmcumeds/81/81i.pdf.

Hutton, R. S. (1945) The Origin and History of Aslib, *Journal of Documentation*, **1** (1), 6–20.

Hutton, W. (2007) *The Writing on the Wall: China and the West in the 21st century*, London, Little, Brown.

International Federation of Library Associations and Institutions (1995) *UNESCO Public Library Manifesto*, The Hague, IFLA.

International Federation of Library Associations and Institutions (1992) *Medium-term Programme 1992–1993*; compiled by the Professional Board of IFLA and edited by Hope E.A. Clement, The Hague, IFLA.

International Federation of Library Associations and Institutions, National Libraries Section (2007) Strategic Plan 2006–2007, www.ifla.org/VII/s1/annual/sp01.htm.

International Organization for Standardization (1996) *Information and Documentation: format for information exchange*, ISO 2709, Geneva, ISO.

International Organization for Standardization (1998) *Information and Documentation: library performance indicators ISO 11620*, Geneva, ISO.

International Organization for Standardization (2003a) *Information and Documentation: international library statistics ISO 2789*, Geneva, ISO.

International Organization for Standardization (2003b) *Information and Documentation: Performance indicators for electronic library services ISO 20983*, Geneva, ISO.

Johnson, D., Johnson, R. and Smith, K. (1991) *Active Learning: cooperation in the college classroom*, Interaction Book Co.

Joint Information Systems Committee (1999) *Adding Value to the UK's Learning, Teaching and Research Resources: the Distributed National Electronic Resource (DNER)*, JISC.

Joint Information Systems Committee (2003) *Developing an Online Information Environment*, www.jisc.ac.uk/whatwedo/themes/information_environment/ie_home.aspx.

Joint Information Systems Committee (2007a) *Information Environment Development Strategy*, www.jisc.ac.uk/whatwedo/themes/information_environment/strat_ieds0105_draft2.aspx.

Joint Information Systems Committee (2007b) *Virtual Research Environments programme: Phase 2 roadmap*, www.jisc.ac.uk/publications/publications/pub_vreroadmap.aspx.

Joint, N. (2007) UK Digital Library Licences and Authentication Systems: national versus local approaches, *Library Review*, **56** (2), 102–8.

Kahn, R. and Wilensky, R. (1995) A Framework for Distributed Digital Object Services, www.cnri.reston.va.us/home/cstr/arch/k-w.html.

Kaplan, R. S. and Norton, D. P. (1992) The Balanced Scorecard: measures that drive performance, *Harvard Business Review*, **70** (1), 71–9.

Karlsen, S. I. (2006) The Public Library: a new version, *Scandinavian Library Quarterly*, **39** (3), www.splq.info/issues/vol39_3/02.htm.

Kim, K.-S. (2001) Information Seeking on the Web: effects of user and task variables, *Library and Information Science Research*, **23**, 233–55.

Kinnell, M. (1992) *Learning Resources in Schools: Library Association guidelines for school libraries*, London, Library Association Publishing.

Kohl, H. (1999) [Speech by German Chancellor Kohl at the opening of Die Deutsche Bibliothek, 1997] Quoted in 'National libraries'. In Line, M. B. (ed.), *Librarianship and Information Work Worldwide 1999*, London, Bowker-Saur, 16.

Kolb, D. A. (1984) *Experiential Learning: experience as the source of learning and development*, New Jersey, Prentice Hall, 68–9.

Kuhlthau, C. C. (1991) Inside the Search Process: information seeking from the user's perspective, *Journal of the American Society for Information Science*, **42**(5), 361–71.

Kvaerndrup, H. M. (2000) Denmark's Electronic Research Library (DEFF): A project changing concepts, values and priorities. In Brophy, P., Fisher, S. and Clarke, Z. *Libraries without Walls 3: the delivery of library services to distant users, proceedings of an international conference organized by CERLIM, 10–14 September 1999*, Library Association Publishing, 121–32.

Lagoze, C. and Fielding, D. (1998) Defining Collections in Distributed Digital Libraries, *D-Lib Magazine*, www.mirrored.ukoln.ac.uk/lis-journal/dlib/november98/11lagoze.html.

Lagoze, C. and Van de Sompel, H. (2003) The Making of the Open Archives

Initiative for Metadata Harvesting Protocol, *Library Hi Tech*, **21** (2), 118–28.

Lancaster, F. W. (1983) Future Librarianship: preparing for an unconventional career, *Wilson Library Bulletin*, **57**, 747–53.

Lehmann, K.-D. (2004) Introduction to the Workshop: rich cultural heritage and its transformation to digital. In *Digital Resources from Cultural Institutions for Use in Teaching and Learning: a report of the American/German Workshop*, Munich, K. G. Saur, 11–13.

Levy, P. (1998) Perspectives on Organisational Network Communities: a review paper for library and information service managers, *Program*, **32** (4), 343–58.

Levy, S. (1999) Wired for the Bottom Line, *Newsweek*, **133** (15), 11 October.

Library and Information Commission (1997) *New Library: the People's Network*, London, LIC.

Library and Information Services Council (1986) *School Libraries: the foundations of the curriculum: report of the working party on school library services*, HMSO.

Line, M. B. (2000) The Lifelong Learner and the Future Library, *The New Review of Libraries and Lifelong Learning*, **1**, 65–80.

Line, M. B. and Line, J. (eds) (1979) *National Libraries*, Aslib.

Lor, P. J. (1997) *Guidelines for Legislation for National Library Services*, UNESCO, www.unesco.org/webworld/nominations/guidelines1_h.htm.

Love Libraries Campaign (2007) *What They Say*, www.lovelibraries.co.uk/quotes.php.

Lyman, P. (1997) The Gateway Library: teaching and research in the global reference room. In Dowler, L. (ed.), *Gateways to Knowledge: the role of academic libraries in teaching, learning, and research*, Cambridge MA, MIT Press, 135–50.

Lyman, P. and Chodorow, S. (1998) The Future of Scholarly Communication. In Hawkins, B. L. and Battin, P., *The Mirage of Continuity: reconfiguring academic information resources for the 21st century*, Council on Library and Information Resources and Association of American Universities, 87–104.

Lyon, E. (2003) eBank UK: building the links between research data, scholarly communication and learning, *Ariadne*, **36**, www.ariadne.ac.uk/issue36/lyon.

McClellan, A. W. (1973) *The Reader, the Library and the Book*, London, Clive Bingley Ltd.

McClure, C. R. and Lopata, C. L. (1996) *Assessing the Academic Networked Environment: strategies and options*, Coalition for Networked Information.

MacCormac Jamieson Prichard (1995) Lancaster University Library Extension and the Ruskin Library. In Taylor, S. (ed.), *Building Libraries for the Information Age*, Institute of Advanced Architectural Studies, 73–5.

McCullagh, D. (1998) Library Computers Logged Off, *Wired*, www.wired.com/news/politics/0,1283,16481,00.html.

McGonagle, J. (1998) *SLA Guidelines: promoting literacy through the primary school library*, School Library Association.

McGreal, R. (2004) Learning Objects: a practical definition, *International Journal of Instructional Technology and Distance Learning*, **1** (9), http://itdl.org/Journal/Sep_04/article02.htm.

McMenemy, D. and Burton, P. (2005) Managing Access: legal and policy issues of ICT use. Chapter 2 in *Delivering Digital Services: a handbook for public libraries and learning centres*, London, Facet Publishing, 19–24.

Mainwood, H. R. (1972) School Libraries in the United Kingdom. In Lowrie, J. E. (ed.), *School Libraries: international developments*, Scarecrow Press, 9–13.

Marchand, D. (1990) Managing Information Quality. In Wormell, I. (ed.), *Information Quality: definitions and dimensions*, London, Taylor Graham, 7–17.

Marchionini, G. (1989) Information Seeking Strategies of Novices Using a Full-Text Electronic Encyclopedia, *Journal of the American Society for Information Science*, **40** (1), 54–66.

Markless, S. and Streatfield, D. R. (2000) *The Really Effective College Library*, Library and Information Commission Research Report 51, Twickenham, Information Management Associates.

Markless, S. and Streatfield, D. (2006) *Evaluating the Impact of Your Library*, London, Facet Publishing.

Melchionda, M. G. (2007) Librarians in the Age of the Internet: their attitudes and roles: a literature review, *New Library World*, **108** (3/4), 123–40.

Mellon, C. A. (1986) Library Anxiety: a grounded theory and its development, *College and Research Libraries*, **47** (2), 160–5.

Miller, P. (2000) Interoperability: What is it and why should I want it? *Ariadne*, **24**, www.ariadne.ac.uk/issue24/interoperability.

Miller, P. (2006) *Library 2.0: the challenge of disruptive innovation*, Birmingham, Talis, www.talis.com/resources/documents/447_Library_2_prfl.pdf.

Milner, E., Kinnell, M. and Usherwood, B. (1994) Quality Management: the public library debate, *Public Library Journal*, **9** (6), 151–7.

Moyle, M. (2006) ShibboLEAP: seven libraries and a LEAP of faith, *Ariadne*, **48**, www.ariadne.ac.uk/issue48/moyle.

Murison, W. J. (1971) *The Public Library: its origins, purpose and significance*, Harrap, 2nd edn, 30.

Museums, Libraries and Archives Council (2004a) *Investing in Knowledge: a five-year vision for England's museums, libraries and archives*, London, MLA, www.mla.gov.uk/resources/assets//I/iik_vision_pdf_5032.pdf.

Museums, Libraries and Archives Council (2004b) *Inspiring Learning for All: detailed framework*, London, MLA, www.inspiringlearningforall.gov.uk/uploads/Detailed framework.doc.

Museums, Libraries and Archives Council (n.d.) *More about the Generic Learning Outcomes*, London, MLA, www.inspiringlearningforall.gov.uk/uploads/More about the GLO's.doc.

O'Reilly, T. (2005) *What is Web 2.0? Design patterns and business models for the next generation of software*, www.oreillynet.com/pub/a/oreilly/tim/news/2005/09/30/what-is-web-20.html?page=1.

Ober, J. (1999) The California Digital Library, *D-Lib Magazine*, **5** (3), www.dlib.org/dlib/march99/03ober.html.

Ofcom (2007) *What is media literacy?*, www.ofcom.org.uk/advice/media_literacy/of_med_lit/whatis.

Öhström, B. (2006) Denmark's Electronic Research Library: evaluation of services through user surveys and usability tests. In Brophy, P., Craven, C. and Markland, M., *Libraries without Walls 6: Evaluating the distributed delivery of library services, proceedings of an international conference organized by CERLIM, 16–20 September, 2005*, London, Facet Publishing, 14–24.

Onwuegbuzie, A. J., Jiao, Q. G. and Bostick, S. L. (2004) *Library Anxiety*, Lanham MD, Scarecrow Press.

Organisation for Economic Co-operation and Development (1995) *Literacy, Economy and Society: results of the first international adult literacy survey*, OECD and Statistics Canada.

Orr, R. H. (1973) Measuring the Goodness of Library Services: a general framework for considering quantitative measures, *Journal of Documentation*, **29** (3), 315–32.

Osburn, C. B. (1997) The Research University and its Library. In Schwartz, C. A. (ed.), *Restructuring Academic Libraries: organizational development in the wake of technological change*, Chicago IL, American Library Association, 238–52.

Owen, J. S. M. and Wiercx, A. (1996) *Knowledge Models for Networked Library Services: final report*, Report PROLIB/KMS 16905, Luxembourg, Office of Official Publications of the European Communities.

Oxbrow, N. and Abell, A. (1998) Putting Knowledge to Work: What skills and competencies are required? In *Knowledge Management: a new competitive asset*, Economist Intelligence Unit, 23–35.

Oxford English Dictionary (2007) *Immersion*, http://dictionary.oed.com.

Parasuraman, A., Berry, L. and Zeithaml, V. (1988) SERVQUAL: a multiple-item scale for measuring customer perceptions of service quality, *Journal of Retailing*, **64** (1), 12–40.

Pask, G. (1976) Styles and Strategies of Learning, *British Journal of Educational Psychology*, **46** (1), 12–25.

Pask, G. (1988) Learning Strategies, Teaching Strategies, and Conceptual or Learning Style. In Schmeck, R. R. (ed.), *Learning Strategies and Learning Style*, Plenum Press.

Paskin, N. (1999) *E-citations: actionable identifiers and scholarly referencing*, www.doi.org/resources.html.

Paye, J.-C. (1995) *Making Lifelong Learning a Reality for All*, OECD.

Pickering, B. (2006) Nature Gives Thumbs Up to Wikipedia, *Information World Review*, www.iwr.co.uk/information-world-review/news/2148074/nature-endorses-wikipedia.

Pinfield, S. and Hampson, A. (1999) Partnership and Customer Service in the Hybrid Library, *New Review of Information and Library Research*, **5**, 107–19.

Powell, A. and Lyon, L. (2005) *JISC Information Environment Architecture: functional model*, Bath, UKOLN, www.ukoln.ac.uk/distributed-systems/jisc-ie/arch/functional-model.

PricewaterhouseCoopers LLP (2005) *Libraries Impact Project*, London, LASER Foundation, www.bl.uk/about/cooperation/pdf/laserfinal6.pdf.

Quality Assurance Agency for Higher Education (2000) *Subject Benchmark Statements: librarianship and information management*, www.qaa.ac.uk/academicinfrastructure/benchmark/honours/librarianship.asp.

Quality Assurance Agency for Higher Education (2007) *Subject Benchmark Statements: librarianship and information management* [in press]. (The 2000 edition is available at www.qaa.ac.uk/academicinfrastructure/benchmark/honours/default.asp, where the 2007 edition will be posted when published.)

Ramsay, K. M. and Kinnie, J. (2006) The Embedded Librarian, *Library Journal*, **131** (6), 34–5.

Ranganathan, S. R. (1931) *Five Laws of Library Science*, Madras Library Association.

Research Information Network (2005) *Strategic Plan 2005–2008, London*, RIN, www.rin.ac.uk/files/RIN Strategic Plan_0.pdf.

Research Information Network (2007) *Stewardship of Digital Research Data: a framework of principles and guidelines: responsibilities of research institutions and funders, data managers, learned societies and publishers*, London, RIN, www.rin.ac.uk/files/Research Data Principles and Guidelines – published draft for consultation.pdf.

Revill, D. (1985) The Measurement of Performance. In Cowley, J. (ed.), *The Management of Polytechnic Libraries*, Gower, 104–34 (the quotation by Charlton is found at p.132).

Rider, F. (1944) *The Scholar and the Future of the Research Libraries*, New York, Hadham Press.

Rowlands, I. (1997) Understanding Information Policy: concepts, frameworks and research tools. In Rowlands, I. (ed.), *Understanding Information Policy: proceedings of a workshop held at Cumberland Lodge, Windsor Great Park, 22–24 July 1996*, Bowker-Saur, 27–45.

Royce, J. (1998) More than Surviving, Thriving in the Information Age: reading as a basis for using information technology efficiently. In Shoham, S. and Yitzhaki, M., *Education for All: culture, reading and information*, International Association of School Librarianship, 177–88.

Rynänen, M. (1998) *Report on the Green Paper on the Role of Libraries in the Modern World*, European Parliament: Committee on Culture, Youth, Education and the Media, www.lib.hel.fi/syke/english/publications/report.htm.

Sanders, T. (2006) Britannica Lashes out at Wikipedia Comparison Study, *Information World Review*, www.iwr.co.uk/information-world-review/news/2152685/britannica-lashes-wikipedia.

Sapp, G. and Gilmour, R. (2003) A Brief History of the Future of Academic Libraries: predictions and speculations from the literature of the profession, 1975 to 2000: Part Two, 1990 to 2000, *Portal: Libraries and the Academy*, **3** (1), 13–34.

Saracevic, T., Kantor, P., Chamis, A. Y. and Trivison, D. (1988) A Study of Information Seeking and Retrieving, *Journal of the American Society for Information Science*, **39** (3), 161–176.

Schement, J. R. and Curtis, T. (1995) *Tendencies and Tensions of the Information Age: the production and distribution of information in the United States*, Transaction Publishers.

Shadbolt, N., Hall, W. and Berners-Lee, T. (2006) The Semantic Web Revisited, *IEEE Intelligent Systems*, **21** (3), 96–101.

Shank, R. (1983) Management Information and the Organization: homily from the experience of the data rich to the information poor. In Lancaster, F. W. (ed.), *Library Automation as a Source of Management Information: papers presented at the 1982 Clinic on Library Applications of Data Processing, 25–28 April 1982*, University of Illinois.

Shedlock, J. and Walton, L. (2004) An Academic Medical Library Using LibQUAL+™: the experience of the Galter Health Sciences Library, Northwestern University, *Journal of Library Administration*, **40** (3/4), 99–110.

Shreeves, S. L., Riley, J. and Milewicz, L. (2006) Moving Towards Sharable Metadata, *First Monday*, **11** (8), www.firstmonday.org/issues/issue11_8/shreeves/index.html.

Shuler, J. A. (2004) Privacy and Academic Libraries: widening the frame of discussion, *Journal of Academic Librarianship*, **30** (2), 157–9.

Smith, N. M. and Presser, P. (2005) Embed with the Faculty: legal information skills online, *The Journal of Academic Librarianship*, **31** (3), 247–62.

Society of Chief Librarians (2006a) *Annual Report 2005–06*, SCL, www.goscl.com/scl_download.ikml?id=122.

Society of Chief Librarians (2006b) *Society of Chief Librarians' Definition of a 21stC Reading Service: (paper prepared) for consultation and discussion at seminar on 27 September*, SCL, www.goscl.com/scl_download.ikml?id=100.

Society of College, National and University Libraries (1999) *Information Skills in Higher Education*, London, SCONUL, www.sconul.ac.uk/groups/information_literacy/papers/Seven_pillars2.pdf.

Society of College, National and University Libraries (2006a) *SCONUL Strategy Statement*, London, SCONUL, www.sconul.ac.uk/about_sconul/SCONUL-strategy.pdf.

Society of College, National and University Libraries (2006b) *Information Literacy*, London, SCONUL, www.sconul.ac.uk/hot_topics/info_literacy.

Sommerlad, E. et al. (2004) *Books and Bytes: new service paradigms for the 21st century library: an evaluation of the People's Network and ICT training for public library staff programme*, London, Big Lottery Fund.

Sotiriou, M. and Gilroy, P. (2004) *Social Epistemology, Meaning and the*

Academic Library, unpublished paper, Manchester, Manchester Metropolitan University.

Spencer, M. E. (2006) Evolving a New Model: the information commons, *Reference Services Review*, **34** (2), 242–7.

Sproull, L. and Kiesler, S. L. (1991) *Connections: new ways of working in the networked organization*, MIT Press.

Steele, V. (1995) Producing Value: a North American perspective on the future of higher education libraries. In Taylor, S. (ed.), *Building Libraries for the Information Age*, Institute of Advanced Architectural Studies, University of York, 1995, 77–80, quoting Sack, J. R., Open Systems for Open Minds: building the library without walls, *College & Research Libraries*, **47** (6), Nov., 538.

Steinwachs, S. (1999) Information and Culture: the impact of national culture on information processes, *Journal of Information Science*, **25** (3), 193–204.

Streatfield, D. R. and Markless, S. (1997) *The Effective College Library*, British Library R and I Report 21, Bristol, Further Education Development Agency.

Streibel, M. J. (1991) Instructional Plans and Situated Learning: the challenge of Suchman's theory of situated action for instructional designers and instructional systems. In Anglin, G. (ed.), *Instructional Technology Past Present and Future*, Englewood CO, Libraries Unlimited.

Su, H.-Y. and Lin, Y. (2006) Enhancing Knowledge-Based Service Quality: a knowledge management perspective, *The Service Industries Journal*, **26** (7), 787–800.

Surridge, R. (1984) The Priorities for Research in Librarianship, *Library and Information Research News*, **7** (27 and 28), 11–16.

Takeuchi, H. (1998) *Beyond Knowledge Management: lessons from Japan*, www.sveiby.com.au/LessonsJapan.htm.

Taylor, A. (ed.) (1993) Introduction. In *Long Overdue: a library reader*, Mainstream/Library Association Publishing.

Tennant, R. (2005) Lipstick on a Pig, *Library Journal*, **130** (7), 34.

Tilke, A. (ed.) (1998) *Library Association Guidelines for Secondary School Libraries*, Library Association Publishing.

Toffler, A. (1980) *The Third Wave*, Collins.

Underwood, P. G. (1996) *Soft Systems Analysis and the Management of Libraries, Information Services and Resource Centres*, Library Association Publishing.

UNESCO (2006) Beacons of the Information Society: the Alexandria Proclamation on information literacy and lifelong learning, http://portal.unesco.org/ci/en/files/20891/11364818989Beacons_of_the_Information_Society___The_Alexandria_Proclamation_on_Information_Literacy_and_Lifelong_Learning.doc/Beacons+of+the+Information+Society_++The+Alexandria+Proclamation+on+Information+Literacy+and+Lifelong+Learning.doc.

University Grants Committee (1967) *Report of the Committee on Libraries* (The Parry Report), HMSO.

University Grants Committee (1976) *Report on Capital Provision for University Libraries* (The Atkinson Report). HMSO.

Usherwood, B. (2002) Demonstrating Impact through Qualitative Research, *Performance Measurement and Metrics*, **3** (3), 117–22.

Van de Sompel, H. and Lagoze, C. (2000) The Santa Fe Convention of the Open Archives Initiative, *D-Lib Magazine*, **6** (2), www.dlib.org/dlib/february2000/vandesompel-oai/02vandesompel-oai.html.

von Baeyer, H. C. (2004) *Information: the new language of science*, Cambridge MA, Harvard University Press.

Wakefield, N. (2007) Bridging the Gap: the Information Skills Training Partnership at Manchester Metropolitan University, *Legal Information Management*, **7**, 63–70.

Watson, L. (2006) The Saltire Centre at Glasgow Caledonian University, *SCONUL Focus*, **37**, 4–11.

Wiegan, W. A. (1999) The Structure of Librarianship: essay on an information profession, *Canadian Journal of Library and Information Science*, **24** (1), 17–37.

Wilson, T. D. (1981) On User Studies and Information Needs, *Journal of Documentation*, **37** (1), 3–15.

Wilson, T. D. et al. (2002) Information Seeking and Mediated Searching. Part 2: uncertainty and its correlates, *Journal of the American Society for Information Science and Technology*, **53** (9), 704–15.

Witkin, H. A. et al. (1977) Field-Dependent and Field-Independent Cognitive Styles and their Educational Implications, *Review of Educational Research*, 47, 1–64.

Wittgenstein, L. (1953) *Philosophical Investigations*, http://users.rcn.com/rathbone/lw1-10c.htm.

Zeithaml, V. A., Parasuraman, A. and Berry, L. L. (1990) *Delivering Quality Service: balancing customer perceptions and expectations*, London, Collier Macmillan.

Glossary

AACR2	Anglo-American Cataloguing Rules, second edition
ADONIS	Article Delivery Over Network Information Systems (Aston University, UK)
ALA	American Library Association
ARL	Association of Research Libraries (USA)
CALIMERA	Cultural Applications: Local Institutions Mediating Electronic Resource Access (European Commission funded co-ordination action)
CD-ROM	Compact Disc Read Only Memory
CEDARS	CURL Exemplars in Digital Archives
CERLIM	Centre for Research in Library & Information Management (Manchester Metropolitan University, UK)
CILIP	Chartered Institute of Library and Information Professionals
CNI	Coalition for Networked Information (USA)
CNRI	Corporation for National Research Initiatives
COINE	Cultural Objects in Networked Environments (European Commission funded project)
COPAC	Consortium of Research Libraries (CURL) OPAC
CRADDL	Cornell Reference Architecture for Distributed Digital Libraries
CSALT	Centre for Studies in Advanced Learning Technology (Lancaster University, UK)
CSCW	Computer-Supported Co-operative Work
CURL	Consortium of Research Libraries
DCC	Digital Curation Centre
DCMS	Department for Culture, Media and Sport (UK government department)
DDC	Dewey Decimal Classification
DEFF	Danmarks Elektroniske Fag- og Forskningsbibliotek (Electronic Research Library) (Denmark)
DL	Digital Library

DLF	Digital Library Federation
DLMS	Digital Library Management System
DLO	Document Like Object
DLS	Digital Library System
DNER	Distributed National Electronic Resource
DOI	Digital Object Identifier
DPC	Digital Preservation Coalition
DREL	Digital Rights Expression Language
DRM	Digital Rights Management
DTD	Document Type Definition
DVD	Digital Video Disc *or* Digital Versatile Disc
EAD	Encoded Archival Description (SGML DTD for archival documents)
EBIP	Evidence-Based Information Practice
EBL	Evidence-Based Librarianship
EC	European Commission
EDINA	Edinburgh Data and Information Access (one of the UK higher education datacentres)
eLib	Electronic Libraries Programme
ERIC	Education Resources Information Center (USA)
ESDS	Economic and Social Data Service
GII	Global Information Infrastructure
GLOs	Generic Learning Outcome
HD	High Definition
HTML	HyperText Markup Language
HTTP	HyperText Transfer Protocol
IA	Information Architecture
IALS	International Adult Literacy Survey
ICT	Information and Communication Technologies
IDS	International Data Service
IE	Information Environment
IESR	Information Environment Service Registry
IETF	Internet Engineering Task Force
IFLA	International Federation of Library Associations and Institutions
ILL	Interlibrary Loan
IP	Internet Protocol
IPR	Intellectual Property Rights
ISBD	International Standard Bibliographic Description

ISBN	International Standard Book Number
ISO	International Organization for Standardization
ISP	Internet Service Provider
ISSN	International Standard Serial Number
JANET	Joint Academic Network (the UK universities' communications network)
JISC	Joint Information Systems Committee
JSTOR	Journal STORage (service which digitizes and makes available back-runs of important journals)
KM	Knowledge Management
LARGE	Leeds Always Reading Group for Everyone
LCSH	Library of Congress Subject Headings
LIRG	Library and Information Research Group
LIS	Library and Information Services
MARC	MAchine Readable Cataloguing
MDA	*formerly* Museum Documentation Association
MeSH	Medical Subject Headings
MIA	MODELS Information Architecture
MIMAS	Manchester Information and Associated Services (one of the UK higher education datacentres)
MLA	Museums, Libraries and Archives Council
MODELS	MOving to Distributed Environments for Library Services (eLib study, including a series of influential expert workshops)
N3	New National Network (NHS)
NaCTeM	National Centre for Text Mining
NBBI	Nederlands Bureau voor Bibliotheekwezen en Informatieverzorging (Netherlands)
NDLP	National Digital Library Program (USA)
NESLi2	National Electronic Site Licensing Initiative (current version)
NISO	National Information Standards Organization (USA)
NLH	National Library for Health
NLLST	National Lending Library for Science and Technology
NLN	National Learning Network
OAI-PMH	Open Archives Initiative Protocol for Metadata Harvesting
OAIS	Open Archival Information System
OCLC	Online Computer Library Center (USA)
OECD	Organisation for Economic Co-operation and Development
OPAC	Online Public Access Catalogue

PC	Personal Computer
PDA	Personal Digital Assistant
PDF	Portable Document Format (proprietary format owned by Adobe)
PN	People's Network
PURL	Persistent Uniform Resource Locator
RDA	Resource Description and Access
RDF	Resource Description Framework
RFID	Radio Frequency Identification Device
RIN	Research Information Network
RSLP	Research Support Libraries Programme
RSS	Really Simple Syndication
RTF	Rich Text Format
SCL	Society of Chief Librarians
SCONUL	Society of College, National and University Libraries, *formerly* Standing Conference of National and University Libraries
SCRAN	Scottish Cultural Resources Access Network
SGML	Standard Generalized Markup Language
SLE	School of Library Economy (Columbia University)
SMS	Short Message Service
SOA	Service-Oriented Architectures
SOAP	Simple Object Access Protocol *or* Service Oriented Architecture Protocol
SRW	Search & Retrieve Web service
SUNCAT	Serials Union Catalogue
TQM	Total Quality Management
UGC	University Grants Committee
URI	Uniform Resource Identifier
URL	Uniform Resource Locator
URN	Uniform Resource Name
VITAL	Value and Impact of IT Access in Public Libraries
VLE	Virtual Learning Environment
VRE	Virtual Research Environment
W3C	World Wide Web Consortium
WAI	Web Accessibility Initiative (of W3C)
WCAG	Web Content Accessibility Guidelines
WSDL	Web Services Description Language
WSIS	World Summit on the Information Society
WWW	World Wide Web

XML	eXtensible Markup Language
XSL	eXtensible Stylesheet Language (a style sheet system for use with XML)

Index

academic libraries *see* libraries, academic
Academic Live (Microsoft) 176
access 30, 32
  as quality attribute 104–5
  see also freedom of access; open access
accessibility 135
  as quality attribute 103
acquisition 57
ADONIS 172
aesthetics
  as quality attribute 102
affect of service 106
Alexandria Declaration (UNESCO) 158
Alexandrian Library 3
  model 55–8
Amazon 11, 172, 194
American Library Association (ALA) 70
Andrew W. Mellon Foundation 200
anxiety *see* computer anxiety; libraries, anxiety
appropriate copy problem 195
architecture *see* libraries, buildings
archiving *see* self-archiving
Ashurbanipal 3
Aslib 46
assessment 136
Aston University Library 172
ATHENS 144
Atkinson Report 58
Audit Commission 36
Australian National Library 22
authentication 84, 143, 144, 150
authenticity 202
authorization 84, 143

Backflip 142
balanced scorecard 203
Bath University 172
Becta 173
benchmarking 75
Berlin Declaration on Open Access to Knowledge in the Sciences and Humanities 30, 177
bibliographies *see* national bibliographies
Bibliothèque Nationale 26
Big Blue 160
Birmingham Free Library 55
blogs 13, 171, 181
A Blueprint for Excellence 40
bookmarks 141–2
bookshops 10
  see also Amazon
Britannica 142
British Library 26, 27, 58
  Business & Intellectual Property Centre 27
  Document Supply Centre (DSC) 60
  Turning the Pages 27, 131
British Medical Journal 47
British Museum Library 22
browsing 149, 150
Budapest Open Access Initiative 30
buildings *see* libraries, buildings

Business & Intellectual Property Centre *see* British Library, Business & Intellectual Property Centre
business excellence 98

California Digital Library 194
Callimachus 3
Carnegie, Andrew 35
cataloguing 23, 187
see also union catalogues
CD-ROMS 172, 179
Centre for Studies in Advanced Learning Technology (CSALT) 154
CILIP 68–70, 158
City Stories Project 180
classification 191
clay tablets 3
clients *see* libraries, clients
clumps 32
Codex gigas *see* Devil's Bible
cognitive styles 147, 148, 153
Collection Description Focus (UKOLN) 193
collections 82, 160, 180
conditional 122
description 80, 123, 134, 193
development 121
interpretation 137
management 134
see also libraries, collections
Comedia 35
Commonwealth Parliamentary Library 22
communication
as quality attribute 105
see also scholarly communication
communities
of practice 54, 154
virtual 135
community libraries *see* libraries, community
competence (quality attribute) 104
computer anxiety 152
Computer-Supported Co-operative Work (CSCW) 131
confidentiality 164
conformance
as quality attribute 100
to requirements 97
connected intelligence 9
consortia 59
Consortium of Research Libraries (CURL) 26, 59
Online Public Access Catalogue (COPAC) 26
Exemplars in Digital ArchiveS (CEDARS) 200
Conspectus 56
constructivism 152
content
access 134
acquisition 131, 134, 172
description 134
digital 33
discussion of 131
identification 134
manipulation 131
selection 134
validation 137
controlled vocabularies 191
COPAC 172, 197
copyright *see* intellectual property rights
Cornell Reference Architecture for Distributed Digital Libraries (CRADDL) 81, 121
Corporation for National Research Initiatives (CNRI) 81
county libraries *see* libraries, county
courtesy
as quality attribute 104
Creative Commons 192
creative producers 6
creativity 13, 114, 132, 135, 179, 207
credibility
as quality attribute 104

cross-searching 196
 see also search and retrieve
Cultural Applications: Local Institutions Mediating Electronic Resource Access (CALIMERA) 129–38, 179
cultural enrichment 36
cultural heritage 16, 23
Cultural Objects in Networked Environments (COINE) 180, 208
currency
 as quality attribute 101
customers
 delight 100
 understanding as quality attribute 105
 see also libraries, customers
Cutter, Charles 64

data mining 183
data protection 145–6
 see also privacy
Data Protection Act (1998) 146
delivery *see* resources, delivery
DELOS 86
Department for Culture, Media and Sport (DCMS) 38, 166, 167
Department for Innovation, Universities and Skills (DIUS) 167
Deutsch Bibliothek 26
development *see* economic development
Devil's Bible 22
Dewey Decimal Classification 191
Dewey, Melvil 64, 67–8
DigiQUAL™ 106
digital libraries *see* libraries, digital
Digital Library (DL) 86
Digital Library Federation 84
Digital Library Management System (DLMS) 86
Digital Library System (DLS) 86
digital literacy 159
Digital Object Identifiers (DOI) 81, 185
digital objects 80, 93
digital pioneers 5
digital preservation 32, 33, 179
Digital Preservation Coalition (DPC) 200
digital repositories 10, 33, 80–1, 84, 85
Digital Rights Expression Languages (DRELs) 192
Digital Rights Management (DRM) 192
digital television 12
disintermediation 116–18
Distributed National Collection 26
Distributed National Electronic Resource (DNER) 32
distributed search *see* search and retrieve
document like object (DLO) 183
document literacy 157
Document Type Definition (DTD) 186
Document Supply Centre (DSC) *see* British Library, Document Supply Centre (DSC)
documents 32
 formats 185
double feedback loop 96
DSpace 30
Dublin Core 189, 198
 Qualified 189
durability
 as quality attribute 101
dynamic collections 121
 content 199

Easterhouse 212
e-commerce 11, 141
Economic and Social Data Service (ESDS) 173
economic development 36
economic impact 108

economy *see* libraries, economy
Edge Hill University 160
EDINA 172
Education Resources Information Center (ERIC) 191
effectiveness *see* libraries, effectiveness
efficiency *see* libraries, efficiency
e-journals 32
electronic journals *see* e-journals
Electronic Libraries Programme (eLib) 32, 79
electronic publishing *see* e-publishing
Electronic Research Library (DEFF), Denmark 174
Elgg 143
embedding 160
emulation 202
Encoded Archival Description (EAD) 190
end-users *see* users
enjoyment 132
Enquire (People's Network) 143
enquiry services *see* libraries, enquiry services
e-print archives 29
e-print repositories 30, 178, 181
e-print services 10
ePrints 30
e-publishing 9–10
EQUINOX 92–4
eScience Grid 168
espida 203
European Web Archive 25
everyday communicators 6
evidence-based information practice (EBIP) 48
evidence-based librarianship (EBL) 48
evidence-based practice 46–8, 209
exclusion 166
expressive richness 155
eXtensible Markup Language (XML) 185–7
eXtensible Stylesheet Language (XSL) 186

Facebook 170
Fairplay (Apple) 192
family history *see* genealogy
features
  as quality attribute 99
federated searching 176, 178
  see also search and retrieve
filtering *see* internet filtering
fitness for purpose 97
Follett Report 31, 209
Framework for the Future 39, 74, 95
freedom of access 164
functional literacy 157
functions *see* libraries, functions
fusion 83

gateways *see* subject gateways
genealogy 179, 208
Generic Learning Outcomes (GLOs) 39
Global Information Infrastructure (GII) 165
globalization 16
Google 5, 17, 62, 93, 142, 146, 148, 194, 195, 206, 207
Google Scholar 10
granularity 181, 183
graphical user interfaces 168
grey literature 30
Grid *see* eScience Grid
Guidelines for School Libraries 43

handles 80, 185
Handsworth Public Library 210
harvesting 197
heritage *see* cultural heritage
House of Commons Select Committee (2005) 41
hybrid libraries *see* libraries, hybrid

immersive libraries *see* libraries, immersive
impact *see* economic impact; libraries, impact; social impact

inclusion 166
individual article supply 61
information
behaviour 146
commons 73
control 106
delivery 207
dissemination 136
environments 173–6
gatherers 6
landscape 80, 122
literacy 44, 63, 157–60, 208
objects 4, 151, 163, 179, 181,
skills 44, 63 *see also* information, literacy
society 6–9
strategies 31
universe 120, 163
Information Environment (IE) *see* Joint Information Systems Committee (JISC) Information Environment
ingenta 61
Inspiring Learning for All 156
instant messaging 143
institutional repositories 85, 137, 207
intellectual freedom 71
intellectual property rights (IPR) 84, 163, 164, 187, 201
intelligence 122
see also connected intelligence
intelligent agents 115
intelligent enterprises 50
interactive television 12
interfaces *see* graphical user interfaces; source interfaces; user interfaces
interlibrary lending 59, 60, 121
intermediaries 114–6, 164
International Data Service (IDS) 173
International DOI Foundation 185
International Federation of Library Associations (IFLA) 23, 158
International Organization for Standardization (ISO) 91
International Standard Bibliographic Description (ISBD) 190
International Standard Book Number (ISBN) 184
International Standard Serial Number (ISSN) 184
Internet Archive 25
internet connectivity 168
internet filtering 71–2
Internet Protocol (IP) 168
addressing 144
interoperability 175, 195
Intute 172, 194
Investing in Knowledge 39
iPhone 14
ISI Web of Knowledge 172, 195
ISO/TR20983 91
ISO11620 91–2
ISO2709 188
ISO2789 91

Joint Academic Network (JANET) 168
Joint Information Systems Committee (JISC) 32, 194, 206, 212
Information Architecture (IA) 82–4
Information Environment (IE) 33, 80, 82, 174
Jorum 173
journals 10, 60
JSTOR 173, 200

knowledge management 49–51, 98, 209
knowledge mediators 78–9
knowledge sharing 135
Kungliga Biblioteket (Sweden) 22

Landmap 173
language 54, 55, 169, 207
games 55
natural 191

Laws of Library Science 61
learning 132, 152, 208
  asynchronous 154
  deep 153
  group 155
  holistic approach 153
  lifelong 209
  models 153
  networked 154
  objects 178
  online 14
  organizations 51, 98
  reflective 155
  serialist approach 153
  society 33
  styles 148, 153; *see also* cognitive styles
  surface 153
  synchronous 154
  see also networked learner support
Leeds Always Reading Group for Everyone (LARGE) 143
Leeds University Library 143
legal deposit 24
Legal Deposit Libraries Act 2003 24
leisureflows 118, 140
LibQUAL+™ 103
libraries
  academic 27–34, 56, 209
  as agents 115
  anxiety 152
  as brokers 116
  buildings 107
  clients 118
  collections 55, 71, 120
  community 64, 140
  county 35
  customers 118
  digital 77–88
  economy 89
  effectiveness 89
  efficiency 89
  enquiry services 130
  functions 133
  as gateways 116
  as guides 115
  hybrid 32, 77
  immersive 63, 206
  impact 89, 106–8
  as intermediaries 114–6
  as mediators 116
  members 119
  mission 113–4
  national 22–7
  patrons 118
  performance 89–109
  as places 106, 209
  as portals 116
  public 34–42, 56, 107, 208; standards 94–5
  quality 98–103
  readers 118
  school 42–5, 209; guidelines 44
  self-renewing 59
  special *see* workplace
  use 148
  users 92, 118–20, 139–62; affirmation of 136–7; expectations 79; perception of service 92; populations 119; profiles 80, 123
  workplace 45–51, 209
Libraries Change Lives Award 179
Library 2.0 115, 171–2, 195
Library Bill of Rights 70–2
Library of Congress 22
  Classification 191
  National Digital Library Program (NDLP) 80
  Subject Headings (LCSH) 191
lifeflows 118, 140, 206
lifelong learning *see* learning, lifelong
link resolvers 195, 211
literacy 208
  see also digital literacy; document literacy; functional literacy; information literacy; media literacy; prose literacy;

literacy (*continued*)
quantitative literacy
The Long Tail 170–1
Loudon County (internet filtering) 71

MAchine-Readable Cataloguing (MARC) 188, 197
Manchester Information and Associated Services (MIMAS) 172
MDA 38, 190
Mechanics Institutes 4
media literacy 159
media transience 16
Medical Subject Headings (MeSH) 191
MEDLINE 47, 172
members *see* libraries, members
memory institutions 199
messaging *see* instant messaging
metadata 178, 197, 202
migration 202
mission *see* libraries, mission
MLA 167
mobile communications 14, 168
models 53
Moore's Law 168
Moving Here 180, 208
Moving to Distributed Environments for Library Services (MODELS) 79–80
Information Architecture (MIA) 79–80, 122
Museums, Libraries and Archives Council (MLA) 38, 58, 135
MyIntute 194
MySpace 5, 13, 133, 142, 143, 206

namespaces 186
national bibliographies 25
National Centre for Text Mining (NaCTeM) 173
National Digital Library Program (NDLP) 80
National Electronic Journal Licensing Service (NESLi2) 173
National Forum on Information Literacy (USA) 158
National Learning Network (NLN) 173, 178
National Lending Library for Science & Technology (NLLST) 58
national libraries *see* libraries, national
National Library for Health (NLH) 47, 167
National Literacy Trust 208
National Preservation Office 38
natural language *see* language, natural
Net Generation 5
Netvibes 142
networked learner support 136
networked learning *see* learning, networked
networking *see* social networking
networks 33
NHSNet 168
Norfolk and Norwich Millennium Library 210
Northamptonshire Black History Project 179

objectivism 152
on-demand publishing 32
Online Computer Library Center (OCLC)
WorldCat 172
online learning *see* learning, online
Online Public Access Catalogue (OPAC) 194, 143, 149
ontologies 170
open access 176
Open Archival Information System (OAIS) Reference Model 202
Open Archives Initiative (OAI) 84
Open Archives Initiative Protocol for Metadata Harvesting (OAI-PMH) 30, 84, 198

Open University 31
OpenURLs 195

packet-switching 168
Panizzi, Antony 22, 64, 208
Parry Report 28–9
passwords 144
patrons *see* libraries, patrons
pedagogy 136, 152
peer review 30
People's Network 37, 143, 167, 212
perceived quality (quality attribute) 102
performance
  as quality attribute 99
  measurement *see* libraries, performance measurement
periodicals *see* journals
persistence 182
persistent identifiers 81, 183, 199
Persistent Uniform Resource Locators (PURLs) 184
personalization 141
Philosophical Transactions of the Royal Society of London 200
Pipes 142
podcasting 143
post-prints 178
pre-prints 29, 170
presentation 83, 134, 135
preservation 57, 83, 137, 199–202
  see also digital preservation
print on demand 15
privacy 145, 164
  see also data protection
problem-solving 147
prose literacy 157
provenance 202
provision layer 83
Ptolemy I 3
public libraries *see* libraries, public
Public Library Manifesto (UNESCO) 36
publishing 9, 132
  see also on-demand publishing

quality
  assurance 56
  attributes 98–103
  management 89, 97, 140
  see also libraries, quality
Quality Assurance Agency for Higher Education 75
quantitative literacy 158

radio frequency identification device (RFID) 211
Ranganathan, Shiyali Ramamrita 62
Rater set 105
readers *see* libraries, readers
reading service 74
Really Simple Syndication(RSS) 142, 171
reliability
  as quality attribute 100, 104
renderability 202
repositories
  see digital repositories; e-print repositories; institutional repositories
research 85
Research Councils (UK) 177
Research Information Network (RIN) 26, 200
resolvers *see* link resolvers
Resource Description Framework (RDF) 25, 188, 192–3
resources
  delivery 32, 78, 79, 80, 151
  discovery 78, 79, 80, 149, 187, 195
  location 79, 80, 150
  provision 79
  release 151
  request 80, 150
  return 151
  use 151
response times 94

responsiveness
as quality attribute 104
retrieval *see* search and retrieve
Robbins Report 31
Round Reading Room 23
Ruskin Library (Lancaster University) 210

Saltire Centre (Glasgow Caledonian University) 73, 140, 210
Santa Fé Convention 30
scalability 174
scholarly communication 84, 85, 114, 173, 176–9
school libraries *see* libraries, school
Scirus 195
Scottish Cultural Resources Access Network (SCRAN) 203
Scottish Library and Information Council 212
Search & Retrieve Web Service (SRW) 196–7
search and retrieve 196–7, 198
Second Life 142, 205
security 199
as quality attribute 104
Select Committee on Public Libraries (1849) 34
selection
for preservation 201
see also stock selection
self-archiving 177, 178
self-renewing libraries *see* libraries, self-renewing
semantic web 8, 169
Serials Union Catalogue (SUNCAT) 26, 60
Service Oriented Architecture Protocol (SOAP) 197
serviceability
as quality attribute 101
service-oriented architectures (SOA) 8
SERVQUAL 105
Shibboleth 145, 185
Short-run Printing Programme (Cambridge University Press) 15
Simple Object Access Protocol (SOAP) 197
situated cognition 153
situatedness 160
Sloane, Sir Hans 22
SMS texting 143
social impact 108
social networking 12–13, 17, 142, 170
social policy 35
Society of College, National and University Libraries (SCONUL) 72–3, 106, 158
Design Award 73
source interfaces 126
Special Libraries Association 46
Spectrum 190
Standard Generalized Markup Language (SGML) 186
stock selection 121
student fees 73
styles *see* cognitive styles; learning, styles
subject classification *see* classification
subject gateways 121
sustainability 174
systems approach 90

tangibles (quality attribute) 104
Tavistock Institute 41
teaching 136
technological determinism 18
television *see* digital television; interactive television
terminology 149
services 83
thesauri 191
Topping Fold Public Library, Bury 140
Total Quality Management (TQM) 97
training 32

Turning the Pages *see* British Library, Turning the Pages

UK Data Archive 173
UKOLN 211
Uniform Resource Identifier (URI) 185, 189
Uniform Resource Names (URNs) 184, 185
union catalogues 60, 197, 198
United Nations (UN) 165
United Nations Educational, Scientific and Cultural Organization (UNESCO) 23, 36, 158
University Grants Committee (UGC) 58
use *see* libraries, use
user interfaces 125
users *see* libraries, users
USMARC 188
  see also MAchine Readable Cataloguing (MARC)

Value and Impact of IT Access in Public Libraries (VITAL) 35
virtual communities *see* communities, virtual
virtual learning environments (VLEs) 14, 63, 118, 206
virtual research environments (VREs) 206
vocabulary control *see* controlled vocabularies

Web 2.0 8, 115, 142, 169, 189, 194,
Web Accessibility Initiative (WAI) 176
Web Content Accessibility Guidelines (WCAG) 176
website design 135
Wikipedia 142
wikis 142, 171, 181
Wittgenstein, Ludwig 54–5, 153
WMA (Microsoft) 192
workflows 84, 118, 140
workplace libraries *see* libraries, workplace
World Summit on the Information Society (WSIS) 30, 58, 165
World Wide Web Consortium (W3C) 176, 186, 188
WorldCat 197
WSDL 197
WW2: People's War 180

Yahoo! 195
YouTube 5, 13, 62, 133, 142, 170, 205

Z39.50 188, 196, 197

The Academic Library 2nd edn
Peter Brophy

An immaculate introduction to academic library management.

MULTIMEDIA INFORMATION & TECHNOLOGY

This authoritative and wide-ranging textbook provides a comprehensive overview of the changing functions of higher education libraries and the organizational cultures in which they operate. It offers an assessment of the impact of such changes on service delivery from both provider and user perspectives, and considers the future role of the academic library.

The second edition has been completely updated, with a new chapter on performance measurement and more extensive coverage of: accessibility; information literacy; portals; digital libraries; copyright; institutional repositories; virtual and managed learning environments; and management of change. Written in a readable and accessible style, the book focuses on:

- the library in the institution
- users of the academic library
- the impacts and opportunities of ICTs
- human resources
- management and organization of resources
- collection and access management
- the academic library building
- library systems and networks
- specialist services
- management and professional issues
- the academic library of the future.

This textbook is an indispensable introduction to the range of issues facing academic libraries for students and new professionals. It also makes stimulating reading for education administrators and academic library managers in both higher and further education.

2nd edn; 2005; 248pp; paperback; ISBN 978-1-85605-527-8; £34.95

Measuring Library Performance: principles and techniques

Peter Brophy

This important book is the first to provide an accessible account of current thinking and research on the evaluation of library services, both traditional and – importantly – electronic. Illustrated throughout with a range of internationally based examples across the different library sectors, it is structured to focus primarily on the intended service user (outcome and impact perspectives), then to look at service management (output and process issues) and the building blocks of services (inputs), and finally to draw together these strands by examining some of the broader frameworks for evaluation that have emerged.

Each chapter features a list of key resources, and the extensive appendices offer practical guidance on data collection methods, the analysis of data and the presentation of results. The key areas addressed include:

- background and theoretical considerations
- user satisfaction and impact on users
- social and economic impact
- inputs, processes and outputs
- staff and infrastructure
- services for all
- standards, benchmarking and the balanced scorecard.

The emphasis on both principles and techniques in this book means that it is perfect reading for busy LIS practitioners but it is also eminently suitable for LIS students and researchers trying to get to grips with this complex area.

2006, 272pp; hardback; ISBN 978-1-85604-593-3; £39.95